# THE PLANTER:

OR,

# THIRTEEN YEARS IN THE SOUTH.

BY A NORTHERN MAN.

---

"For much, and too often, we on one side, have cowered before the unseemly bearing of those who have assailed us. If there has been *any* of this giving ground, it is more than enough, it is more than was due; and it is time that we should repel all such violences."—Restoration of Belief.

---

PHILADELPHIA:
H. HOOKER, CORNER OF CHESTNUT AND EIGHTH STS.
1853.

## ADVERTISEMENT.

It is the proud boast of abolition authors and senators, that the literature of the age is all on their side. There let its infidel philosophies and licentious levities forever remain. When its destinies shall have been fulfilled, that literature will be found to have done much to settle men's minds in submission to God's Providence. People will then see and feel strongly that it is due to justice and truth, that the forged drafts on their imaginations must be protested. This boasted literature represents the condition of the Southern slave as enormously wretched; and the true facts appearing will be received as evidences of the enormous wickedness of abolition literature. The time is approaching for the reaction to commence. This truthful little work is designed to accelerate it, by showing that the world abounds with worse evils far, than Southern slavery, even as falsely represented by its calumniators. If it do a little to arrest the progress of error, and to induce the public mind to think soberly as it ought to think, the object of the writer will be attained.

# TABULAR VIEW.



1*

## CHAPTER VIII.

THE WEDDING—CHRISTIAN SLAVES—SLAVERY A MISSIONARY INSTITUTION.



## CHAPTER IX.

PLEASURES OF SLAVERY.



## CHAPTER X.

DRAYTON ISLAND.



## CHAPTER XI.

ADDRESSED TO ALL SUCH PERSONS AS DESIRE TO KNOW WHAT ARE THE REAL MERITS OF THE QUESTION OF NEGRO SLAVERY.



## CHAPTER XII.

SAVAGE CONDITION OF AFRICA.



## CHAPTER XIII.

SOUTHERN NEGRO HAPPINESS IN CHILDHOOD AND AGE.



## CHAPTER XIV.

PREJUDICES OF EDUCATION, AN APOLOGY FOR ABOLITIONISTS.

CHAPTER XXI.

SLAVERY OF THE POOR ABOLISHED ONLY IN THE SOUTH.



CHAPTER XXII.

NEW ENGLAND.



CHAPTER XXIII.

"DESPERATE ROW."



CHAPTER XXIV.

SPIRITUAL STATE AND PRIVILEGES OF SOUTHERN SLAVES.



CHAPTER XXV.

A CHAPTER OF LACONICS.

# CHAPTER I.

## AN INTRODUCTORY TABLE TALK.

It was on the eastern bank of the Upper Delaware, in easy view of where, on both sides, the rocky hills are separated from the rocky river by the well paid labor of men, who had been sent to us by European misrule and oppression. So—though woes await the oppressor—so good cometh out of evil.

It was a cold morning; and it was made more dreary by the falling, driving, and beating, sleet and snow. In contrast with the almost summer-like weather that had immediately preceded it, for invalids particularly, its character approached almost even to the hideous. But even then and there, a comfortable and thankful little family party was cosily seated around a breakfast table. It was in a small stove-room. Adjoining it was a kitchen, not less comfortable. It was occupied by a neat handed and newly and warmly clad Irish girl,—a good natured and faithful creature. She was one of the survivors of a packed cargo of emigrants from the almost desolated Connaught;—the daughter of a family, by oppression separated for the ever of this world.

The breakfast party consisted of the host, the wife, the sister, two young daughters, and the Doctor;—a favorite and friendly guest. He was an old acquaintance of the host; and had been with him through the hot sands and deep swamps, and many trials and perils in the far South, when perils there were real and not imaginary. In many labors, the Doctor had aided him. In many sorrows, he had wept with him. In many joys he had rejoiced with him. Of course, then, the Doctor was almost more than at home, in the retirement of his friend, on the banks and among the hills of the Delaware. Therefore, naturally and suitably he introduced and opened the following

DIALOGUE.

THE DOCTOR. Taking from his pocket a newspaper:—"Ladies; here is something highly important; and of special interest and concern to yourselves."

WIFE. In a semi-apparent alarm:—"To us? How, Doctor?"

DR. "To the women of this country, the noble and the simple women of England,—from duchesses down to plain misses,—address a petition to aid them, in the charitable work of subverting the institution of southern slavery;—or, at least to begin with, so to interfere with it as to prevent its '*frightful results.*'"

SISTER. "What frightful results? Are the negroes starving to death, like the poor people of Ireland and Scotland? and even of England and Germany?"

FIRST DAUGHTER. "Or are they turned out of their cabins, and hunted away from their homes, as our good Peggy says the poor Irish women and children are, by thousands upon thousands; and that they may never get back to them, their poor hovels are all burnt down to the ground?"

SECOND DAUGHTER. In tears: "Oh! I hope my dear old black friends who were so good to me; and Uncle Raphe, who used to carry me before him to school on the poney, are not turned out of doors to suffer!"

HOST. "No fear of that, my daughters; they are no doubt as unsuffering and comfortable this cold morning, as even you could reasonably desire them to be. But,

Doctor, let us hear what it really is that the noble ladies of England want of our republican women; and what are the frightful things they have discovered in the condition of our southern slaves?"

THE DR. Having very solemnly read the Address: "Shall I read all these titles and names?"

WIFE. "Certainly, Dr., let us hear them; by all means."

THE DR. "There then, you have them, ladies; from the Duchess of Sutherland to Mrs. Rowland Hill."

SISTER. "Mrs. Charles Dickens, inclusive. I wonder if Mrs. Charles Dickens has read Oliver Twist and the Bleak House? They might point her to other work to be done, nearer home, than our Southern States; where there is no poor Oliver '*to want more,*' nor poor homeless Joe, who could not have had less."

THE DR. "Mrs. Charles Dickens reads the COURT JOURNAL, and attends the aristocratic opera; and probably, sometimes goes to the Royal Chapel; and she must not therefore be expected to read, or to know any thing about such little dirty and starving humanities as Oliver Twist and poor Joe."

WIFE. "Of course not. And as her husband *insulted* our country, it is not wonderful that she should embrace such an illustrious opportunity to add an *injury* to the insult."

THE DR. "Well, ladies, what is your intention to do in this matter? Of course, so polite a communication on a subject so important, must not be silently neglected."

HOST. "No fear but that the convention women will have a special general convention, for the express objects of concocting a suitable and learned Reply to the Address of the Convention at Stafford House; and the organizing of a female crusade to unite its power and influence with that of the aristocratic organization on the other side of the water.

THE DR. "Yes, doubtless; and they will thereby confirm the women of England in their pernicious delusion with regard to the frightful results of our southern slavery. But would it not be kind and useful to undeceive them?"

HOST. "It might, indeed, be kind and useful; if *possible.* But how is it to be done?"

THE DR. "You might write a book to show, what you so well know of the condition of the slaves; and that the thus declared views of female England are preposterous. Yes, sir; write a book; and tell and explain at large, what are the comforts and privileges of the southern negroes in slavery, so called; and show how surpassingly better they are off, than the Africans at home;—the free blacks of any country;—and indeed, of the poor white laborers of Europe; or even than tens of thousands of them in our own country."

SECOND DAUGHTER. With enthusiasm, "O, yes, father, *do* write a book."

FIRST DAUGHTER. Quietly: "I wish you would write a book, dear father; if it be only to tell the good ladies of England, how *very* much they are mistaken about the slaves not being allowed religious privileges."

WIFE. "But can it be, Dr., that they are sincere in what they say of the '*frightful results,*'—*interdictions,*—*separations,*—and the like? Can we reasonably suppose educated and sensible women in such ignorance of a matter, so easy to obtain full and complete knowledge of? I can not easily suppose it."

THE DR. "Madam, did you never hear of people who *studied* ignorance?"

WIFE. "I think I never did, Dr., did you?"

THE DR. "Certainly, madam; I have known plenty of them;—plentier than blackberries—students of ignorance on almost all subjects. And on this subject, in particular, you may find all over the country, men and women by tens of thousands, who study hard, in their way,—to learn every possible objection against negro slavery;—which they carefully teach their children among their first and last lessons,—and not less hard do they study to shut out, from their thoughts and knowledge, every consideration that might in any way tend to remove, or palliate their objections. And that is what I call studying ignorance."

HOST. "So it is indeed, Dr.; and very well explained. And in the matter of our southern slavery, you think the ladies of England are proficients in that science?"

THE DR. "No doubt of it. Slavery by name, is a very unpopular subject in England; and the people are carefully taught that it is the most frightful thing imaginable; in order to keep them quiet under the far heavier yoke of their *real* slavery. And so long and zealously have the teachers been thus employed deceiving others, that the retributive justice has overtaken them at last, of being themselves deceived into believing and loving a lie. And so is it, in a large measure, in our own country. Learn the views of the first ten persons nearest you. Begin with your next door neighbors; and you shall find them all familiar with the popular objections to slavery; and not more than one, in the whole ten, at all familiar with any thing that may be urged in its defence. And this general *prejudice*, the natural result of thus studying ignorance, is termed public sentiment."

HOST. "Dr., *you* must write the book."

THE DR. "No indeed; not I. Once on a time, a book was about to be written, when I heard that in reference to the design, a certain man had said, 'O that my adversary *would* write a book.' And the book was never written."

HOST. "That you might not gratify an adversary?"

THE DR. "Perhaps, partly that. More largely something else. But to get back to where we ought to be: Your missions in two of the southern states; and your travels over most of the others, with your eyes and ears open, have supplied your portfolio and memory with the materials; and you are bound to put them together into a book."

First Daughter. "Dear father, do write a book; and tell the English ladies and every body else, about the beautiful churches which we saw in the south and south-west, built for the slaves; and about the Sunday schools; and how well the slave scholars behaved and learned; and how happy and good they were; and how sweetly they sang the lovely hymns that dear mother and aunty taught them to learn by heart. Do, father, write the book. It will make the good dear ladies of England very happy indeed to know that the slaves of the south are so well off as we know they are; and are so kindly treated and taught, as we know they are. Please, dear father, write the book."

Sister. "By all manner of means, brother, write the book."

Host. "And what say you, wife?"

Wife. "Certainly, write the book; and make the Doctor help you?"

The Dr. Looking through the window into the storm; "Gladly would I do what I could; but I reckon I am off for the south again before many days."

Host. "Indeed, Dr., and why this sudden move?"

The Dr. "This sudden snow storm."

Wife. "The Dr. will surely not leave us so. Don't fear?"

Host. "Suppose then, Dr., after due deliberation, the work of the proposed book be entered upon; how shall I proceed? Please sketch me an outline."

The Dr. "Well; let us think about it a little, seriously. How would this, or something like this, do? In the first place, to show that the slaves of the south,—*physically*, *socially*, and *morally*—or spiritually, if you rather, though I understand them as identical, or including each other—are, in all these things, in a far better condition, than are the negro race in any other condition. This you may easily enough do. In the second place; that the results of emancipation have been, and are in general, frightfully cruel,—even murderous,—by forcing the poor creatures into the arena of a gradual and painful extermination. And thirdly; having established firmly these facts, and amply multiplied your defences by the use of select materials from a world full of them;—then, "carry the war into Africa." Teach the aristocracy of England what the people are anxious they should know; viz., that JOHN BULL IS A GREAT SLAVEHOLDER, AND A VERY HARD MASTER."

HOST. "Is not that pretty high ground, Doctor?"

THE DR. "Yes; but it is good and solid ground—sure footing—and if you would do any good for the cause of God's Providence, and of man's progress, you must take it, and stand on it firmly and fearlessly. The appointments of His Providence, God will surely vindicate, and make the truth to triumph. He can steady His own ark; and He will do it. And woe to the faithless and the presumptuous doubter who would put forth his hand to help Him."

HOST. "Doctor! Doctor! what is your drift?"

THE DR. "Portward, with a strong arm, a firm heart; without which no harbor can be made in this storm. Abolition, or intervention, is but a comparatively small lever of a huge engine that has been put in motion to disrupt every conservative institution of the age; and as it has been shown in other lands, how it could shake thrones into fragments, and again re-erect them with blood and bones; in our own land it has shown too, how it could upheave the masses like an earthquake, and rock the solid pillars of the Union."

HOST. "Dr., do you indeed, apprehend any such danger to social order, as your words may seem to inculcate?"

THE DR. "Danger? Yes, sir; I see, and *feel* it too. Dr. Thornwell says, eloquently, 'The parties in this conflict are not merely abolitionists and slaveholders—they are atheists, socialists, communists, red republicans, jacobins, on the one side, and the friends of order and regulated freedom on the other. In one word, the world is the battle-ground—Christianity and atheism the combatants, and the progress of humanity the stake.' I believe him. And, in this money and mischief loving age, I *do* apprehend danger. Not of the final issue; but of overwhelming calamities to the millions of mankind guiltless of the strife; and of a long and disastrous countermarch of Christian civilization."

HOST. "Dr., do you perceive any thing of an alarming character in this lady-movement in England?"

THE DR. "Yes, sir: we may talk lightly of it; newspapers may sport with it; shallow thinking people may laugh about it, till they crack their sides; but, seriously, it presents to my mind a phase of the subject of a most appalling character!"

HOST. "As how, pray, my good Doctor?"

THE DR. "As indicating on which side in this conflict, the power of Great Britain may arrange itself."

HOST. "But do you think there is danger that England will take part with the confederacy enumerated by Dr. Thornwell—atheism and its allies?"

THE DR. "It looks very like it. What is the British Parliament, with a few exceptions, but an aggregated mass of reckless trimmers? Among these women who are thus put forward on the platform of agitation, are conspicuous connexions of nearly, if not quite, every ruling family in Great Britain; and wives of the most influential commoners. Perhaps, very few of them know what they are doing; but nothing is plainer than that they are imbuing the whole nation with the fell spirit of a universal and atheistic revolution; compared with which the world has never seen a revolution. It is therefore now too late to go gingerly into the contest. When an atheistic universal prejudice is called the public opinion of the civilized world, and the cause of truth is placed under the ban of it; it is then too late for temporising;—too late for studying the *expedient*, instead of the right. England holds in her hand a mighty weight, which thrown into any of the world's scales, may give it a preponderance; and she must not therefore be allowed, unrebuked, to feed a powerful faction of our country,—a sworn brotherhood to subvert our institutions, —with female flattery; nor to call off the eyes of the rest of the world from her own frightful evils, to fix them, with scorn and hatred, on an institution of ours, which excites her envy."

HOST. "Her ENVY, Doctor?"

THE DR. "Yes, certainly; her *deadliest* envy."

HOST. "How, Dr., I may not understand you, rightly?"

THE DR. "She has been at a great national expense to add many ten thousands to her pauper population; to ruin her West Indian possessions; and to reduce to beggary and vagabondism, their inhabitants, white and black; and to restore something like a balance, she would bring our southern states into the like condition; though she must be blind not to see, that it would add two millions more to her pauper population, from the three millions and a half, whose subsistence is derived from the manufacture of cotton. It would however be no more blind than much of her legislation has been.

"That's not all; though quite enough. Our slaveholding states have no starving poor. They have no poor taxes. They have no workhouses. What a contrast to her condition; with her millions of laborers and citizens, on the very verge of beggary; toiling to support millions already over the verge.

"Yes, sir; it is my opinion that British envy helps to keep up and encourage this wicked agitation; and that to it, we are indebted for the grave discussions of antislavery philosophy;—the solemn instructions of transcendental and pantheistic pulpits;—the light effusions of the poet and the novelist,—male and female, on both sides of the wide water. For British fame, and for British gold, the abolitionist writes, and preaches, and sings. And in popular assemblies, and in legislative halls, he pours out his wrathful vials of execration and contempt, on the institution of slavery, to tickle the open ear of British envy, for British praise, and British pay."

HOST. "Dr., are you in a fine frenzy? or is it possible that you have been speaking right words in truth and soberness? Is it possible that you are right?"

THE DR. "Possible, sir? It is certain. I have been behind the scenes. I have smelt the tarred ropes and the tallow candles. And to my alarm and indignation, too, I have learned that there is a countless no-party party, yet unorganized perhaps, that gives to the abolition faction both countenance and sanction, with very much comfort; at the same time that they profess their antagonism to it. Among these are all such,—again to quote Dr. Thornwell, —as cannot find in their hearts to join in the violent maledictions which zeal for humanity has piled upon the slaveholders; but never venture upon a plea of justification in their defence. They pity their dear southern brethren. They lament their lot. They admit their case to be bad,—desperately bad;—but then, they think them not *so much* to blame as the abolitionists represent them to be. 'They curse them in their sympathies.' Of this party, it may almost be said, JOAB is their leader."

HOST. "Do you think this party numerous, Doctor?"

THE DR. "As to its numerical strength, you may be safely referred to certain prominent members of both branches of our national legislature, which have been sent there by it; and to certain popular newspapers represented there; and which contend, in words, with about equal force, for and against abolitionism;—or rather against the abolition party. Some time since, one of these double-faced newspapers had prepared a bitter draught for the party, but before commending the cup to their lips, extracted all its bitterness, to make more bitter, a cup for a great lamented senator, to punish him for the proposition, that '*under the present circumstances of civilization, the slavery of the south, is not a curse, but a blessing, to the negro.*' For this, by a prominent anti-abolition newspaper, the author was held up to scorn and execration."

HOST. "How strange that such a proposition should be denied by any one at all acquainted with the comforts of the southern slave, and also with the wretched condition of the northern free negroes, generally!"

THE DR. "An eminent and popular writer, in a late number of a Washington paper, under the head of southern slavery, in reference to the Stafford House movement, which he condemns in manly terms, takes some pains, at the same time, to have it very distinctly understood, that he is not 'defending' the institution, and that he is 'no friend' to it. The faction demon gloated and chuckled over it delighted; and greatly was his delight increased by the plaudits of several eminently respectable anti-abolition papers, which copied it, and praised its dignified moderation."

HOST. "But, my dear Doctor, you do not condemn moderation."

THE DR. "Certainly not. I would be moderate in all things; and advise others to be so. I am not at all disposed to condemn or blame such writers and editors. Some of them are known to me as most worthy men who would not knowingly do any wrong thing. And if they are sincere in their halfway views, as here presumed; and if they honestly suppose, as here also presumed, that they are bound to publish them, they are right in doing so. It is doubtless, in some way, best that they should. But whether they intend it, or no, they are giving countenance, and adding strength to the abolitionists. Of this I am confident; and so is the faction into whose hands they are playing."

HOST. "I think none of them will agree with you, Dr., that they are auxiliaries of abolitionism."

THE DR. "I suppose not. And therein lies much of the danger. Nor will the authors of several portentous volumes of the same character, and from the same platform."

"On quite another, and higher platform, I hope you will take your stand, and give us a book that shall indicate its author, as an unflinching, conscientious, and unqualified believer in the Bible;—a lover of his country, and of its blood-bought constitution;—a friend of the human race, of every condition and of every color."

HOST. "DR., I really wish *you* would write the book. You shall have all my accumulated materials. And these, with your clear notions of what you think it should be, and with your retentive memory of your own experience and observations in the south, would enable you to do it well, and with ease and rapidity."

THE DR. "I reckon it is much easier to *tell* what a book should be, than to make it what it should be. You know I can talk, much better than I can write; and if it may be said without offence, I think you can write better than you can talk. So then, go on with the book, you write, and I will talk. But, before you begin to write, let me talk a little more. What memoranda have you of our southern experience; and of your own, before I joined you?"

HOST. "With certain preliminaries; I have some notes of my voyage and its adventures;—of my stay of a few days in Charleston, and what there I saw of the condition of the slaves, so incomparably better than I had expected;—of my passage to St. Augustine; and of there finding but one unhappy negro, and he a free one;—of the visits to the plantations, where they were anticipating holiday delights;—of the wedding party that you wot of, when the negroes were almost too joyous to be happy;—and of our boating party up the river to Lake George and Drayton Island."

THE DR. "One of the most delightful incidents of my life; and among its pleasantest memories. *There* was seen negro happiness in perfection."

HOST. "'THE PLEASURES OF SLAVERY,' I have entitled my account of it."

THE DR. "Excellent. Appropriate, and graphically descriptive. You can soon make a right sort of a book, with such materials. By the way,—our visit to the Sea Islands, you must not forget. It almost ought to be a book by itself. I remember it as if yesterday; and I will help you if you need any help of memory."

HOST. "Thank you, Dr., I accept the offered kindness. At your leisure I will read to you my Sea Island notes."

THE DR. "But, as in the character, somewhat of a scribe for the ladies, I believe you should begin the book, with a chapter or more, directly addressed to the ladies of England, on the subject of their address to the women of

America. And it might not be amiss to appropriate a few pages to the Earl of Carlisle, in his character of abolition editor."

Host. "Certainly, Doctor; neither the noble ladies, nor the ladies' noble editor, must be forgotten."

The Dr. "Well; now I think you will do. Go at it. And I will try what may be done with the dog and the gun, in the way of a game dinner from the fields and the woods."

The Doctor withdraws to prepare for his sport; the daughters take Peggy with them to put the study in order for work; the ladies remain to restore order to the breakfast room before resuming the daily needles; and the host prepares his feathered armor for the engagement;— a true labor of love,—battling for the truth.

## CHAPTER II.

### TO THE "WOMEN OF ENGLAND," CONCERNING THEIR APPEAL TO THE "WOMEN OF THE UNITED STATES OF AMERICA," FOR AID IN THEIR INTERVENTION TO REVOLUTIONIZE AN INSTITUTION OF OUR COUNTRY.

Ladies of England:—

Rarely, with more painful sympathy, have I been exercised, than for your unhappy mistake, with respect to the social and spiritual condition of the African slaves in our country. And to relieve the heavy weight of sorrow for their imaginary sufferings, which is bearing upon your afflicted hearts, I hasten to correct the sad and saddening error, into which you have been so unkindly beguiled.

It rejoices my aged, but still warm heart, that through much labor and sufferings, and through many perils, I have become so well able and prepared, by a long series of years, passed in the south among slaveholders and slaves, to set your disturbed hearts at rest, with respect to the social and spiritual condition and privileges of the slaves of our country.

When I mention the fact, which I trust will not be quite uninteresting to you, that for more than thirteen years I was a Christian Missionary in several of the slave-holding states, it is hoped confidently, that you will receive kindly, and to your great relief, what I have imposed on myself as a duty to communicate to you.

How you have been misled into the belief, that the slaves of our country have no sacred social privileges; and are not taught in the religion of the Gospel, nor allowed to be taught, is of minor importance. It is sufficient to know the unhappy fact, that such is your no doubt sincere belief.

Ladies of England; pray pardon me for saying, what need not long remain to be proved, that you have been very grossly and most wickedly imposed on. Who the impostor may be, is of less concern. Would to God!—with fervent reverence be it spoken—would to God! that the poor white people of Europe, and even of our own country, had their personal comforts, and their social rights, as well secured as have the slaves of the south: and above all, that their souls were as faithfully and efficiently cared for!

You speak, ladies, of "frightful results of negro slavery, even under kindly disposed masters." From this allusion, and from the notice of your amiable interference with the system, in the Manchester Guardian of December 1st, and other newspapers of your country, there seems show of reason,—without violence of inference,—to suppose your movement to have been impelled by a popular romance of a countrywoman of ours; who, it is said, is "a sort of divinity in the aristocratic *boudoirs* of the British metropolis."

If the inference be not sustained by the fact, in your kindness and Christian charity, you will pardon it;—if it be, it may be no unkindness to communicate to you, in what estimation that strangely popular romance, is held by a very large majority of the respectable Christian communion to which that lady belongs by inheritance and education, as well as by profession; as indicated by its chief literary organ, one of the most able, and widely circulated religious newspapers in America.

Thus speaks THE NEW YORK OBSERVER:—

"We have read the book, and regard it as antichristian.

We have marked numerous passages in which religion is spoken of in terms of contempt, and in *no* case is religion represented as making a master more humane; while Mrs. Stowe is careful to represent the indulgent and amiable masters as without religion. This taint pervades the work, just as it does the writings of all the modern school of philanthropy. It is certainly a non-religious, if not anti-evangelical school. Mrs. Stowe labors through all her book to render ministers odious and contemptible, by attributing to them sentiments unworthy of men or Christians."

Ladies of England;—pardon me;—is this the school in which you have received willing instruction to interfere with our affairs, and to encourage our infidel calumniators? And is this the book, made up as it is mostly of deceptive fictions, seditious sentiments, and most offensive scoffs and sneers at things sacred!—is this, indeed the book, which has so filled the cup of your indignant charity, that "you cannot keep silence," nor withhold the blazing torch from Mrs. Stowe's man of straw?

Indeed, Ladies of England, forgive, pray, this little outburst of honest indignation. KNOWING, as I do, most undoubtingly, that the book is a vile and mischievous calumny from beginning to end, it is found as impossible for me to speak of it with cool indifference, as it is for you to keep silent, believing it to be a true statement of the "frightful results of negro slavery." Ungrateful is the task, but it may be needful, to show briefly that it is entitled to no regard as an authority on the subject of which it treats.

> "For me, I cannot bolt it to the bran
> As can the holy Dr. Augustin."

I cannot think of entering upon the painful and revolting task of dissecting this putrid body to expose all its sources of poison. It might disable me quite for my pleasant labor of love, in exhibiting to your happy eyes the reverse and bright side of the subject. For, as you shall see, if you will deign to look, that even slavery, through grace, has its bright side.

> "Next to Sincerity, remember still,
> Thou must resolve upon Integrity."

It might be useful to show, how this bold woman has used unblenchingly, and unscrupulously, every popular element, to make her romance acceptable to a corrupt age, in which,—not common vices, merely, but even crimes of every dark shade, find their defenders and advocates, in such multitudes, as to make emperors and kings,—black and white, of their chiefs. But room only for passing allusions, or little more, may be allowed.

This miserable thing of sin, cannot be examined with any discrimination, without discovering on its every page, that it has taken up among its destructive elements, every popular and infidel ultraism of the age,—sensual, social, political, philosophical, and religious.

It flatters every phase of modern reform;—every feature of every faith, which freely admits antislavery and abolitionism into its creed.

It censures, blindly, the government of the country; and it arrogantly denounces its acts in the most jacobinical and rancorous spirit. Your own radical authors and declaimers cannot go beyond it, on even their own superior vantage ground.

The execution of the laws of the land,—even its organic laws, embodied in the constitution at the foundation of the nation,—it bitterly and treasonably execrates.

In morals, it is shamelessly profligate.

It ministers to the licentious passions of the age, by gross allusions to illicit desire and indulgence, and it makes itself a guide-book to the market-place of abomination, for the use of travelling roues from the north.

In religion, it occupies the seat of the scorner and the hypocrite. At the same time that it affects great religious fervor, it showers the most offensive odium on the whole body of the ministry of every name; and fulminates special anathemas towards all who show the slightest reluctance to join in a seditious and infidel crusade against "Cæsar" and against "God."

Among the minsiters of the Gospel most distinguished for high character and deep learning, there are very many; —and *millions* of intelligent laymen, who religiously believe; and meekly, and in the fear of God, declare their belief, that the Bible fully sanctions the institution of slavery.

All these, Mrs. S. virtually presumes to denounce as unworthy of common civility. And she would have them answered in no other, or more courteous style, than with a laugh of scorn. She holds them in too deep contempt to speak of them, even decently. And to condescend even to say *to* one of them, "stand by thyself,—come not near me, for I am holier than thou!" she seems to imagine it would be too much honor for her greatness to confer!

Trusting in her own righteousness, she evidently despises all, whomsoever, that belongs not to her own school of the Pharisees.

In fine, in her abuse of the Bible, and the clergy, it is certainly not too much to say, that she has, not only trenched on the domain of Fanny Wright, but even shown a superior title. With a far bitterer venom than Fanny, she has shown less regard for modesty and candor.

The friends of Mrs. S. cannot plead for her even the miserab lemerit of fanaticism; which may be truly and honestly urged in favor—if so it be—of the extravagancies of very many of the most honest of her party.

"Fanaticism," says Jeremy Bentham, "never sleeps, it is never glutted. It is never stopped by philanthropy; for it makes a merit of trampling on philanthropy. It is never stopped by conscience, for it has pressed conscience into its service. Avarice, lust, and vengeance, have pity, benevolence, honor,—fanaticism has nothing to oppose it."

Some of these frightful features of fanaticism are conspicuous in her character; but though with the peculiar talent of enlisting the fanatical element in her cause, for personal profit, she is not a fanatic. She may not, perhaps, be reasoned with any more properly, than if she were a fanatic; but it is because she is rendered unconscionable by her vanity and cupidity, her arrogance and ambition;—if not also by the addition of even lower vices of mind and heart;—but she is not a fanatic.

Please now, Ladies of England, look at a few particulars of her performance, and plainly may you perceive, that it is entirely unworthy of your belief or regard; not to say your admiration.

Alone, as a weapon of offence in the hand of the political demagogue, in his battle against truth and right, was it intended to have value; and surely it has no other possible. As such instrument of mischief and ruin, dear to the enemies of our country, and to all who would break down its institutions of every kind,—trample upon the religion of the Bible,—fill its pulpits with infidel lecturers, —make an eternal separation of enmity between your nation and ours;—as such it may remain in use, by the popular and efficient aid and countenance of the women of England, until the land of the South shall be drenched with the blood of both white and black,—sparing, perhaps, a sufficient number of the latter, to establish another Haytien Empire, with another QUASSIA, to take a daily imperial bath in the blood of his sable subjects!

By the way, Ladies, *en passant*, are you so deluded as to imagine the masses of the Haytiens, the population in gross—in as happy a condition as the negroes of our South?

As a literary work of art, this popular novel, in the eyes of all candid persons whose personal knowledge of facts enables them to judge advisedly of its character, it is abhorrent to every principle of truth and taste. As a work of art, in its untruth to nature, it is a mere monster of deformity! But of necessity, you, Ladies of England, do not perceive its monstrosity; because you are unacquainted with the true facts of the subject. You know that your own great novelists present facts of fancy that are true to nature; and you are deceived into the unhappy belief that so does Mrs. Beecher Stowe.

You naturally thus judge, because her work is thought to be popular at home; where, you suppose, people ought to know whether or not it be true to nature. It is not popular at home, but as a political missile only, with those who wish to throw it into the ranks of their opponents, except indeed with the mass of novel readers, who generally know no more of the South, than they know of Siberia;—thousands of them even less.

You know that your Bulwer, and Dickens, and Warren, and Kingsley, your late Chancellor of the Exchequer, and such writers, have not overdrawn, the horrible pictures of crime, and poverty, and degradation, and oppression, in your own country; and it is therefore not strange, but natural, that you should receive as true to nature, Mrs. Stowe's paler pictures of suffering among our Southern slaves; whom hunger never leads to crime; as it does very largely the poor of Europe, and even of our own country.

Had Mrs. S. laid her scenes on this side of "Mason's and Dixon's line," and drawn with truth the crimes and sufferings of the free negroes here, whose vices and miseries are crowding them into our penitentiaries and lunatic asylums, she might have produced a work of art, which would have secured to her a lasting and a fair fame; though it would have given her less of money, and less of popularity of numbers and RANK; but it would not have been suited by its subject, to the purposes of the unscrupulous political demagogues and disorganizers of the age, for whom her book has been written *especially*.

Or she might have drawn from the immeasurable mass of facts connected with the terrific increase of crime and prostitution in our great cities; and so have presented a work true to nature, as known in cities, every where, that should have done good police service as a guide book, through the highways and byways,—the broad avenues, and dark alleys,—trodden by tens of thousands on their route to the gallows,—to the penitentiary,—to the asylum, —to the pauper's pallet,—to the Cyprian's den, or to the suicide's grave!

In such work of truthfulness, she might have indulged to the full, in her love of the horrible, by reproducing, with embellishments to her taste, the mangled remains of Adams and Parkman; and from the life and writings of their murderers, she might have revealed to what class of religio-philosophers they belonged;—for they were both men of mark. Or she might have found in the police records of any of our cities, ready to her hand, in distinct outline, plenty of conjugal murders; infanticides by hundreds; and arraignments of thousands of children and adolescent youth of both sexes;—and told us of their training. Such works, well done, could not but do good to the public, whatever they might do *for* the author.

Alas, she chose another subject; and so has she handled it, as to make her book a firebrand of destruction, of so deadly a character as to throw in deep shade the veriest infidel and seditious publications of the last hundred years.

But a word more of it, as a work of art. I trust you will be no longer deceived, Ladies of England, into the absurd supposition, that this novel, like those of your own great artists, presents facts with fidelity,—in its abuse of the South,—for there is scarcely such an instance of any kind, in the whole book. It is full of false assumptions of the most mischievous character, and manifesting a wicked and malicious intention to deceive the unwary and the unknowing. It is not necessarily here intended to charge her with such reckless wickedness, as these hard words, which I did not make, ought to express; for, being bred in a school which *compels* conscience into its service, and confounds it with feeling, enthusiasm, education, prejudice, party-spirit, and I know not what, so called principle of a "higher law," of their own make, she may be very conscientious in her measures of mischief, and think even that she is doing God a service. So thought Uzzah, no doubt; and so did your own Guy Fawkes; so did the conscientious authors of the massacre of St. Bartholomew's. So did *not* their victims;—so did *not* the British Parliament;—so did *not* God. Uzzah died for his presumption; Guy, for his intention; and the St. Bartholomew assassins are

"Damned to everlasting fame."

## CHAPTER III.

### TABLEAUX VIVANTS.

"Look here upon this picture, and on this."

AND now, having made this only, but ample apology for Mrs. Beecher Stowe,—in the spirit of the only one that even Omniscience could discover for the misguided, on an ever memorable occasion,—we proceed to another look at her celebrated work, already famous in its "frightful results."

Let it be viewed as a panorama, or as a picture gallery. Select for special notice, some of its most conspicuous groups, and single pieces; and examine their claims to be true to nature.

Look at these *tableaux vivants*, in the mansion of Shelby, and in the cabin of Uncle Tom.

"Look first on this, and then on that."

Can both be true to nature?

See Tom and Chloe, the incorruptible, and the excellent; and the reverenced, loved, and trusted, undoubtingly, by their master and mistress; and all but adored by their only son; who is all but adored by his parents—young "mas'r George"—the intelligent, loving, energetic boy:—and little Mose and Pete are in the corner;—the little negroes, to whom Mrs. S. ascribes flashes of wit that would not have shamed even Foote and Sheridan.

Leaving these little sable wits on that intellectual eminence, let us look at Aunt Chloe, feasting young "Mas'r George," at her own table.

*This* group is true to nature. I have more than once been delighted with such pleasant scenes as this good old negress feasting a pet young master or mistress,—both parties joyous exceedingly;—but, O, never, never, on the same domain where the mansion scene could happen by any possibility.

Skilfully wrought out and presented is this contrast, to suit the tastes of all such credulous lovers of the marvellous and the horrible, as are able to swallow any absurdity, for the sake of the pleasure of indulging their morbid appetites.

The beautiful and natural cabin scene prepares the credulous reader to be as much and as deeply shocked, as even Mrs. S., or any other abolitionist can reasonably desire, by the revolting caricature exhibited in the mansion. But the party will all believe it; or, effectually school themselves, if need be, to believe it; because they love to have it so. And many other simple-hearted, honest and benevolent people, not perceiving its absurdities, have been already shocked into horror and indignation, and all uncharitableness, by the miserable and wicked fable.

An agonizing sense of necessity secures the ready faith of the abolition faction, in every abominable fiction of this sort. It can neither consist, nor subsist, but by the most intemperate use of such garbage.

Writers of the Stowe class; and kindred *reverend* Lecturers against the Bible, who declare themselves atheists to a God who sanctions slavery; and senators who deride the Constitution, are as indispensable to their existence as a faction, as was Voltaire and his school, to the cause of infidelity, and the infidel party in the last century. He too, was a, so called, PHILANTHROPIST!—A Theophilanthropist!!!

Voltaire's works and his school have followed him. But their nefarious influence is yet felt around the globe. In other, and even christened forms, his disciples, in some bad sense, are busied, day and night, at their native and congenial work of political mischief, and social ruin.

They have already done much;—perhaps,—God, in mercy, grant it,—the most of what they may be allowed to do, to subvert the blessings of our revealed religion, by ignoring its Divine history; and to subvert our government and laws, by deriding the Constitution and sapping its foundation.

But should they succeed in their untiring and ruthless efforts to bring the constitution under the contempt and abhorrence of the millions, whose faith in the Bible they have shaken; they may finally overturn our government, and bring about a revolution, compared with which, the old French revolution was a mere village brawl!

Glance we now our mind's eye on the mansion scene. It is too disgusting an invention for more than a glance.

A table with wine and dessert of fruit, &c. The master of the mansion, a refined and intelligent gentleman, accustomed to the best society, seems unconscious of the incongruity of his situation at the table, and familiarly conversing with a negro trader of the very coarsest dimensions of vulgar brutality! A bad specimen of a universally detested class! Strange, is it not? Has he *dined* with that refined host? O yes, and he is now taking wine and fruit with him in the most familiar manner!

Nay, in the style of the vilest slang, the brute of a guest is telling the host incredible lies about incidents of his trade—things that in the South would soon rid the world of such a monster—and he is listened to with undisturbed courtesy!

Still more strange,—he proposes to buy Tom; and is allowed to retain his seat! Incredible! Worse yet;—the master consents to part with the incorruptible and faithful Uncle Tom, to this brute! but he cannot endure the sight of Tom's "taking off," and must absent himself! It is an unsolved mystery why he should particularly want Tom, a man quite too old for the slave market; but Tom he *must* have.

There comes, springing into the dining-room, a little yellow boy of four years old; and though declared impossible, as he is a pet of the lady, whose maidservant is its mother, the insatiate wretch must have the child too; though too young for his business. And, with agonizing reluctance the master consents! Amazing!

But passing over the brute's "undisguised admiration" of the child's mother, and Mrs. Stowe's voluptuous description of her charms, which so fascinated him, we proceed to the question, how these things, so strange, are to be explained, to make the tale plausible, of the despotic powers of the vile negro trader over the master of these slaves?

Did his life, or that of any, or all of his family, depend on his submission to this ruthless tyrant

Oh, no.

What then? Had he the planter so completely in his power that, unless he submitted to his whim to have Old Tom and little Henry, he could so ruin him at once as to reduce himself and family to beggary?

Nothing of all this.

What then?

Why, he held a promissory note against him. And by the time that the planter could grow two crops, he might force the payment of it. So much; no more, is the planter in the trader's power. Such is the slight foundation on which Mrs. Stowe has erected the main building of her showy and admired edifice.

And as it is not therefore necessary for the distracted mother of little Harry to run away with her child, and to cross the Ohio river on floating ice; nor for the conscientious and peaceable Quakers to fight in her defence; nor for Uncle Tom to be whipped to death in an "ogre's den," we may retire from the contemplation of these TABLEAUX VIVANTS.

But the author herself seems not fully to trust in this kind of logic, but to introduce it for the sake of embellishment; for she is careful throughout the narrative, and to declare as much in her preface and concluding remarks, that such cases of cruelty, as the separation of mothers and children, are by no means uncommon;—a mere every-day, matter of course affair! It is terrible to think of, that persons can be so depraved by party prejudice and rancour, as to allow themselves in such malignant calumny.

By the statute laws of the State where this scene is laid, no child, until over ten years of age, may be separated by sale from its mother. Such a sale would therefore be illegal and null; or rather perhaps equivalent to the emancipation of the child, at least. And people who suppose that such rights of slaves are not protected by the law are greatly mistaken; and still not less greatly are they mistaken, if they suppose the slaveholders are not generally vigilant to see that the laws are not violated.

But Mrs. S., not satisfied with calumniating the people of the South, presumes also to libel even the laws themselves. She would have it believed, that every one of her "frightful results of slavery"—every abuse of the institution—were sanctioned by law. What can be more daringly wicked? Was it not enough, by a cruel silence, tacitly to deny the existence of laws securing the rights and privileges of slaves wherever slaves are found in our country?

No; for her and her party, it was not enough. The

laws themselves must be compelled into their hard service. The book is full of malicious and impossible inventions; but, to my mind, this seems the most gravely wicked;—if indeed, among infinitely abhorrent things, it be not an absurd attempt to find the basest.

Hear this; and try to imagine any thing on the pages of the most diabolical calumniator, more diabolically calumnious?

"Whoever visits some estates, and witnesses the good-humored indulgence of some masters and mistresses, and the affectionate loyalty of some slaves, might be tempted to dream the oft-fabled poetic legend of a patriarchal institution and all that; *but over and above the scene, there broods a portentous shadow—the shadow of law.*"

How impossible, after reading this, thoughtfully, not to find one's imagination wandering far back to the garden scene, where innocence was perfect, peace undisturbed and happiness unalloyed? It was the blessed lot of a loving and loyal pair, until one entered the garden, and envied them, and plotted their ruin. It was DIABOLOS! THE SLANDERER! "The father of lies!"

He,—and not the law, under which they lived and loved; and but for him would still have found themselves protected in their possessions by that law,—*he* brooded over them as a portentous shadow—the shadow of death!

"The shadow of LAW," brooding over such a scene of patriarchal happiness, and ready to descend upon and make it a scene of misery! She would so have her duped victims to believe. But what law in particular is to do this Satanic deed?

Is it the law, which forbids the separation of mothers and children, and secures this blessing to the slave as it is no where secured to the poor hireling—the slave of stringent circumstances, which are daily separating parents and children?

Is it the law, which enjoins on the master to provide comfortably for slave children, and for the sick, and for the aged, as no law provides for the poor in any other condition?

Is it the law which provides that no slave shall be made to work more than a moderately prescribed number of hours? A law that the poor white man, under the despotic rule of his hard fate, would be unable to avail himself of, if made in his favor?

Or, is it the law which empowers and commands the magistrate to find a better master for an ill-treated slave? Is it either of these laws? But did Mrs. S. know of the existence of such laws? Aye; and that they are in force, and faithfully executed. Not better was it known by the first enemy of our race, that our primal parents were under a law divinely adapted to their peculiar circumstances to secure their happiness.

So much for Mrs. Stowe's "Shadow of Law." Ladies of England; is it not rather a rose-colored shadow? Does it not seem more like the brooding of a good, than of an evil spirit? This, however, is one of her bashful slanders. Alas!—a fact too shocking to be contemplated!—this terrific calumniator defames our Southern States, by charging them with being in a *conspiracy* against both justice and humanity! She charges all their executives, legislators, and judges, with the most awful and devilish corruption;—a corruption,—that, perhaps, no other human mind than her's was ever able to conceive, or to imagine! In most unmistakable terms, she frames the horrible slander,—worthy of the prime Slanderer himself,—that the laws of the South are "*so arranged*," as to allow masters to murder their slaves! Hear her:—

"Facts too shocking to be contemplated occasionally force their way to the public ear, and the comment one often hears made on them is more shocking than the thing itself. It is said, 'Very likely such cases may now and then occur, but they are no samples of general practice.'"

In passing to our main point,—is it indeed, more shocking, so *to say*, than *to do*, what is too horrible to be thought of? Let it be applied to the case of the murder of Dr. Parkman, in Boston; or to that parallel case in New York; or to any of a thousand mangling murders which the last year's newspapers recorded; and its absurdity will be transparent. I cannot think it very shocking,—if wicked at all—to say, and to hope, that the cases of men being murdered and dismembered by educated gentlemen of high standing in the community, in payment of a debt, are very rare and uncommon cases!

"If the laws of New England," she continues, "were so arranged that a master could NOW and THEN torture an apprentice to death without a possibility of being brought to justice, would it be received with equal composure? Would it be said these cases are rare, and no samples of general practice?" I should hope, indeed, it might be so said, without any shocking offence. If Dr. Webster's science had not been at fault as much as his purse, even he might have escaped.

But her slanders and insinuations, with her admirers, pass for arguments. If arguments, wherein is found their cogency? Are the laws of the South "so arranged" that a master may indeed openly murder his slave with impunity? Intentionally, *so arranged?* That is certainly her meaning. So, doubtless, she would be understood;—and then, the words yet remain to be invented, which may at all duly express the indignation and horror that such a calumny ought to excite!—must excite, every where, out of an "Ogre's den" of the malignest fanaticism!

Surely, she could not have presumed to find credit any where else; and least of all among the noble, and educated, and Christian ladies of England! And has her noble editor found no difficulty in the endorsement of so horrible a calumny?—and knowing as he does, that it *is* such calumny? Has madness fallen on the nobility and gentry of England, indicative of a coming destruction? May Heaven, in mercy, defeat the omen!

What! are all the Governors, Legislators, and Judges, so diabolically depraved, as to so conspire unanimously against justice and humanity, as to have framed,—" so arranged"—a system of statute laws for each and all the Slave States, as to allow masters, without fear of punishment, to murder their slaves? Are elections and appointments of executive and judicial functionaries so made as to secure the administration of the laws in accordance with such arrangement?

How deplorable must be the state of mind and heart of a human being who can imagine such wickedness!—such an extended and populous territory of deliberate murderers! What a reproach on the age or country in which such malignity can be popular! The subject is too revolting to dwell upon. It is a *fact too shocking to be contemplated*, that such a malignant calumny can be believed, and praised, and munificently rewarded!

It would be very strange, should it never happen, that a bad master, of an ungovernable and cruel temper, in a paroxysm of malicious passion, take the life of an offending slave, under circumstances in which the felony might be concealed. Perhaps, more strange still would it be, that there should be no such bad tempered men among the great body of slave-holders.

Wicked and bad tempered men are found every where; and every where the wicked do wickedly; and whoever, in any capacity, is under their rule, from the wife and child, down to the servant and the domestic animal, may suffer even death from their inhumanity. Such husbands have murdered their wives, and escaped unwhipt of justice; and such masters their apprentices and employes; and such superiors their subordinates, in every capacity and relation of life. And often, no doubt, do they escape detection and punishment. But who before ever heard of the laws of a country being so arranged that the guilty might go unpunished?

Can any thing possibly go beyond this? And yet, the ladies of England profess to believe it, and are organising a crusade to correct it; and the Earl of Carlisle has endorsed it with his noble name and title, and given it currency, by sealing it, perhaps, with his hereditary coat of arms! Does the noble Lord, also, disclaim political motives? Perhaps so; but woes will befall my country if such disclaimers are allowed as sincere and satisfactory.

Ladies of England; it is here believed and hoped that you have been beguiled into this injurious crusade against your friends; and that, not willingly, have you thus put yourselves in the wrong. If so, then, for your own, and for your country's sake; let your recantation be prompt and public, that otherwise inevitable "frightful results" may be avoided. On this side of the water it is clearly enough understood why your powerful influence has been thus employed; but in this, I hope respectful and friendly communication, it is taken for granted, that, *personally*, you have no political or sinister motive; nor other than humane and Christian motives.

But I must not leave Mrs. Stowe, till she is made to confess with sufficient precision, for all practical purposes, that she has deceived you into the unhappy notion that the slaves of the South are not allowed to be taught in the Gospel nor to enjoy Gospel privileges. How was it with Uncle Tom? His story is very edifying as regards this question. It is of incalculable value in several views of it. Fairly understood, it completely destroys its author's theory of the unmitigated evil of slavery; and it shows clearly, that the notion of the Women of England about the *interdiction*, is without foundation to rest upon.

Tom is represented to be, not only in a general sense, a Christian man, with a Christian family, but, an *eminently* Christian man—"a man of incorruptible fidelity, piety, and honesty." Nay, conclusive to the point: "The incorruptible fidelity, piety, and honesty of Uncle Tom, *had more than one development to her knowledge*." No doubt. Any where in the Slave States she might have found very many such developments.

But how is this?

Let us pause a moment and think!

Does she mean by this explicit declaration of personal knowledge, of an indefinite number of such incorruptible, faithful, pious, honest men, as Uncle Tom, that so much good can come out of such a Nazareth as Southern slavery?

How then can it be the altogether and horrible evil,—the "Ogre's den," which herself and school-party declare it to be?

Such results are certainly *not frightful*. An institution which can turn out a great number of such good Christians, must really have some good in it.

Ladies of England; please think of this; and be comforted by the assurance of your illustrious American sister, that many are the good and happy Christians among the Southern slaves; and, anon, I will delight your grateful hearts with *real*, truthful pictures—pictures of what I have seen—of happy Christian slaves in such multitudes as shall rejoice you with the pleasing conviction, that in their Christian privileges, of pastoral care and instruction, they are peculiarly, and uncommonly happy.

In passing, as a fit conclusion to this brief notice of the spiritual privileges of the Southern peasantry—there may be said, in anticipation of a more extended survey, what may astonish, but delight, the pious Ladies of England, that of the whole body of Southern slaves, a greater proportion of them are blessed with Christian privileges, than of the population of London, or New York; and that of those who profess to believe the Gospel, a far greater proportion are communicants in good standing, than of any people of our country, or of yours.

And now, Christian Ladies of England, pray be happy in the reassurance, that no such awful system obtains, on this side of the Atlantic, and most certainly not, either by statute or by custom, among the slaves of our Southern States, as "interdicts education in the truths of the Gospel and the ordinances of Christianity." Where else soever, to any race of man the Gospel is denied or withheld, it is not there. To whomsoever else the blessings and privileges of the Gospel ordinances are interdicted, they are not to the slaves of the South.

## CHAPTER IV.

### "A DEEPER DEEP."

"The weakness of man can never make that straight which God hath made crooked.—THORNWELL."

IT seems by their address, that these distinguished Ladies consider slavery as *inconsistent with God's Word; with the inalienable rights of immortal souls;* and with the pure and merciful spirit of *the Christian religion!*

Is it indeed so? Is this really your meaning, ladies, that slavery, *per se*, is inconsistent with God's Word? And that under any and every modification of justice and of mercy, slavery is more than other subordination,—more than poverty and its evils—inconsistent with the Christian religion?

If so be your meaning, your reading or understanding of God's Holy Word, differs much from mine; and not from mine only, but from all your own great divines and commentators; and from all Christian antiquity. I need not quote your own great teachers to show their agreement with the Bible in teaching the people that the government of masters, as well as of fathers, is an appointment of God, and therefore to be honored. In this connection, I say nothing of the authority of husbands, lest you erroneously suspect a desire to weaken your disclaimer of political motives.

That the Bible is full of recognitions of the institution of slavery; and of its charaeter as an instrument in the hands of God to chasten the idolatry of His chosen people; and to punish the nations that forget Him, in order to bring to their remembrance that doubtless, "verily there is a God that judgeth the earth,"—the Christian women of England, of all ranks, cannot require to be informed or reminded.

Here, therefore, I may be content with a short quotation from one of your late excellent divines, to exemplify how it is recognized in the Christian Scriptures, and still understood by Christian teachers of great wisdom and piety.

The late worthy and Rev. Mr. Nicholls, of Queen's College, Cambridge, in one of his most valuable works, "HELP TO THE READING OF THE BIBLE," thus notices the Epistle to Philemon.

"Philemon, to whom St. Paul wrote this Epistle, was an inhabitant of Colosse, and probably owed his conversion to the Apostle. Onesimus, his slave, had run away, and wandered to Rome, where he met with Paul, then a prisoner there, through whom he was converted to Christianity. The object of this Epistle, of which Onesimus was the bearer, was to persuade his master to receive him back, not merely as a slave, but with feelings of esteem as a fellow Christian. To accomplish this, the Apostle uses the most skilful address, touching with the greatest delicacy, yet with much force, on those points which were most likely to influence Philemon."

"We have here," as Paley remarks, "the warm, affectionate, authoritative teacher, interceding with an absent friend for a beloved convert; aged and in prison, content to supplicate and entreat, yet so as not to lay aside the respect due to his character and office."......While Onesimus, as a Christian, became the Apostle's son, and Philemon's brother, "*this in no respect interfered with the civil duties he owed to Philemon as his master.*"

It will be here perceived—profitably it is hoped—how the celebrated Dr. Paley, the Divine, and expositor of

Scripture, differs from Dr. Paley, the anti-slavery politician, and author of a system of moral philosophy, not inaptly styled "THE SELFISH SYSTEM,"—a great authority with abolitionists. V. also, Whitby, Tomline, McKnight, Grotius, *et al.*

But perhaps I may not understand aright the language of the Address of the Ladies of England. I wish it may be so on this point. Perhaps they may intend to speak only of the abuse of the institution, and not of the institution itself. If so, they will please pardon this diversion, which even so, may not be quite useless. Perhaps only to the *fancied frightful results,* they allude as not being in "accordance with God's Holy Word; the inalienable rights of immortal souls; and the pure and merciful spirit of the Christian religion."

If so, their unfortunate credulity is only to be commiserated. Not that there are no evils resulting from slavery. This it would be folly to pretend. Even "frightful results" are not denied. But if that is to be allowed as an argument against the institution, what institution is safe? What social, religious, civil, political; or of any other character, can bear such test?

In the abeyance of the institution of matrimony, civilisation could not exist. But countless thousands fall victims to its abuse. From ecclesiastical institutions, the most "frightfnl results" have ensued; but shall they be abolished, therefore? The institutions of Government and laws are indispensable. But do not "frightful results" flow from them in even rivers of blood? No other institution on earth may bear such test any better than the institution of Slavery.

The Women of England speak feelingly of "laws of our country which deny to the slave the sanctity of marriage; and separate at the will of the master, the wife from the husband, and the children from the parents."

Ladies; no doubt, from this movement of intervention, you believe that such laws exist in our statute books. And perhaps you suppose they are acted upon to the disruption of many slave families. It is not so, ladies, Christian masters encourage, and not deny to their slaves, "the sanctity of marriage, with all its joys, rights, and obligations," and never, "at their will," separate the wife from the husband, and the children from the parents. If it be done, it is their "strange work," not their willing. In my mission to the South, I married many pairs of slaves, who were in no more danger of being separated than any lord and lady of your land;—where, even *such* things have *sometimes* happened. In every case, in which I thought there was danger that man might put asunder what God had joined together, the masters were required to *obligate* themselves to prevent their being sundered. Pray believe this, ladies, for your comfort and for the correction of your erroneous belief drawn from the mischievous and unprincipled calumniators of our country and its institutions.

Families, in the Providence of God, both white and black, are lamentably often disrupted and dispersed. But for one family that is broken up by the institution of slavery in the South,—and that one by the visitation of God, the misfortune of the master, or the crime of the slave;—there are hundreds separated among free people, by cupidity, or other vice or crime, or by the oppressive power of poverty. Of the tens-of thousands of poor Irish labourers employed on our canals and railroads, &c.,—driven from home by an oppression worse than slavery,—a very small proportion have all their families with them; and very many of them never can have.

Ladies, unless your celebrated Mr. Dickens be as reckless a romancer as our Mrs. Stowe, your own institutions of Jurisprudence, alone, disrupt and ruin, in person and estate, many more families than do our institutions of

Slavery. But the fancies of romance aside, the authenticated facts communicated by your Parliamentary investigations of the working of your poor laws, and even of your poor-house reports, tell of such cruelties as are utterly unknown to our system of slavery, and in such numbers as to make any heart but one of stone to bleed, if not to break!

Aye, Ladies of England, finally,—pray your pardon if any thing offensive to your tastes be found herein;—if our slaves were made to endure but the tithe of the cruelties that are visited continually on the poor of Europe, in hardships, in family disruptions, in destitution of every comfort of life; in famine, in starvation, in carelessness for their souls, as well as for their bodies, then well might the Women of England unite in appeal to the Women of America, to interfere for their amelioration. But even then, would it not seem as reasonable for them, to raise their voices of sympathy, and to employ their full and jewelled hands of charity, to relieve their own poor, down-trodden, and suffering people?

Ladies, permit one parting word of sound counsel:—

"To do good, and to distribute, forget not; for with such sacrifices God is well pleased."

"Be merciful after your power;" and "provide for the sick and needy."

And when none nearer require your aid; O then, come, and help us; and what you lay out "shall be paid you again."

# CHAPTER V.

## MEMORY OF THE SOUTH.

VERY pleasant is the memory of having found comfort, where discomfort was expected to be found, and joys, where sorrows were looked for; and happiness, where I had been taught that only misery could dwell. This pleasure of memory is a boon of great value to my declining life, in my almost solitary retirement, in the narrow valley of the upper Delaware. It is usually obedient to my behest, too, to cheer my solitude; and never more pleasant, than when it revives some of the unlooked for scenes of the sunny South, among the joyous children of the Sun in servitude; with whom I had been taught to look for unhappiness alone. Almost twenty years ago, my thoughts were turned towards the South, in the hope of benefit to a constitution impaired by the wear and tear of northern life, to which it was not originally well adapted. By the urgent suggestion of many anxious friends, I should have gone South, long years before; but that from an unfortunate prejudice, I had contracted a loathing dislike of the Southern institution of slavery.

I had seen misery and suffering in many and dreadful forms among the poor; and often with added oppression by the less poor, and by the rich. Often had I seen women and children turned out of doors; and their little furniture sold by the law, to pay the rent of the wretched habitation, from which they had been ejected, and thrown upon the cold charity of a cold world. And, in my frail health, I trembled with the painful apprehension of seeing more cruel things at the South—chains and lashes and mangled limbs—human beings treated as beasts of prey!

Often had I seen the unhappy laborer in a vain and sad pursuit of leave to toil for food and fuel, to save his poor wife and children from hunger and cold; and I have seen the grateful tear bathe his honest and hardy cheek, when gratuitous relief was urged upon him. Recently had I witnessed the sweeping death by cholera, breaking into the abodes of poverty, unresisted; and gorging himself unrebuked, and undisturbed by the also well-fed mortals around—*calling themselves Christians!*

By some strange and unhappy, but perhaps not uncommon illusion, I had been impressed by the false and injurious notion, that a cruel bondage of the southern slave was an *addition* to all these sufferings of northern poverty.

It was with neither views nor hopes, of finding relief from the illusion, that, on an early day in November, with trembling reluctance, I stepped on the deck of a ship bound for Charleston; where I looked to witness the very horrors of slavery. Among the passengers,—some going in pursuit of health, and some returning to their homes to enjoy its possession,—there were several agreeable southern ladies; and three southern gentlemen, of characteristics too well marked, to be easily forgotten. One of them was a no mean poet—now a celebrated and favorite author, in both prose and poetry; the others, a father and son, of the best class of planters. The poet had been making a northern tour for *amusement,* in the primitive meaning of the term. The father had accompanied his charming family, for the improvement of their mental and physical health by travel; and the son, an intelligent, robust, gentle, and joyous young man of twenty, had passed a portion of the season in superintending the work of a piano maker in the erection of an instrument for his own use. He had with him a German teacher of music and mathematics.

So unexpectedly pleasant was our voyage, that some of us, outward bound, would willingly have protracted it. On the third day, having passed "Mason's and Dixon's Line," the general conversation of the passengers, easily and naturally fell into the discussion of Southern Slavery. Some of us turned away from the subject with deep distaste, as one that should be *tabooed* in every promiscuous company; lest some super-sensitive philanthropist should perchance be too painfully shocked.

At that time, blinded by a sickly and ignorant prejudice, I should have vied with the rabidest of abolitionists in gloating over the down-trodden law of the land and of all lands, tolerating the abominable thing. This, per se, is not a pleasant memory. It is humiliating, to be obliged to admit, among the happy things of memory, such a justly mortifying recollection of a disgraceful and degrading prejudice. It even makes me shudder to think of it!

But then, I find a miserable comfort—still a comfort—in the knowledge, that far greater, wiser, and better men, have been not less deeply involved in the same palpable darkness. When Wilberforce, and Clarkson, with their illustrious compeers; and the whole body of Friends—among them many wise and excellent persons, come up before my mind's eye;—and when I think of all these, as devoting their lives and talents, and making great personal and pecuniary sacrifices, to abolish negro slavery;—when I remember Johnson's toast of 'Success to the next Jamaica insurrection;'—when I hear, above the thunder of the Mountain of the Decalogue, the maxim of Dr. Channing—'Any thing but Slavery!'—and now, especially, when the titled, and other excellent women of

England, are found weeping over the fictions of negro sufferings, and with bleeding hearts, appealing to the women of America, to aid in the holy cause of softening them; I feel boldness to look back on my former self with less of displacency.

But to return from this digression to the conversation on the ship's deck. It soon became animated, and unexpectedly interesting. My attention was irresistibly arrested by the strangely sounding declaration of the father, before named :—

"Had I my life to live over again, and could I advisedly make my choice, to be either the master of a large number of good slaves, or the slave of a good master, so far as the ease and comfort of life are concerned, I am sure my judgment would prefer the latter. I cannot say I should so choose," he added; "for pride, or vanity, or some other folly or vice, might influence me to choose less wisely."

He was one of the most sober, calm, and sensible of men, and from his character and manner, it was impossible to question his sincerity. He was gazed at by many of us with surprise; but not unmingled with reverence; for he had already been received among us as the true and accredited representative of all that is excellent in man :— piety, purity, honesty, and benevolence.

"You present an even stronger case than does the author of the 'West India Journal,' M. G. Lewis," said the poet, "in favor of the negro's condition in slavery."

"What says the Monk?" said the younger Mr. R. "In 1816, he thus wrote, what, unfortunately, remained till this year, in manuscript, in consequence of his death, on his return voyage two years later :

"If I were now standing on the banks of Virgil's Lethe, with a goblet of the waters of oblivion in my hand, and asked whether I chose to enter life anew, as an

English laborer or a Jamaica negro, I should have no hesitation in preferring the latter."

"That was saying very little in commendation of the condition of the slave," remarked an English Chartist; "for I would prefer to be of the race of the Baboon, than be of the degenerate race of English laborers,—man, woman, or child,—dwarfed and deformed, as the mass of them are physically; and mentally and morally depraved almost to the level of the brute; and many of the less miserable below, by hunger, hardship, and hatred. But the declaration of Mr. R. surprises me."

"And some other of our fellow passengers," respectfully added the poet, "seem to look on your declaration as coming in a *questionable shape.*"

"It is quite true," remarked one of the northern invalids, "we have been accustomed to hear slavery spoken of far otherwise than as a desirable condition; and for one, I should feel myself obliged by an explanation of the paradox, that the condition of a good slave of a good master, is happier than that of the good master of a good slave."

"Such, I believe," replied the venerable man, "were not my words, exactly; for they would contradict one of my most cherished and favorite principles;—that the truly good are equally happy in all conditions or stations of life. My meaning was,—perhaps not as definitely expressed as it should have been—that, as far as comfort is concerned, the condition of the slave is quite as desirable as that of the master,—the master and man both being what they ought to be in their respective stations. And this may be easily explained and verified; paradox as it may seem, or sound."

In an *aside,* by a passenger,—"nothing can make slavery desirable."

"Yes, *comparatively;*" in an under tone, said the poet, "and generally, if not always, for the negro race."

The momentary interruption was not observed by Mr. R., and he resumed:

"Perhaps the most satisfactory explanation I can give, may be in the way of personal narrative of my experience."

All ears were open, and attentions riveted.

## COMFORTS OF SLAVES.

"At my first coming to manhood, I was the only son of my mother, and she a widow. My father had died and left her with four children, myself and three younger sisters. During her life, as the widow of our father, she was to remain in the proprietorship of the estate and head of the family. When their school days were over, so long as they should remain unmarried, my sisters were to aid me in the management of the estate and household, under the eye and approbation of our mother; and when married, with her consent, certain legacies were to be paid them from an accumulated fund, and from the produce of the plantation; but not by infringement on it. It was not to be diminished in size, nor the number of the people, by sale or purchase, to be either diminished or increased.

"It had been the unvarying rule of my father, that no negro child was to be taken from the personal care of its mother until ten years old; and no old man or woman be required to work after seventy. This rule was to be religiously pursued. It has been, and will be; and under it we have a dozen or more old people, all things considered, more comfortable than I expect to be, should I live to their age.

"By a provision in my father's will, the system was to be forever continued, of allotments of land to each family of negroes, equal to an acre for each member, betwen ten and seventy, with time to work it equal to half a day in every week; that the Lord's day might never be desecrated by secular employment.

"In addition to their allowed exemption from labor for their owners, by early rising to their prescribed tasks, they could gain more than ample time for all the purposes of their own culture. By this pleasant arrangement, which is usual among the planters of my acquaintance, the enterprising and industrious portion of the negroes, by early rising, have the most, if not all of every afternoon in the cropping season to work their own grounds; or if this is not required, to do extra work, if they choose on the plantation, for which they receive full pay. In fact, several fine fellows on my plantation, by the aid of the exempts of their family, for months together, eat their breakfast after finishing their day's work. The negroes prefer late breakfasts.

"The cabins, or rather cottages, of all these are, at the least, as comfortable as their master's mansion; and if they are so disposed, as well supplied with extra comforts, which they are not less able than he to procure. The income of several of them this year will be not less than from fifty to seventy-five dollars.

"In addition to their ample allowance of meat, bread, and vegetables, my negroes may supply themselves at pleasure, with fish, clams, oysters, &c., or with game from the woods or shores. Their living is therefore not only abundant, but if they choose, luxurious. The ugly fear of want, they know nothing about. In a bad season, many a planter may find himself embarrassed to provide ways and means; but no such embarrassment ever reaches them. Whatever else may fail, their food and raiment must not fail, though ruin descend on the master. Nothing is more common, than a stress of circumstances in unfavorable seasons, to make it necessary for the family of whites on a plantation, to deny themselves many a common indulgence, that the negroes may not be denied any of their usual comforts.

"Another circumstance in their favor is not less obvious

or striking. All told, including about thirty distinct families, there are, of our out household, or plantation negroes, about two hundred. Among so many of all ages, from infancy up to very old age,—from seventy to almost a hundred, five or six of them—there are few nights in the year, in which I am not disturbed,—often more than once—to attend to some complaint of indisposition, and to administer remedies. When I am abroad, which is seldom, that not easy office is in the special charge of a competent person specially employed for the purpose; and with authority to call a physician at discretion. But not one of those negroes is ever disturbed of his rest on account of any sickness of myself or family. All their rights and rests are inviolable. And now," said the good man, blushing as if he had been unaccustomed to talk so long at a time, and owed an apology to us;—"And now, I hope the paradox of the slave having a more comfortable life than the master, is satisfactorily explained." And he left us to join his family in the cabin.

No statement that he had made; no word that he had spoken, was doubted by any of us.

By several of the northern passengers, frank declarations were made that they had received some quite new ideas, and new impressions, of southern slavery.

"But," said the poet, "you must not expect to find all masters like Mr. R. He has always felt his great responsibility deeply, as a Christian master of slaves; and with his best powers and faculties, he fulfils its obligations, faithfully and affectionately. Among all the apostles, there was but one St. John."

"And but one Judas," interposed a bystander.

"True," continued the poet; "and if there be not found among slaveholders,—as I think there are not,—a greater proportion who shamefully and cruelly betray their trust, there would seem no good reason for the wholesale condemnation of the institution; which we are so often pained to hear, knowing as we do, that the laboring negroes of the South are so far more comfortable than the laboring poor, both white and black, at the North."

"And yet," said one, "Slavery is still slavery."

"Yes; and poverty is still poverty; and misery is still misery; and evil, of every kind, is still evil; and it is likely, for a long time to come, to remain so. Every condition of life has its own peculiar evils; and that would seem the most desirable which has the least and the fewest."

# CHAPTER VI.

## CHARLESTON.

DURING several days detention in Charleston, awaiting a passage to the Land of Flowers, we had the advantage of seeing slavery in various aspects. The working of the system was found by us, northern strangers, very different from the anticipations with which we left home. At our landing we found no lack of drays and coaches; but happily, an entire absence of the boisterous and angry competition, among the drivers, which so annoys and often terrifies, at least the female portion of northern travellers.

At the hotel, without blustering or noise; and in quiet cheerfulness, the servants of the house—all slaves—attended to us courteously, and in the apparent spirit of cordial hospitality. From what we had heard on shipboard, and from all that here appeared for days together, we began to have dreamy thoughts of the Southern slave, as rescued from the curse of the fall, in a peculiar and almost paradisiac sense; unknown to other conditions of human life!

So extremes meet. Too soon we found ourselves undeceived. Some of the evils incident to our fallen race, cleave still to the lot of man in all conditions. A scene, such as at home we had been accustomed to think of with unmitigated horror, presented itself:—an auction sale of negroes. The very thought was revolting! Happily, we looked in vain for the barbarous pictures and incidents that so often we had heard and read of

It was a solemn, but not a barbarous scene. Hundreds of people were collected; but not a smile even appeared on any countenance; nor one uncivil or discourteous remark heard. Men spoke in whispers to each other. The voice even of the auctioneer was subdued and respectful, exceedingly. It appeared like any thing else than an ordinary northern auction sale, of even the furniture of a ruined family, such as, alas, I had often been so unhappy as to witness.

The slaves were intelligent and very neat looking house-servants of a family fallen into a melancholy embarrassment. Their late head,—a man of munificent benevolence, had died insolvent. The servants seemed sorrowful, but not overwhelmed. Some tears they shed on perceiving the approach of a young man in deep mourning. He was the much-loved surviving son of their late master. He had come from his weeping mother and sisters, with words of comfort for them, which caused their old Christian mother to exclaim with clasped hands and lifted eyes, 'Thank the Lord! thank the Lord!' and, adding, as she looked with piety and love on the younger ones, 'I told you, my children, that the dear Lord would not forsake the widow and the fatherless, nor the faithful servants, of our good master.' And their silent tears fell fast at the name and thought of the 'good master,' gone to the better Master.

The consoling message, brought them by the young man, informed them that they were to be sold together, to remain in the city; and that the privilege had been secured to the family of a repurchase without advance. The pleasant result was, that they were purchased by a friend of the family, and sent quietly away with their young master, to gladden the *sad hearts* of the mourning widow and her fatherless family. It was a scene of much interest and feeling; but by no means an uncommon one in the generous South.

This sober and feeling scene of the drama passed away; and another of a quite different character came forward upon the stage. Some half a dozen—a whole family of field hands, came forward;—real Guinea negro looking ones,—laughing and joking, and playing monkey tricks with one another. In this manner and spirit they mounted the stand; were at once sold off in a lot; and they marched off with their new master in apparent delight, full of fun and frolic. Yet they were going from the easier work of a cotton, to a sugar plantation; which, though heavier labor, is a negro's ideal of paradise on earth.

As there are ofttimes compulsory removals and dispersions of people, of a very painful nature, in every other condition of life; so, undoubtedly, like evils await and befal the negro slave. But yet I am quite confident—and have the fullest right to be so—that the enterprises and necessities; the artificial conventionalisms,—the vices and crimes of northern life, cruelly disrupt more families, and effect more unwilling and unfortunate removals, by a thousand times, than southern slavery ever does. This in passing to a happier theme; and in ill accordance with the unfortunate notion of the Duchess of Sutherland and her associates, that the slaves of the South are interdicted, by their condition, the privileges and blessings of the Gospel and the church.

With much of surprise, and with high and grateful pleasure, I learned practically, that in Charleston, no class of people whatsoever, had more spiritual privileges, or pastoral care, than the slave population; and that none better availed themselves of them, or more heartily enjoyed them. Beautifully blessed was the sight, when, on a Lord's day, I beheld, of more than a hundred colored communicants of that class of Christians—models of cleanliness, and patterns of reverential propriety—partaking at the same sacred banquet, of the consecrated elements, with their masters and mistresses! And in every church in the city—now many more than then—the same grateful scene may be witnessed; and in several of them, in very far larger numbers!

Surely, great is the error of the women of England, in supposing that southern slavery is that awful system which interdicts to any race of man, or any portion of the human family, education in the truths of the Gospel and the ordinances of Christianity! But this greatly interesting subject of the SPIRITUAL FREEDOM of the southern slave, here but alluded to, will be found more at length discussed under its proper head.

## CHAPTER VII.

### PASSAGE TO ST. AUGUSTINE.

In our pleasant passage of three days to St. Augustine, we witnessed with wonder and delight, the sublime, enchanting, and most gorgeous phenomenon, of the descent of a protracted shower of meteors, which frightened and alarmed so many people on the night of the 13th Nov., 1833. It was a glorious sight beyond any thing our eyes had ever beheld, or ever again are likely to behold in this world.

A brief description of it may not be quite uninteresting. The previous sunset was remarkable, and a fitting herald of the approaching wonder—the coming glories of the night.

As the sun descended to near the horizon of the blue waters of the ocean, it seemed quite shorn of its own radiating beams, and to be set as a crimson picture in a metallic frame of alternate, divergent bars of gold and bronze. In that glorious setting, it seemed to sink slowly, and with majestic beauty and splendor into the azure water. It was to merge on the morrow with added glory.

In the night we were called on deck to behold what seemed much to alarm some of our crew and passengers,—a shower of gold, and silver, and purple fire, falling from a clear blue sky—thousands of meteors, of the kind commonly called falling, or shooting stars; yet varying in color from silver to purple, and in apparent size, from that of an apparent star, to nearly or quite that of a full moon!

They seemed to start from their high home in the very

zenith of the heavens, and there to separate, following in their descent the imaginary curved lines of an immense dome. Thus, for hours, these brilliant meteors were constantly descending and flying athwart the horizon.

In the depth of the night, when several of the larger class were in full blaze at the same time, the stars became invisible; and some of the crew declared "they *must* be stars that are falling." With gradually diminishing glory, this brilliant phenomenon continued till nearly sunrise. And what a sunrise followed! As he had gone down into it, the glorious orb of day ascended from below the ocean wave, with a majesty well becoming the grandeur of the display which had heralded his advent.

All the works of God are wonderful, sublime, beautiful! but never before had I been so conscious of the full influence of their wondrous sublimity, or of being entranced by their surpassing beauty, as when on that broad ocean of blue, under a sky of blue, pouring forth myriads of such beautiful things.

## ST. AUGUSTINE.

The scene had well prepared me for the approaching spectacle on shore. A narrow passage, between two long and narrow islands, took our little craft over the bar into the snug harbor of St. Augustine; and there in quiet repose lay before us the old city, embowered in orange trees loaded with their golden fruit. It was a quite novel and most luxuriant view;—a foreign scene brought home to our own country. It was a very pleasant surprise. Nor did the pleasure pass away with the surprise. A delightful refuge from the boreal storms, was that old Spanish town;—a soothing rest, it offered to the grieved and care-worn soul and shattered frame. But, alas! in two short years came the killing frost, and the desolating war; and its comforts and its quiet, and, all its goodliness passed away, never again to be restored! An hundred frostless winters may bring back the glorious old trees loaded with twenty barrels each of the rarest varieties of the orange; and the towering oleander may spring up; but the old population, in their old Spanish houses, of various tongues and nations, and all living in loving harmony, and happiness, may never again be hoped for.

Yes, they were indeed happy. Avarice and ambition seemed quite unknown among them; and good-natured simplicity appeared to be the rule of social intercourse, with most rare exceptions. And of all that happy population, the negro slaves seemed most happy.

Not easy to be forgotten, is my first definite vision of the contrast between the two conditions,—negro slavery, as it exists in our South, among the good and generous —a mere *quasi* bondage, strongly resembling that of the freed-man of ancient Rome,—and of negro freedom—a mere *quasi* liberty, without the protection of the freedman,—manumitted, but not forsaken;—still under the shielding patronage of his former master.

Besides the prevailing gold and green, and rich aroma of the orange tree, the gardens and hedges were fragrant and brilliant with many colored and sweet flowers. Various birds were singing in all directions. The saucy mocking bird was mimicking all the rest; and occasionally pausing in his song to laugh the caged parrots out of countenance. But the loudest music, was the laughing, and whistling, and singing of the negroes proceeding to their easy tasks of the day.

It was a panoramic vision. It was a delightful morning walk through the old city;—a little exploring ramble, to learn its strange and pleasant peculiarities. My cicerone was an intelligent little boy of twelve summers,—the only son of my host, a principal man of the territory.

We threaded the narrow streets and lanes. We passed through, and around the PLAZA, or public square. We deciphered the marred inscription on the last remaining monument erected in honor of the Spanish constitution, in the centre of the square. This is a simple little obelisk of some ten feet high; but not destitute of historical interest. On his restoration to power, the infamous Ferdinand, with one foot on the constitution, and the other on the necks of his subjects, commanded all memorials of it to be demolished.

The people of Florida were no longer his subjects; and the little monument, carefully and lovingly wrapped up in a nice bit of bunting, with some stars and stripes upon it,—still stands the only memorial of the kind, that the people of Old Spain, some forty years ago, had a paroxysm of love for constitutional liberty!

We passed through the old Castilian gateway, (which ought to have been preserved,) into the spacious court of the antique Spanish Government house, long since replaced by a modern Court-house of fair dimensions, and fronting the plaza; on the opposite side of which stand the markets. On the two other opposite sides, stand an old and spacious Roman Catholic, and a pretty and modern Protestant church. On the square, and around all these public buildings, young negroes, with here and there a young Minorcan, or Spanish boy, were seen at play, or sucking oranges, or sugar cane. And I sighed to think of the hard lot of the thousands of little boys in the North, shivering in the cold and dwarfed by toilsome labor!

But Governor Seymour says, "Our ideal of a respectable man is one who thinks only of his business, and works himself to death." Under the guidance of such an ideal, if "the boy is" to be "the father of the man," he must go early to his task, that he may be prepared for such respectability. And thus multitudes are worked to death, to prepare them for working themselves to death! Return we now to our own ramble among a people happily ignorant of our northern "ideal of respectability."

Through gardens and orange groves, we made our cheerful way. The morning air of that delicious climate acted as a much needed healing balm to both my flesh and spirits. I was happy; and I rejoiced to behold on all hands, unmistakable manifestations of happiness, at every look around me. My little companion and guide seemed to know every body, and every thing; and to enjoy, very highly, the pleasure of answering all my questions; and of pointing out to me every thing rare, curious, and beautiful. I remarked to him, that all the negroes we met, seemed very cheerful and happy. He replied:

"Yes, sir; I believe they are almost always laughing and singing, only when they are eating or sleeping."

"But, William, don't they have to do a great deal of hard work?"

"No, sir; they always seem to make play of their work;—like those fellows yonder in the trees, picking oranges to send to New York, and throwing them at each other's head."

"On the plantations, William, they say the negroes have very hard work."

"May be, on some plantations they have to work hard; but I was out to Hanson's the other day to see them making sugar; and all the negroes seemed to make a frolic of cutting and toting the cane. I have seen some poor white men seem to work very hard; but I don't remember to have seen negroes seem to work very hard."

In the course of our ramble we met a black man who appeared care-worn and gloomy; sad and sorrowful; and not as well clad as were usually the people of his color. And I said, "William, that man looks unhappy. I am afraid he has a hard master." He replied:

"O sir; he is a free man; and a bad fellow, people say."

My heart sank within me. A free man; and yet not only worse off, but worse than a slave!

A free man, who is a bad fellow, whether black or white, has *indeed* a hard master. For some reason, not yet discovered and made clear by Anti-Slavery philosophers, this kind of hard master, who rules with a rod of iron over all bad fellows—all vicious people of all conditions and sexes,—seems the most hard on the poor free negroes. He scourges them without mercy, and without measure. In droves, he sends them, through the cold and dark avenues of vice and crime, to the scaffold, to the penitentiary, to the lunatic asylum; or to die of debauchery, or of cold, or hunger; in a filthy ditch, or a filthier cellar or garret! Poor, unhappy creatures! how cruel to throw upon them the weight of a responsibility, which not one in fifty is found able to walk uprightly under! How less cruel than death towards them are the northern States, which persuade and help them to *steal* the burthen; and then scourge them from their borders, because they are unable to carry it, and know not what to do with it?

This is a painful subject; and I will only add,—if, to exterminate the African race from our country, be the real object of the Anti-Slavery party, they can adopt no wiser course, than to encourage their flight from their protectors; to resist the fugitive slave law; and to induce the largest possible number of free negroes to stay in, and hang about the cities and villages of the North.

How very strange does it seem, that in Christian lands, and by Christian people, slavery is spoken of as Christianity never speaks of it; and that among the philosophers of our age, the term is limited, as it was not limited by the philosophers of old?

By the Great Teacher, Himself, we are taught that, "Whosoever committeth sin is the servant, or slave of sin." And by the letter and spirit of His religion, though you may scorn to call any man master on earth, you may still be in a galling and a degrading bondage. You may be rich as Crœsus, learned as Bacon, and versed in all the knowledge of the profoundest statesman, and able to solve every question, of civil and political liberty, and yet be slaves; and under the sway of a more cruel tyrant than ever wielded an earthly sceptre.

The real slaves among the southern negroes form but a very small proportion of the real slavery of even our own country; the Bible and philosophy being judges. As the Bible teaches, they only are truly free, who, in bondage to Christ,—servants of God,—have and live by this truth, which only can make free indeed—free from sin, free from the bondage of Satan, free from the wretched servitude of the world—all else are slaves indeed; and not merely in name—slaves to their own lusts, to the world, and the devil;—all harder than Egyptian taskmasters.

And what says the wisdom of the wise heathen? "Who is not a slave to lust, avarice, ambition, or fear? No bondage is more grievous than that which is voluntary." So says Seneca; and the greater Plato, "Count no one free who is intent to indulge wicked passions. They serve more cruel masters, than do slaves by inheritance or purchase who are bound to obedience."

"All wicked and covetous men are slaves," says Tully.

## PLANTATION NEGROES.

Having had strange things brought to my ears on board ship; having seen the slaves of Charleston in the enjoyment of apparent enviable happiness; and having seen but one unhappy negro in St. Augustine, and he a free man, my prejudices against slavery, as injurious to the negro race, were becoming feeble, when I had occasion to make a journey of some days through the interior. I wandered a good deal about the country among villages and plantations; but I found no materials to repair the breaches so unexpectedly made in my tower of anti-slavery, that would at all stand the weather.

I went into the cabins of the slaves, and I found them luxurating on more plentiful and better food than I had ever found general among the laborers of the North—either white or black. In many cases—perhaps every one, of honest thriftiness—their own fowls supplied them with chickens and eggs; and their own cows with milk and butter. Of bush swine—the very best for the far South—some of them had scores.

The Christmas and New Year's holidays were near, and extra preparations were every where being made for distinguishing this great season of festivity. Exclusive of the vicious indulgences which marked the ancient pagan feast, the Christmas season, to the Southern negro, is a real Saturnalia. Only for large pay, or for real love, and then as a special favor, will he lend his aid even to keep the system in motion of his master's household.

"But of what value are all these privileges and pleasures to people deprived of the privileges and pleasures of religion?"

We shall see if such deprivations belong to their condition.

## CHAPTER VIII.

### THE WEDDING—CHRISTIAN SLAVES—SLAVERY A MISSIONARY INSTITUTION.

On the first day of Feb., with some northern friends, I was at the celebration of a double marriage, some thirty miles from St. Augustine, in the interior. The May-like weather had already filled the country with spring flowers and fragrance. From the piney woods, with here and there a little oasis, of oaks, magnolias, palms, or bays,—hiding places of the deer, and wild turkey,—we passed suddenly into an extensive orange grove,—each tree a study of grace, color, beauty, and perfume, beyond the reach of art. The grove was fenced and diversified with long extended hedges of lemon, lime, and other tropical growths.

Through a more lovely avenue, than, on this earth, we shall ever again pass, we came to the cottage built, and modest mansion. It was on the banks of a broad and beautiful river; and almost literally covered with the freshly bloomed *rosa multiflora*. By many species of the fruit-trees of various climes, in full flower, the buildings and lawns were begirdled and decorated.

With polite cordiality, we were received by the numerous white family; and, as connected in their minds, with the coming happy event, with the most joyous delight by the negroes. All in sleek health and neatly dressed, their joyousness seemed natural and unalloyed.

We arrived in the early morning and passed the day charmingly. Not the smallest of the charms of the day, was that of the pleasure to witness the various delightsome amusements of the sable subordinates of the establishment, to which their superiors contributed in no stinted measure.

In the early deep darkness of the evening, the marriage came off; and no sooner were the solemnities closed in the deepest and most reverential silence, within and without, than the whole outer atmosphere seemed in a blaze of light and beauty, and filled through all its space with sounds of huzzas and of songs of joy and gladness. There was not one present, even of the household, who was not manifestly surprised. It was the entire invention and work of the negroes themselves.

The long evening passed off with unmarred and chastened hilarity. All acted well their parts; but best of all, the black party. The delightful, and gratefully satisfied air with which each one of them saluted the new married pairs,—"Wish you joy, Mis'r Col. and Mas'r Major; wish you joy, Miss Caroline and Miss Leonora; and may the Good Lord bless you all;" though a rather lengthened affair, it was highly and solemnly interesting.

Our enjoyments, in the house, of the evening festivities, were not slight nor tasteless; but still poor and vapid, compared with the apparent, and undoubtedly real pleasures of the negroes on the illuminated lawn, brilliant with the beauties, and fragrant with the sweets of nature and of art.

On the following day, most of the wedding party crossed the broad river on a visit to some interesting relatives of the wedded ones—a very highly respectable old family; who had never sold a slave, though they had a considerable number; nor had the present generation ever purchased one. Their negroes had no more fear of being sold than have our children, nor were they in half the danger of being separated.

They seemed a happy family, and well to deserve to be; but unless all signs fail, and all appearances deceive, the happiness of the negroes was most complete and unqualified. The negroes, on both sides of the river, on the beautiful plantations belonging to very intelligent descendants of old British settlers, were themselves uncommonly intelligent negroes ; and no doubt our abolition friends to a man and to a woman, would have pronounced them all well worthy and well prepared for freedom and self-management. But when I think of their happy condition, in contrast with the miserable and life-long struggle for subsistence, of our free negroes of the North, I am hardly able to imagine a more cruel act than it would have been to emancipate them. But of negro emancipation more hereafter.

Making our parting salutations to our agreeable friends, who were all of the Roman Church, we early returned with the wedding party, in order to examine a number of candidates for baptism among the slaves of our host. Through grace, and the enlightened instruction of their pious and excellent master, it was most gratifying to find them all—so far as man may be allowed to judge—unusually well prepared, in spirit and understanding, for the solemn rite. And with a large number of young children and infants, in all more than fifty, they were baptized in the evening.

Had the pious duchesses and ladies of England been so happy as to witness that solemnity,—the master and mistress, in fervent Christian love and devotion, taking on themselves the most solemn obligations of sponsors for their slaves,—I think it would never have come into their imaginations, that the slaves of our South are precluded from the privileges of the Gospel and the church. Alas ! the wrongful notion, that at least the plantation negroes are denied religious privileges, is by no means peculiar to the ladies of England

It is rather extensively supposed, that in southern cities, the slaves have some religious privileges; and that a few avail themselves of them; but the question, or an equivalent for it, may often be heard in the North,—"are not the plantation negroes heathens?"

I wish an unqualified negative could be given to that question. But I am afraid that among the country negroes, some of whom are so unfortunate as to have practically heathen masters—but not in a greater proportion than the *sons* of the North have such fathers,—I am indeed afraid, there are not a few slaves who are little better than heathens, though not altogether, as were their forefathers in Africa.

Yet in all my rambles for thirteen years through our Southern States, I have never found nor heard of, as I can remember,—and assuredly not among the negroes born in our land,—such utter blankness of mind with regard to religion, as is often found in our northern cities among white people; and as found described, as not uncommon, in a large portion of the modern literature of Europe; and,—sorry am I to be obliged to say it—especially of England, whose voice is so loudly heard, calling us to our duty towards our neglected slaves, and to a greater care for their souls.

Both children and slaves are, no doubt, in the North and South, too much neglected; and too few of us care, as we ought, for their souls; but from an extensive personal experience, from correspondence, and from authentic documents, I am confident that the amount of practical heathen infidelity among southern slaves, bears even a very small proportion to that which may be found but too easily, among the population of our cities, and many of our rural districts.

In remarkable and striking coincidence with the developements in England of the brutal atheism of numerous white savages, as described by the late Chancellor of the Exchequer,—some years since, there were reported and published cases in one of our own cities, of persons of various adult ages, and of both sexes, who were utterly ignorant of the meaning of religion—without any sense of religious and moral obligation, and who had never heard of the Saviour!

Over the revolting accounts of their beastly characters, let the curtain fall, while we ask the harrowing question, 'Is the case better now?' The very latest intelligence from the same city, says, "The increase of the population far outruns the increased means of religious instruction." And in refence to this very statement, a religious paper of another of our large cities, says,—"Is it better with us?"

Should any one desire to know whether the slaves of the South are spiritually better or worse off, than the tens of thousands of the uncared-for in our cities, and the hundreds of thousands in the greater cities of Europe, let him examine the statistics of crime and degradation in those cities; and then let him inquire of the devoted men employed in the hard and trying work of city missions; and he will learn of cases of heathen darkness in ample abundance, to solve the awful problem of the frightful increase of crimes of the most abhorrent character. Indeed, crimes such as no code of penal laws ever contemplated, have already become so frequent in large cities as scarcely to excite surprise!

Yet, in all our great cities, this terrific state of things is overlooked, and quite lost sight of, by men and women, who organize crusades against an institution afar off, which utterly excludes, and makes impossible such frightful abominations of crime and beastly degradation.

And from the Greater Metropolis of England,—where the uncared for, but by the police, form a population of white savages equal to the whole population of one of our small States—a wailing lamentation comes across the broad ocean, over the condition of our slaves, who are incomparably both better and better off—not merely than her white savages and starving paupers—but than a very large majority of her hard working laborers chained to the block of their cruel fate, and lashed by their wretched condition to perform an amount of toilsome work, the half of which the hardest master never dreams of exacting from a far better fed slave!

And then how unkindly offensive is the calumny that the slaves' souls are uncared for, in connection with the real facts of the case, that in many portions of the South, extending over very large districts, and containing many ten thousands of the colored race, all of them are enrolled by name as belonging to Christian congregations; receiving regular stated instructions; subject to religious discipline; and participating in all gospel privileges. Of the entire population of any of our northern States, there is probably not a greater proportion than among the slaves of the South, in the full enjoyment of those priceless privileges. And what is the proportion of the human beings in London, who are so blest?—or of the great manufacturing towns of Great Britain?

Abolition Authors and Editors; Legislators and Lecturers, hold and teach that slavery makes man a brute; by depriving him of all rights and privileges. Let this be granted, and taken as a true definition of slavery; and what follows? Why, inevitably this follows, that there is a smaller proportion of the Southern negroes in servitude, who are slaves, according to this their true definition, than of this, or perhaps any other country called free; for there is a smaller proportion of them brutalized by vice, crime, and infidelity;—the only true brutalizers—that is, there is a larger proportion of them made "free indeed," by the TRUTH.

Perhaps, on the face of the whole earth, there may not be found a promiscuous body of people, of equal numbers, having a greater proportion to whom faithful instruction is given in the religion of the Gospel, nor of whom a larger proportion reverently honor its holy ordinances.

I have before me Journals of Conventions in the South, and Reports from various Ecclesiastical bodies, which show that in many parts, the proportion of colored members is greater than that of the whites; and reporting a great number of Christian marriages of slaves, by clergymen who would shrink with horror from desecrating the solemn rite by joining together parties who were in danger, or likely to be sundered by man's arbitrary authority.

With our adversaries, however, all this may go for nothing. All this may be sneered at as not worth the glance of a thought, by the transcendental, or infidel abolitionist, who holds up to our view his own notion of a man—the Lockean two-thirds of a man; the Lord Monboddo man; the featherless biped; or the man of the atheist philosopher, who lacks nothing but himself of being a man—and says, boldly, "If you make him a slave, you make him a brute."

To pass untouched the questions, how much such man wanted of brutality before, or what he lacked of being a real man; I will propound a somewhat different question, viz.—who may dispute or deny the conclusions of the abolition philosopher, that first allows his premises; and standing on the same platform of materialism, denies that there is a *freedom indeed*, which no earthly condition can enslave, or affect, for evil or for good?

Of this freedom indeed,—which knows no "higher law," but the HIGHEST, only; and which is possessed by many thousands of Southern slaves, who pity and pray for their masters, and for all others who are so unhappy as to have it not,—those poor Africans could have known nothing; save for the mysterious, but merciful Providence, which placed them in their condition, so deplorable in the eyes of the ignorant, the faithless, and the fanatical.

## SOUTHERN SLAVERY, A MISSIONARY INSTITUTION.

Allow it then to be asked of the Christian who duly prizes this highest freedom, to consider of Southern Slavery as a *Missionary* Institution for the conversion of the heathen. In this light let it be candidly looked on for a passing moment, and you cannot fail to contemplate it for ever hereafter, with other feelings than abolitionism would excite in you.

But, that you may be able to judge, understandingly, of the missionary character of African slavery in our country, you must first learn something of what other efforts have been made, and are being made, to Christianize heathens.

At an expense of more than FIVE MILLIONS of dollars, and of many valuable lives, in the course of more than fifty years, all the Missionary Societies of our country, of all denominations, are able to reckon up in gross, some fifty thousand converted heathen in various parts of the world. If, as we will rejoice in hoping, they are truly emancipated from the slavery of heathen idolatry and superstition, and made *free indeed*, it is a great and blessed work. May it go on, and without interfering with our home duties.

Look now at what the institution of Southern Slavery has done in this department of Christianizing the pagan portion of mankind.

There may be some hundred thousand or more of the present race of Southern slaves, who come from Africa, involved in the deepest darkness of a brutal paganism;—many of them even cannibals. And still in heathenism, did I never yet find one of that old race; but very many of them, have I known, who were rejoicing in the truth that had made them free. Among them, indeed, I have found some of the most spiritually-minded persons that it has ever been my lot to meet, in any condition of life. Many of them have since gone; and daily are they going to the "rest that remaineth for the people of God."

Would they have become Christians in their own land? I ask not an answer. God knoweth.

But what of the field of the faith now among the slaves of the South? How many are partaking of, and rejoicing in, its fruits?

Fifty thousands or more?

As many as all the Missionary Societies and Boards of Missions in our whole country, can reckon up converts from heathenism?

Aye, more than double that number can be claimed as converts by each of several of the churches of our country; and from authentic accounts and various statistics, now before me, I have good reason to suppose, that more than half a million of the slaves of our South are regular members of Christian congregations; while of infidel heathens, properly so called, there are probably very few, if any!

What a contrast is here presented! Foreign missionary zeal, at great cost and personal sacrifice, has rescued from heathenism about the tenth part of the number that Southern Slavery has added to the Christian church; at the same time that, of the dead and the living, it has rescued from heathenism, not fewer than a hundred times the whole number of foreign converts!

Let these facts stand by themselves, for more easy examination and scrutiny.

## CHAPTER IX.

### PLEASURES OF SLAVERY.

Is it a Paradox? We shall see.

By the millions of the North it may be considered as paradoxical to speak of the pleasures of slavery; and by one hundred and fifty thousand men, and a somewhat greater number of women, it may be denounced as a very gross absurdity. We shall see.

It is not more remarkable than true, that the most, if not all, of good-natured and candid travellers, and sojourners in the southern portion of our great Republic, speak of the slaves as enjoying more of contentment and pleasure than do people in other conditions of life. And such is undoubtedly the fact. That some of them run away, is no more of an argument against their general contentment, than it is an argument against the general contentment of the people of New England, that they sell and leave their pleasant homes to dare the horrors of a voyage round the Horn, Isthmian fever or assassination; or an overland journey to California, in search of gold, and mark the miles with graves and bones instead of milestones, and guide posts.

But not so much of the contentment of the slave, as his pleasure—his joyous pleasure,—something of a higher order than mere contentment, am I now to speak. The Southern slave is a joyous fellow. In willing and faithful subjection to a benignant and protecting power, and that visible to his senses, he leans upon it in complete and sure confidence; as the trusting child holds on to the hand of his father, and passes joyously along the thronged and jostling way, where he would not dare to be left alone. The poor free negro, like the child alone in the tumultuous throng, with no hand to lead and protect him, is usually sad and melancholy. Not so the slave of a good master. His are the thoughts that make glad the heart of the cared-for child, led by paternal hand.

The abolitionists say, they are thoughtless, and *therefore* gay and joyous. If they mean this literally, then are they greatly in error. Of deeply corroding and distracting thoughts, such as make lunatics of multitudes of the free negroes of the North, and not a few of the white races, they may be said to be *thoughtless*. Generally they have none of these to depress their cheerful and laughing spirits. To have to chew the cud of bitter thought, most rarely befalls them. They have not to think and be anxious about what they shall eat, or what they shall drink, or wherewithal they shall be clothed; or kept from the horrors of pinching frost, when the cold winter comes; or how it may fare with them in the winter of old age, when they can no longer work.

None of these things, which make sad and sorrowful the days, and horrible the nights, of the poor of other lands, ever disturb their minds. How great a contrast between the two conditions in this respect! And hence, of all people in the world, the pleasures of the Southern slaves, seem, as they really are, most unalloyed.

With a visible power to depend on for protection and support, perhaps no other human condition whatsoever can be a more happy one than that of good and virtuous servants to good and virtuous masters and mistresses. At their easy tasks, and in the enjoyment of their varied pleasures, their thoughts are not of anxious cares, but of how happy they are. This is indicated both in their sacred, and in their secular songs; and not seldom in the grateful way of practical sympathy for poor and virtuous white people in their neighborhood.

## BOATING PARTY.

It was on an early day of the February of that remarkably delightful sunny winter which followed the mysterious shower of blazing meteors; when three gentlemen left St. Augustine for the St. John's river, with the exciting object of making a boat voyage up the stream to Drayton Island, in Lake George.

The morning ride from the ancient city to the noble river, was through sixteen miles of an atmosphere, resonant of vernal music, and perfumed by myriads of flowers, whose coral lips were rapidly opening to the genial sun. A happier little party has rarely passed over that quiet, and almost desert,—not long after made unquiet by the rifle crack of the Indian; and its sand and its flowers stained with the blood of inoffensive travellers, and of its few peaceful inhabiters. Than,—till decoyed into the death-snare by the assurance of peace, when there was no peace,—the cheerful and happy Weedman;—what passer across that plain ever found, any where, more cordial hospitality, than with him and his primitively simple family? Who ever saw any thing in Weedman, or in any one of his Germano-Spanish family, but the most delightful simplicity of goodness? Who ever saw any thing more simply beautiful and picturesque, than that almost immensity of a man—the ever cheerful and loving father, and gentle master, leading afield, or to the cowpen, his numerous happy sons and daughters, and two or three laughing negroes? I never did. But, alas! insatiate war gave that peaceful man, and a portion of his family to the Indian tomahawk; and broke up that happy home, where the weary and the benighted traveller had ever found kind and generous hospitality; and where dwellers in the man-made town were wont to visit, to be refreshed by a draught of nature, where

"God made the country."

Should these lines fall under the eye of any survivor of that long gratefully remembered family, let them be accepted as a trifling tribute due to the memory of the murdered father, whom the author esteemed as one of the best and kindest of men; and also as a cordial thank-offering to his household for the many pleasant hours enjoyed among them, in their once cheerfully simple, and therefore happy home, untimely desolated. To others, who have never heard of the Weedmans, nor of their humble home on the Picolala road, far away from the haunts of men, I have only to say, pardon this little detour to drop a tear of memory on the bloody grave of an honest man, a noble work of God;—happy in himself,—happy in his family,—happy in love to his God, and to his kind;—nor less happy in being the master of a few faithful slaves, whose *pleasures were not a paradox.*

Of the three gentlemen, with their small crew of black boatmen,—one a dweller in the land of flowers, was the patron, who generously provided the pleasure; one was "the Doctor," who had been in the South but a few weeks; and the third a sojourner of several months.

The Doctor had visited the South imbued with a northern notion that all the slaves were determinedly biding their time, for any—even the most desperate—chance to free themselves from their condition. Haunted by this absurd notion, and seeing ourselves outnumbered by the slaves, who, as he probably supposed, were only *making believe* happy and joyous, he secretly expressed some alarm of peril from them, when we might be far away and completely in their power. He was quite right in thinking that, easily they might dispose of us in the broad river, or lake, or on the lonely shore; and with the well appointed craft flee down the river into the open sea, and escape, with scarcely a possibility of detection.

To his great relief, but utter astonishment, he was perfectly reassured by a laugh at his ridiculous fears from the experienced citizen of the country; and his sober declaration that he never felt safer than when surrounded by southern slaves; and that it is a great mistake to suppose them anxious to change their condition; as not one in fifty of them would accept of their freedom, if offered it. In proof of this,—to the Doctor—astounding declaration, he named many instances of such offers, and among them, to two of our own little crew.

"When a good chance offers, of which there will be no lack during our excursion, Dr." said our friend, "talk with that man George on the black mule, about the condition of the slaves in this country; and particularly get him to tell you his own story of choosing to remain in his present condition. And when we have nothing better to talk about, and we are all in a humor for it, I will tell you some amusing anecdotes of Dick Downing; and especially of his spirited rejection of the boon, for which your northern abolitionists seem so positive that every slave is painfully longing."

"Thank you;" said the doctor, "I never had any of the furor of the abolitionists about me; for I never could believe the slaves of the South as badly off as our miserable free blacks; but I had somehow imbibed the notion that they were, generally, if not every one, very anxious to be free."

"It is quite a mistake, Dr., as you will easily find out by staying a few months in the South, with your eyes and ears open."

"I begin to think so already:" he replied cheerfully.

And we rode on quietly, to the tranquil shore, where two years after I "saw another sight." But let not the tranquil present be disturbed by the future trump of war.

With our fine, roomy and staunch boat, well stowed and stored for a week's voyage, we launched out upon the young Flood. As to a Naiad, or genial fairy Water Sprite, come to their aid, the negroes gave her a melodious song of grateful welcome. In the song, which was any thing but classical, save only in the association, there was nothing like an allusion to the mythological water nymph; which, perhaps, as in their capacity of boatmen, they may have heard her often spoken of by classical passengers, was the more remarkable. It was doubtless a mere natural coincidence. Nature is Nature every where; and the free imagination,—there is none freer than the southern slave's—is ever employed in the poetical work of personifying her works and wonders; not the least striking of which are the tides of her many waters.

After a few hours made easy by her efficient help, we met the retiring tide on the current, when more power was required at the oars. The negroes perspired freely; and our sympathies suggested a landing on an umbrageous and flowery bank, enriched by a native orange grove, in both fruit and blossom. There our watermen, as handy as happy, spread our cloth for dinner, on a gorgeous carpet of the little red lily, and the creeping sensitive plant; in the deep shade of a large magnolia, where the golden fruit would hang over our heads.

The Dr., who had looked to see the men lie down in the shade, to rest their tired limbs, was delighted to find them apparently far less weary than their passengers, and with mirth and high relish, enjoying the much praised refreshment which had been so liberally provided.

On the second day, having been rather disturbed through much of the night, by their songs and laughter around their blazing fire, our sympathies for their toil at the oars was not particularly painful. Indeed every night they seemed by no means so weary as we were; and during the whole excursion, they manifestly enjoyed it as though it had been entered upon and prosecuted for their special gratification. It gave *us* pleasure, to the full amount of our capacity for enjoyment, but, with all our supposed advantages, the much greater amount of real pleasure very plainly fell to *their* lot.

What most surprised us in the negroes,—strangers till then to their peculiarities—was their remarkable talent of improvisation. Their extemporaneous songs at the oar, suited to various scenes and occasions and circumstances present, induced the natural feeling that our boatmen were a set of rare geniuses, selected by our generous friend for the purpose of giving us additional pleasure and surprise. It was afterwards found that extemporaneous singing was not uncommon among them.

The negro boatman of the South seems inspired by the improvising muse whenever he seizes the oar; and especially if it be to row a company of agreeable people on a party of pleasure. If there be young ladies of the number, they may be quite sure to be introduced by the muse, and to receive not only compliments, but admonitions.

Farther to pursue this subject, though it may conflict with the unity of the narrative, there may be told a brief story of a case of improvisation, on a subsequent occasion, of a very striking and characteristic nature; and by no means a bad illustration of the scope and power of the poetic muse.

At the time alluded to, there was an unmarried planter of large property in the country, whose character was not at all enviable, as either a Gentleman or a Master; although he had received an education which should have made him a model in both characters.

A party of ladies and gentlemen were passing down the river on the retiring tide, and the oarsmen had little other labor but to keep time with their oars. After a low preparatory talk among themselves, they entered upon an extemporaneous song of considerable length, and not without artistic merit. The chorus had evidently been concerted among them; for the whole united in it at the first recurrence, so as to make the shores reverberate it, and particularly the last word—the name of the victimized planter. He was described by the leader of the music, as a rich and handsome young man, with fine house and gardens;—horses and carriages; and all desirable things for comfort and elegance. But all these advantages are represented as more than counterbalanced by bad qualities of heart and conduct, described and exemplified to excite abhorrence. And all the unmarried ladies, *by name*, one after another, are warned not to be tempted by his wealth and splendor to marry him; because bad masters make bad husbands.—"Don't you marry * * * * *." The name in itself was replete with melody, and its structure and vowel sounds wonderfully adapted to musical effect. I know of no name in our language to compare with it in musical sound; and when it came back in echo to our ears from the distant shore of the broad St. John's, the effect was wonderful. Could I give that name it would far better illustrate my meaning than I can describe it. It must not be. Long since his race of unhappy profligacy had been run; but surving relatives of worth and excellence might be wounded by the needless reminiscence.

Return we now to our little party on their way to the charming Lake George.

The kind and generous friend, to whom we were indebted for the excursion, had been so long accustomed to the improvising talent of the negroes, though a gentleman of literature and taste, as to have lost sight, it would seem, of the fact that it was peculiar, or any thing worth observing. He so expressed himself in reply to our remarks of surprise and pleasure.

"But," said the Doctor, "have you ever fallen in with it elsewhere among uneducated people?"

"Though common enough with the negroes, I can't say that I have," he replied; "nor among educated people either, in fact, unless, perhaps, occasionally, at a pretty well advanced term of a convivial party."

"Then, sir, how, pray, are we to account for it among the negroes, with whom you say it is not uncommon?"

"Really, I have scarcely ever given the subject a thought; except, perhaps, when many years ago I may have been somewhat more poetical than now."

Said the doctor with great interest and earnestness:—

"It appears to me a very curious fact,—indeed a phenomenon, worth many a thought; and deep and searching ones too."

"Perhaps so, Dr., and I recommend it to your critical and learned investigation."

"I think, indeed, that some serious labor and research may worthily be given to the subject. But a word or two more about it, now, to begin with. Have either of you gentlemen ever found it among free blacks?"

We, of course, both answered in the negative.

"Nor did I, and if among people of the same identical race, but in a different condition, it be not found, the conclusion is inevitable,—is it not?—that it is a peculiarity of the condition."

"It would seem so, Dr., most clearly. But what then?"

"What then; do you say? Much: very much, then. It is a wonderful example of the divine system of compensation. In his providence, God has taken away their freedom, and given them poetic souls; as He enabled Milton to compose the Paradise Lost—the greatest of Epics, to compensate him for the loss of his eyes. By the way, I wonder if Horace was not the better poet—the best of his age in my opinion—for his slave blood? To become such a poet, I would have the metaphorical chain fastened on my limbs to-morrow; as I would give my eyes to be able to create another Paradise Lost."

"Dr., your enthusiasm for poetry is delightful; but it seems rather extravagant to talk of Horace and Milton in connexion with negro singing. And why not do honor to blind Homer as well as to blind Milton?"

"I am not so sure of Homer's, as of Milton's blindness. I did not intend any thing like a comparison of Horace and Milton, with these poetic slaves; but perhaps they may not less enjoy the favors of the muse, which she confers on them, than did those great poets her greater favors. Whatever may be the measure of its capacity, whensoever the afflatus of the poetic spirit fills the soul, it elevates him above its earthly condition, whatever that may be; and fills it with all the happiness it can hold."

"That may all be, Dr.; but what is there, think you, in the peculiar condition of the slave, inducing the visits of the muses?"

"His condition relieves him from the corroding, carking, anxious cares which tend so powerfully, and, in general effectually, to bar out poetical thoughts and feelings from the minds and hearts of almost every body else, save only the heaven destined genius, whose flame, even calamities and tortures can not quench, or smother. Their minds at ease about ways and means, and the like, full play is given to their imagination; and the imagination of the joyous runs naturally in a poetical and musical channel. But for overburdening cares and harassing anxieties, poetry would be almost the common language of our human race.

"Nothing is more plain, than that the slave is not a thoughtless being, as the abolitionists affect to suppose; but his thoughts are not of distracting cares and apprehensions, if he be honest and faithful, but of enjoyment and pleasure. As these men well exemplify, theirs is a *life* of conviviality. That's it; depend on it. The secret is out. They can't help singing. It is the outburst of a pleasurable emotion, that makes its own songs when required for an occasion. Yes; that is it. And a happy discovery it is, that far overpays me for ten days and nights of sea-sickness."

"Then, doctor, you are no longer in fear of an attack of rebellious indignation from the negroes, in order to break their galling chains?"

"No, indeed. They are too joyously happy, ever to be cruel; unless under the influence of some malign fanaticism; and should that calamity befall them, their extemporaneous singing, and the great happiness of heart it so demonstrably indicates, will be for ever at an end."

## CHAPTER X.

### DRAYTON ISLAND.

WHEN we arrived at the beautiful island of our destination, the doctor had become nearly as joyous as the negroes themselves. And then we had the pleasure to look on another phase of the obnoxious system of human brutalization, well adapted to deepen the favorable impression made on his perhaps too susceptible feelings.

For the purpose of propagating several rare and valuable varieties of tropical plants, from the ocean islands and other foreign regions, the proprietor of Drayton Island had placed on it a little colony of two or three families of his own household, under the deputed patriarchal oversight of the senior, and mostly, the progenitor, of the colony; a grave old man, who had been rescued many years before from the cruel tyranny of a savage African master. We landed on the shore of the island at the opposite extremity from the settlement. Hence, we rambled through the plantations and nurseries of tropical plants and trees, defended from ungenial winds by the indigenous forest, bursting into spring beauty and sweetness, and made more paradisiacal by the unrivalled bird-music of the south, mingling with the soothing murmur of the pine leaves—like "the aggregate of many gentle movements of gentle creatures"—and with the ceaseless ripple of the surrounding lake. The little birds that love the ground, hopped along before us; and gorgeously resplendent clouds of ten thousands of paroquets, sailed high over the silvery lake in their everlasting robes of green and gold, reflecting in the blazing sun more than every color of the rainbow.

Entranced by such varied charms, too soon, as we felt, we came to the home of the sable islanders. We had feared to find ourselves there, too rudely precipitated from the height to which our pleasurable emotions had been elevated. Our fears had been groundless. The happy condition of humanity that opened on our view, was but adapted to confirm and make practical, so to say, our previous and pleasant experience. At their easy and pleasing garden work we found these happy people. They smiled upon us a kind greeting from among the orange, lemon, and lime trees; all starred over with white blossoms, relieving most charmingly the deep ground of rich green leaves of every shade of that grateful color.

From their own provision-grounds, which they were planting with corn, okra, potatoes of both kinds, cassada, arrow-root, melons, and other delicious southern vegetables, they had come in to enjoy a luxurious two hours, with the late breakfast, which the southern negro best likes, and especially, as on the present occasion, when he may extend a welcome hospitality to the friendly stranger.

"Well, well," said the doctor, "this seems to me to realize an ideal of some *dream*, that some time or other I have had; unless, indeed, I am now dreaming!"

"You are not dreaming, doctor. This scene, and this island, and lake, and life scenery, are all real."

"I think so. And if so, living in harmony and love, as these people seem to, and in such delightful circumstances, in this genial and lovely climate, if any human condition may be happy, what can interfere with the happiness of these people?"

"Not their condition as slaves, I should think, doctor."

"No, indeed; for if not slaves, they would have no

such paradise of a home—a home, such as any man or woman ought to be ashamed not to be happy in."

"You are quite right, doctor; and how finely is here illustrated the proposition of our own great Shakspeare, communicating the blessings of a lowly station:

'"Tis better to be lowly born,
And range with humble lives in content,
Than to be perk'd up in a glistering grief,
And wear a golden sorrow.'

"Yes. 'Tis better; and very graphically, as well as beautifully, it is told by the inimitable poet. For the favored individual 'tis no question better. But to carry on the great scheme of the world's Divine Government, that, in the good time of the Great Ruler, man may again walk uprightly, some *must*

'Be perk'd up in glistering grief,'

and some must wear *golden*, and many more must wear *iron* sorrows."

"And when that good time shall come, doctor, will there be any slaves?"

"No; but of God. Nor will there be any starving paupers; nor will there be any imprisoned or punished criminals; nor ignorant and vicious unbelievers, requiring to be taught that 'doubtless there is a God that judgeth the earth.' But until that good time shall come, to abolish the institution of slavery, might be no whit wiser or better than to abolish almshouses, penitentiaries, penal laws, schools, and churches."

"Then, doctor, we must wait and work."

"We must wait and work; drink of the brook in the way, and seek for a higher good, than yet attained by our race; and learn lessons of wisdom from the pleasures of slavery."

## GEORGE,—THE NEGRO WHO WOULD NOT BE MORE FREE.

On our return down the river, the Doctor enquired of George about his refusal of freedom. George seemed not disposed to be very communicative on the subject, and rather to evade it as something not agreeable to his recollection. He merely said, he had seven hundred dollars which he had offered to his mistress for his freedom, and that she had advised him to consult with some of his friends on the subject, and if they thought it best for him, she would comply with his proposal. The friend, to whom George applied for counsel, dissuaded him from the purchase of what he would be better without; and that if he could have his freedom for nothing, even, it would be a bad bargain for him.

But happily, to remedy the taciturnity of George, that friend was present; which fully accounted for George's embarrassment, at which he smiled, and said to George, "May I tell the story?" "Yes, Mas'r," said George, "if you like; but it makes me ashamed."

"You should not be ashamed, George," said his friend, "for having come to a wise conclusion. Let others be ashamed, who act less wisely."

George hung down his head, as though there were something connected with it which he remembered unpleasantly. It was not, however, as once the Doctor seemed half to suspect, that he regretted not having closed the bargain with his mistress; but that he had been so unwise and ungrateful as to propose it.

"Well," said the friend, "this is George's story about buying his freedom."

George had always been a favorite servant of his mistress—an excellent widow lady;—and she had therefore allowed him many privileges; such as a large allotment of negro ground, and to do jobs for people, when he could get good pay; and asked from him in return little more than enough to remunerate her for keeping him,—often less. Well, in this way, after a while, George had accumulated, I know not how much more than seven hundred dollars. So much he offered his mistress for his freedom. She thonght it best for George to retain both his money and his home; and told him so; but added, that if his friends—the gentlemen in the neighborhood—thought it best for him, he should be gratified.

Being nearest, George first applied to me, and stated the case. And thus we talked it over.

"You have seven hundred dollars, George?"

"Yes, Mas'r."

"And you wish to purchase your freedom with it?"

"Yes, Mas'r."

"George, how many free negroes do you know?"

George thought over the question, a little, and answered,

"About twenty, I guess, Mas'r."

"About twenty, eh, George? And how many of them do you think have seven hundred dollars?"

George looked up as if struck with a new idea, and answered:

"Not one, I 'spect;—not all put together."

"So then, George; *their* freedom has not been a very profitable concern to them; eh, George?"

"No, Mas'r; that's true enough. But I——"

"Take care, George; and don't belie your character of a modest and sensible fellow. As a free negro, you would not have been better off now than the best of them—Tom Butler—who has been free for ten years, and has not ten dollars to his name. Give up this foolish notion of yours, George; or in ten years, when you are no longer a young man, you will be no better off than Tom Butler."

"Do you think so, Mas'r?"

"I do, George. And do you know, that your good mistress paid a doctor's bill on your account, two or three years ago, of more than a hundred dollars?"

With marked surprise, George replied:

"No, Mas'r; I didn't know that."

"But she did, George; and very few, either masters or mistresses, would have had the great kindness not to have told you of it; especially as it was not in her employment that you got sick. And who nursed you, George, during that long illness, which you brought upon yourself by exposures to which you had not been accustomed in the service of your mistress?—Who nursed and took care of you then, eh, George?"

With moistened eyes, George replied,—

"My good missus. She was with me, by night and by day."

"And as a poor free negro, do you think you would have been as well cared for, George? Think over these things, George; and of how much comfort you may have in your old age, in your nice cabin and garden, with your children and grandchildren about you; and with money to supply all your wants beyond your allowance. Think coolly of all these things; and of how good and kind a mistress you have, think too; and then if you choose to give seven hundred dollars to boot between her and Mistress Freedom World, who don't care a pin for you; and would look on and laugh while you were dying of sickness, or want; then leave your good old mistress and try the new one."

"Thank you, Mas'r," said George; "I now see what a fool I have been. I'll go tell missus; and be a good nigger to her."

"That's right, George. Now you talk like a sensible and good fellow. Let nobody persuade you to fool yourself out of a good home and good friends; and to pay dearly for it into the bargain."

"Was it about so, George?"

"'Bout so, Mas'r;" said George, with some emotion, that did him great credit.

Some little time elapsed before George could sing again; but then it was with renewed vigor and joyousness. Was not George, think you, at the least as wise as the negroes who run away to freeze or starve in the wilds of Canada?

## CHAPTER XI.

THIS CHAPTER IS DEDICATED AND SPECIALLY ADDRESSED TO ALL SUCH PERSONS AS DESIRE TO KNOW WHAT ARE THE REAL MERITS OF THE QUESTION OF NEGRO SLAVERY.

What is the condition of the negroes in their native Africa?

It would seem that we ought to be able, advisedly and rightly, to answer this question, before too rashly we condemn the Divine Providence, through which a portion of them have been forced away, and held in bondage in other lands. If they are better off than they would have been in their native land, it was then a merciful and a gracious providence which removed them, by whatever agency. If they have been taken from the happy homes which many poets, and some philosophers, would have us believe, then surely a great wrong has been done them. In his late noble colonization speech, Mr. Everett has rather bowed to such poets and philosophers, than to authentic historians, and reliable travellers.

Execrable is even the thought, that we may do evil that good may come; but the Great God, who judgeth the Earth, is able to bring good out of even the extremities of evil. Let it be willingly granted, then, that the slave-trade is at, or very near the extremity of evil; and let us see if the goodness of His power has not been manifested in educing good, to some millions of Africans from this extremity of evil, as, perhaps, in our ignorance of the matter, we may deem it. He seeth not as we see. In passing this only to such as believe in Him, as revealed in the Bible.

The subject shall be introduced by the simple narrative of an incident, which, to several others than myself, was a very deeply interesting one. My readers may also find some interest in it, at second hand; yet no pen—certainly not mine—can at all bring it home to the mind of a reader, with any thing like the thrilling effect experienced by us who were present, with all our senses alive to the scenery, and to the scene

## THE NEGRO SUNDAY SCHOOL.

It was in the far off South. On the elevated bank of a noble river, and in full view of both shores, stood a beautiful edifice, erected for the worship of God. In the cool of a Sunday Summer morning, with a few white people of both sexes, there were assembled about an hundred blacks, of ages, from under five, to over sixty. They had come to receive religious instruction in a Sunday school, which had been lately instituted for their special benefit. More than with mere willingness,—gladly had they assembled to meet their kind and devoted teachers. An affectionate address was made to them on the important object in view,—their improvement in Christian knowledge and happiness.

In plain and simple language, suited to their intellects, they were made to understand what was required of them. They were told what advantages and comforts would accrue to them, if they acted well their own easy and delightful part.

I suppose that the outlines of Christianity, as a divine system of grace and morals, known only to such as receive it, are not often better delineated, than they were on that lovely morning, to those children of the Sun. The great truths of the gospel are seldom put with more simple skill of familiar illustration, than they were by the superintendent, or head teacher, of that negro Sunday school. Nor have I ever witnessed an apparently more kindly and feeling reception of them.

They were all slaves; and to help them thankfully to accept of the good which was offered them, in the form of religious instruction, that they might in some degree appreciate it, so as to insure their continuance in well-doing, in the pursuit of the best knowledge, it was thought desirable to induce their thankful contentment with their condition. In no condition of life will the restless and discontented make much progress, in either mental or moral improvement.

They were questioned about their knowledge of their origin; and of how they came to be in their present condition. With the exception of a few old people, who were born in Africa, and brought away in advanced youth, or maturity, they seemed quite in the dark on the subject of their origin, and the land of their ancestry. In language adapted to the occasion, a brief general account was given them of their progenitors coming from Africa, sold into slavery by their own countrymen.

And now, said their friend and teacher, we will see if we cannot make this matter more plain and interesting to you. For this purpose we will try to get the story of his coming to this country from one of these old men, who was born in the country of your forefathers.

Addressing himself to a happy old African, the teacher said, familiarly, Daddy Cudjo,—as he was usually called,—will you tell these people and children, the story of your leaving Africa; and how the people live there? It may be good for them to know how they happen to be here; and that they are better off, as you have before told me, than are the people and children of Africa.

But Cudjo was not accustomed to public speaking on such occasions; and instead of complying with the request, he would doubtless have blushed, had his complexion allowed of such an exhibition of modesty. Therefore to get at what was wanted from the old man, a conversation, in this wise, was entered upon and pursued. Cudjo had never learned well to use the English tongue. Some Africans never do. Like instances are found among other foreigners.

"Cudjo, how old was you, when you came from Africa?"

"Do'n know, mas'r."

"Do you think you were fifteen, Cudjo?"

"Do'n know, mas'r,—mebby so."

"Well, how big were you?"

"'Bout 's big 's dat boy Sam, dar'."

"Very well. And how old are you, Sam?"

"Mose fourteen, mas'r," said Sam; at the same time showing about that number of the whitest kind of teeth.

"Then, Cudjo, you were about fourteen, perhaps?"

"S'pose so, mas'r."

"Then you can remember very well about your home, and how you came to leave it?"

"Yes, mas'r, 'member *bery* well."

This was said with a strong emphasis on what he meant for very, and it aroused the wakeful attention of all present; and especially the younger portion, whose curiosity was excited with the expectation of something wonderful.

"Cudjo, did you live in a village, or in the country on a plantation?"

"Lib in big town, mas'r. Nobody lib in country dar'."

"Why not live in the country, Cudjo?"

"Enemy all roun' 'bout."

"And what sort of town was it that you lived in, Cudjo? Tell us something about it and the people who lived in it."

"Berry big town, mas'r. King lib in it, all he big men

lib in it, an' all he fine lady, an' great many Spearmen, an' great many poor people 'longing to the King an' big men. Bery, *bery* big town."

According to Cudjo's description of the town, or kraal, and from his comparison with towns with which he was acquainted, as Charleston and Savannah, it may have contained several square miles. Of the town, or kraal, of the Zoola Chief in eastern Africa, Mr. Isaacs, who was often in it, says, "I should think it would exceed three miles in circumference, and includes within its space fourteen hundred huts. The King's palace is situated at the head of the kraal, on an eminence, and comprises about one hundred huts, in which none but girls live, as men are not allowed to enter the palace,"—or harem.

The Zoola Chief, with a powerful savage army, and in possession of thousands of square miles of territory, from which he had nearly exterminated the former possessors, and held the residue in bondage, had no occasion for large walled garrison towns, like Cudjo's King, who was surrounded by ferocious enemies.

"But, Cudjo, if all the people live in the town, how do they get provisions to eat?"

"Ebery one grow sweet taters, an' cassada, and groun' nuts, an' melon, an' quash!"

"Do all the people live on vegetables, then?"

"Yes, mas'r, 'cept King and big men, an' soger. Them go out an' fight, an' git slaves, an' cattle an fish an' game."

"And how came you to be taken from such a town, Cudjo? Did an enemy get in and steal you in the night?"

"O no, mas'r, town strong—fence all roun' wid brick."

"With brick, Cudjo? Was the big town walled round with brick; such as we have in this country?"

"Not zacly, mas'r. Not little red brick; big brick,

bake in sun, mas'r. Wall bery tick, bery high; brier and prickly pear on top. Nobody get ober."

"Then you were outside, when taken!'

"Yes, Mas'r, outside."

"But how came you on the outside and unprotected?"

"My uncle, my mudder's brudder, say, 'Cudjo, come go see my brudder.' Him lib in fort little way off in de ribber, an' catch fish for de king. So me go wid uncle. In bush, big man wid long spear jump up hine' log, ketch me—carry me off."

"But where was your uncle at this time, Cudjo?"

"Him run away."

"Cudjo, did you never suspect that your uncle had sold you to the big spearman, and took you out to him to carry you off?"

"Me hab sometime bin tink so, Mas'r. Me tink him steal me from my mudder,—him bad man;—him sell own chillen, an' two wife."

"And what did the big spearman do with you, Cudjo?"

"Him take me off two tre night, wid more boy,—sell me to nudder black man wid much spearmen wid him. Him had many, many boy, an' gals too."

"And what did these new masters do with you and the rest of the boys and girls?"

"Dem car' us off, long, long, way tow'rd sun set, an' day sell us to white man in big ship."

"Cudjo, had you ever before seen white men?"

"Nebber, Mas'r, nebber."

"Did you know there were white men before you saw him you were sold to?"

"No, Mas'r, nebber hearn o' one."

"And what did you think of him, Cudjo, when you first saw him?"

"Me been tink him de debbil, Mas'r."

"And what did you think the white man was going to do with you?"

"Me tink him gwine eat me, Mas'r."

At these answers all the white teeth present were shown, with other demonstrations of merriment.

"When you were first taken from your uncle, what did you think the spearman would do with you, Cudjo?"

"Me tink him gwine sell me to him king, or some udder big man."

"Why did you think so?"

"Caze, Mas'r, my king, an him big men buy boys, an' gals, an' people."

"And what did they do with the people they bought?"

"Make 'em work, an' make 'em fight."

"Were many of the people slaves there, Cudjo?"

"Mose all, Mas'r, 'cept de king an' him big men.'

"And were not the big men slaves to the king?"

"'Spose so, Mas'r. King make em kill one a nudder, sometimes, when him angry."

"How did the masters treat the working and fighting slaves? Were they kind to them; and feed and clothe them well?"

"No, no, Mas'r. Bery hard work; bery little eat; no clo'es—plenty lashing—some time kill."

At this all the white teeth are covered, and some sighs and groans heard from the old women. The teacher proceeds with affectionate solemnity,—

"Well, we have no more time now for Cudjo to tell us about Africa. You have all been quite attentive. And you have learned that you have no reason to be sorry that you are here, and not in that wicked land, where there is no Sunday,—no rest for the poor—no peace—no safety—no hope of a better world beyond the grave. At another time, perhaps Daddy Cudjo may tell us about the bad and foolish and cruel superstitions which they have in Africa, instead of the blessed religion of the Gospel.

"And now, my friends,—now, children, we are to worship the good God, our heavenly Father; and you must be very sober and attentive, and pray for the poor heathen who know nothing of a Great Father in heaven. Pray that they may learn to know and love Him.

"And I know you will be very thankful, that your lot is fallen in the pleasant land where the blessed Saviour, our Lord Jesus Christ, is King."

"Yes, Mas'r; tank de Lord! tank de Lord!" ejaculated a venerable old African woman, in a neat clean dress and white turban.

"Tank de Lord! tank de Lord!"

How its thrilling tones appealed to all hearts to be thankful! In my mind's ear, it is sounding still.

The exercises of the Sunday School were closed by an appropriate hymn sung by the blacks. With the aid of the female teachers, principally their young mistresses, they had thoroughly committed it to memory; and with their teachers, they sang it heartily, and not without taste. I have never since been more pleased with any thing of the sort than with that negro Sunday School. The impression it made, it is most pleasant and profitable to revive, deepened too, as it was, by the public worship that followed.

In age, how the memory of the heart loves to dwell on the oases in the general desert of life, as guide-marks, through the wilderness, to the green fields and living waters beyond!

And now pass we on from the "negro-talk of Daddy Cudjo, to other, and more classic sources of information, about savage Africa—the land and legitimate mother of slavery.

# CHAPTER XII.

## SAVAGE CONDITION OF AFRICA.

It seems a very common notion, not at all confined to abolitionists, that the confessedly miserable condition of the African masses at home, has been produced by the slave-trade of civilized nations. Nothing can be more incorrect. The exact reverse seems to be the undoubted truth. The slave system of Africa is either the true mother of all African slavery elsewhere, or, all such authority as the world has ever held to be good authority, is actually good for nothing.

Long years—perhaps thousands—before African slavery was introduced any where in the rest of the world—at least on this continent or the neighboring islands—in Africa itself it existed in its most cruel and loathsome forms.

The foreign slave-trade, perhaps, has never, at any time, penetrated into the far distant central districts of Africa; and yet, there, according to the most trustworthy authorities, reaching back centuries before our era, and especially, according to modern authorities of unquestionable veracity, slavery not only prevails generally, but is of the very character in all its horrors, that some, at least, of our abolitionists seem best to love to think of it as existing in the South.

In Africa, slavery is a system of unqualified, and unfeeling tyranny. It is an oppression in which the slave has not accorded to him, even the immunity which the laws of civilized countries extend to brutes! And what is the proportion of the people in this wretched condition—slaves to the most savage of monsters?

MUNGO PARK, whose truth, I believe, was never called in question, and who had the best of means to know what he stated, estimated the slaves, by hereditary bondage, to be, at least, three-fourths of the whole population.

LANDER says, "four-fifths of the people are slaves." In these estimates, probably neither of these travellers reckoned the multitudes of women in the harems of the chiefs; whose life, even, is never secure from the capricious tyranny of their savage masters, for a single day. Sometimes scores of them are sacrificed at once for no cause but some ferocious freak of the tyrant; or to indulge his savage appetite for the strong excitement that blood only can allay. When these tyrants perish, naturally or by violence, which is most common, their hundreds of widows, as an English missionary to South Africa calls his slave girls, "*are hurried to an untimely end, and their carcasses given to beasts of prey, which tear them limb from limb and drag the bones to their dens.*" Wolves and hyenas abound in Africa; and their principal food, as many travellers have supposed, is murdered human flesh! As stated by the last authority—the Rev. Mr. Kay—the chiefs among the negroes, have entire command of the persons and property of the people, who are not called slaves; and that a man dare not deny even his *wife*, if demanded by his chief. And let it be remembered, edifyingly, that these accounts of the Africans at home, are given by an English missionary, in relation to tribes of savages in South Africa, and under the protection of the British authorities; and to some extent amenable to British rule. But they are darling negroes, and not vulgar white laborers, and paupers; and so the sceptre of British royalty is laid on them delicately. Mr. Everett says "they are not savages;" but Mr. Kay speaks of "every page of African history" as showing the native African savage as of the very worst character of savages—the numerous tribes and clans continually feeding the vengeful flame, with strifes, contention and bloodshed—the native troops, mustered either to pillage their weaker neighbors, or to retaliate upon some thievish aggressor!—"Such is the estimate of human life, that the death of a female by violence attracts little attention."

In other and very distant parts of the continent, the same ferocious savagism obtains, as all authorities declare; and that no where human life seems of any appreciable value. Imagination, even, is at fault, in every attempt to add a darker hue to the pictures given us by Mungo Park, and other truthful travellers, of the cruel and bloody tyranny of the chiefs, warriors and slave holders in the interior of Africa.

Towns are taken;—the chief ruling family, with all the old, infirm, and unavailable population are slain; and, if not eaten as food by the conquerors, are given to the beasts and birds of prey; and the residue are enslaved. If they find themselves with more slaves than they can employ, and cannot sell them, the surplus are butchered. He speaks thus of the African system of slavery:—"It is evident from its nature and extent, that it is a system of no modern date. How far it is maintained and supported by the slave traffic, which for two hundred years, the nations of Europe have carried on with the nations of the coast, it is neither within my province nor in my power to explain. If my sentiments should be desired concerning the effect which a discontinuance of this commerce would produce on the manners of the natives, I should have no hesitation in saying, that, in the present unenlightened state of their minds, my opinion is, the effect would be neither so extensive, or so beneficial, as many wise and worthy persons fondly expect."

Such are the statements and views of the wise and worthy Mungo Park, of the character and condition of Africans at home. They have certainly not been made worse by a removal to our country. They would hardly be benefitted by finding their way back.

Another, and independent testimony, that the slave-trade of Europe neither introduced slavery into Africa, nor stimulated the ferocity, nor cupidity, of its native savages, is found in the character and customs of

## THE ZOOLUS OF EASTERN AFRICA.

Less than thirty years ago, this numerous and powerful tribe, first saw an individual of the white race. "The King had always thought there was no other land than that which himself and his people inhabited, and that he was the only great King in the world." So writes Mr. Isaacs, who, with a few other Englishmen, sojourned for several years in the Zoolu country, and became familiar with the King and people. They were cast away, and they lost their vessel on the coast, in about 30 degrees S. Latitude. One of them was an officer of the British Navy, Lieut. King. This gallant and magnanimous young officer, on the 26th of August, 1825, set sail from the Cape of Good Hope, in search, says the Lieut., of "an old friend of mine, a Mr. Farewell, an East India merchant, who had been absent for more than sixteen months, on a very hazardous speculation, to the Eastward, amongst the natives, who, it appeared on my former voyage on the coast, *had never seen a white person.*"

Mr. Isaacs' book is a journal, embracing a space of nearly seven years. In addition to the accounts of hunts and journeyings through a savage country, abounding with broad and rapid rivers, where boats were unknown and undreamed of, until introduced by his party, to the astonishment of the natives, his Journal contains little less than enumerations of almost daily savage atrocities, the moving spirit of which was mostly the terrible Chief of the tribe,—"an insatiable savage monster of cruelty," says Lieut. King.

Before the first white man had ever landed on his coast, he had conquered most of the surrounding tribes, and slain all the vanquished, save a few picked men to whom he had given their lives for their services, so long as he might choose to spare them.

This Chaka the *Great*,—as well may he be styled, in allusion to other conquerors so called,—had never heard of the slave-trade; had never sold a slave, but had murdered them by thousands!

"All the males of his broad dominion were under the most severe military discipline; always under arms; and for the most trifling offences against the King,—no matter at what distance from him—were immediately put to death, and their bodies left to gorge the wolf or hyena; or perchance, if near a river, thrown to the crocodiles and fishes!"

While the King remained at home in his palace, which consisted of a hundred huts, scarcely a day passed without an execution. He had been absent on a campaign in which he had destroyed the last tribe, that for a long time had dared to resist him. Says the Journal, "He appears to have destroyed in this last encounter, nearly every human being of the tribe, man, woman, and child. The King ISSECONYARNA, with a few men alone escaped,—to a pit within the bushes,—secreted until the merciless Zoolus had retired from the field. Isseconyarna had been an inhuman tyrant, and now had received the punishment due for his many vices and cruelties."

Conscious of growing old, and that the color of his wool was beginning to witness against him, the King was usually melancholy; from the certainty that it could not be long before a successor would be sent by the army to trample his gray hairs in the dust, and give his body to the beasts. Old age on the throne is an abomination to the Zoolus.

But after the feast of blood, with which he had regaled himself in his last campaign, Chaka retained an unusual cheerfulness for several days. The agreeable excitement, however, passed away, and his appetite for human blood returned upon him. He easily, and soon, found means to appease it for a little while.

He suspected, or pretended to suspect, that the purity of his seraglio had been violated in his absence. The dreams and visions being related, by which he was not only certified of the fact, but also of the guilty parties, with savage cunning, he has them all decoyed into a suitable enclosure, and there, to the number of one hundred and seventy, girls and boys, concubines and slaves, barbarously murdered! But the details of this wholesale carnage may not all be omitted.

"The King, at first, beat his aged and infirm mother, with inconceivable cruelty; and to the astonishment of all, as he had even manifested towards her a strong filial affection. He then became in such a violent and savage rage, that, knowing his want of temper to discriminate objects, and apprehending something for my own personal safety, I withdrew to my hut.

"Every thing being ready for the bloody scene, to complete this massacre of unoffending beings, he called his warriors and told them that his heart was sore; and that he had 'been beating his mother, 'because she had not taken a proper care of his girls.'

"He ordered the victims to be brought to him. He began by taking out several fine lads, and ordering their own brothers to twist their necks. Their bodies were dragged out and beaten with sticks until life was extinct.

After this refined act of cruelty, the rest of the victims were indiscriminately butchered. When all was over for *this* time, he asked me with a smile of exultation, 'why I did not assist in killing the UMTAGGARTIES?'—people not fit to live."

His majesty then addressed his warriors,—squatting on their hams in token of submission:—"You see we have conquered all our enemies, and killed a number of umtaggarties; I shall now consult UMBEAH and find out the rest. To morrow I shall kill all who have offended in my reign; there will then be nothing wanting to make you and me happy."

"The King then retired to his palace; and the people to their huts to take certain roots, for having killed their relatives:—these they say prevent their grieving; which is punished with death. I have known several instances of people having been suspected of crying for the loss of relations, and by the King's order put to death on the instant."

This wretched savage had not been hardened by the slave-trade. He had never heard of it.

The day after the slaughter,—"the King appeared much more lively and in better spirits than yesterday." He told his warriors that "hitherto they had witnessed deaths of common people, but they would soon behold that of chiefs.

"The wolves were to be seen in large droves, making hideous and deafening howls round the kraal, attracted by the blood of the preceding day."

The entry of the next day says,—"I was disturbed early this morning by the cries of a man knocked down just behind my hut, and taken away to be killed. He was the King's chief domestic. I could hear him distinctly thanking the savage monarch as they were beating him to death!"

Why did he not sell him into slavery? He had never heard of that more deeply condemned method of punishment. "At noon two of the adopted daughters of this execrable monster, and one of his chiefs, were dragged through the kraal and executed with similar barbarity."—"The King spent the afternoon in dancing with his people." And this chaka is but a fair specimen of a negro in power beyond the reach of the African Slave-trade.

And now that like instances of atrocious tyranny are reported by all travellers beyond where the slave-trade has penetrated, how unreasonable is the prevailing notion, that the miserable condition of the Africans at home, is the fruit of any foreign influence! Where the slave-trade has never reached, and where it has been destroyed, the same horrible custom prevails of sacrificing human beings on the graves of the King's relatives.

Chaka's old mother, whom he had beaten for not taking proper care of his girls, dies, and a whole village is destroyed by fire and sword; not a single life spared nor a vestige of its habitations.

The King of Dahomey thinks he can do no better with his surplus population than, to water the graves of his ancestors with the blood of thousands of them, and with their bones to build and decorate the palaces and temples of his capital!

An Ashantee King buries his mother, and at her grave, three thousand human victims are slain, and two hundred slaves weekly, for the three following months!

Are these the results of our southern slavery? Nay, the condition of no body of slaves among any civilized nations on earth, can be exaggerated even by the most imaginative among rabidest abolitionists, so as to reach any thing like a parallel to the condition—not of the slaves only—but of all the subject people of pagan and savage Africa! If not savages, as Mr. Everett declares; what are they; something worse?

The fiction of poor old Tom of the cabin excites and sustains the sympathies of the multitudes who are ignorant of the undoubted facts that constitute volumes of proof, that in the land of his ancestors he would have been even more cruelly treated, as thousands of his race are daily. The wretched Legree would make but a poor figure of an apology for a tyrant, by the side of an African King.

Bad enough, certainly—far too bad—the fancied horrors of the plantation of Legree—himself its most miserable and degraded slave; but how tame and amiable, when viewed in connection with a camp, or a palace of a savage African chief!

If that was justly represented as an "ogre's den," by what horror of horrors, can one of these be typified, by even the imagination of a Milton, a Dante, or a Salvator Rosa?

## THE SHILLOOKS.

By our own Bayard Taylor, the truthful and tireless; the fearless and the faithful African traveller; still bearing the marks, I suppose, of a tropical sun—we are informed that the Shillooks of the White Nile, in Central Africa, comprise a savage negro kingdom of some three millions. They are a nation of robbers and murderers. They have no respect for the rights of others, or for one another, but as such rights are guarded and defended by superior might.

They have gained some notions of civilization from Turkish and European Traders; but it has not improved their morals. That such intercourse with the harpies of civilization is not wont to improve the morals of savages, the people of our Continent require no additional authority, above that of the experience and history of a few ages.

As shown by an incident related by our traveller, in a letter dated "Islands of the Shillook negroes, White Nile, Jan. 24, 1852," they are accustomed to seizing upon people as slaves, whenever they find them, if they possess the power to effect the object. The incident alluded to is curious and interesting; and very graphically suggestive of the characteristics of the savage Shillooks. The Turkish Sultan, or whatsoever, they may imagine the Sultan to be —they seem to hold in profound awe and veneration. Their awe of his mighty power, they doubtless derived from the Turkish traders, who had threatened them with his displeasure.

Mr. Taylor's guides and attendants were acquainted with this circumstance of the Shillook's terror of the Sultan's wrath; and, for their own, as well as for his protection, they introduced him as the son of the Sultan. But for this stratagem, on their part, he would have been plundered to a certainty; and probably murdered. And with this protection to himself, he came near losing a very necessary member of his suite; to save whom the young Sultan had to appear in the new character of a polygamist. "As we were leaving, the sailors informed me that one of the Shillooks, who had come down to the boat while I was seated with the Shekh on shore, took a fancy to the fat, black slave, who cooks for them, and expressed his determination to take her. They told him she was one of the Sultan's wives, and as his Majesty was now the Shekh's friend, he dare not touch her. "Oh," said the Shillook, "if she is the Sultan's wife, that is enough;' and he immediately returned to the shore. I forgave the impertinence of the sailors in passing off such a hideous creature as *one* of my wives, in consideration of the adroitness with which they avoided what might have been a serious difficulty."

He says too; "The rais informed me that the Shillooks

frequently sell their women and children; and that a boy or girl can be bought for about twenty measures of dourra."

Of these Shillooks, comprising a twentieth part of the negroes of Africa, all are slaves, under savage oppression; or tyrant masters; and yet, compared with a large proportion of the remaining nineteen twentieths, they seem gentle and merciful.

Are then the African negroes at home, better, or better off, than our southern slaves?

## CHAPTER XIII.

### SOUTHERN NEGRO HAPPINESS IN CHILDHOOD AND AGE.

In poetry, and in other sentimental literature, many fine things are sung and said on happy childhood. But it has been my lot never to have seen it general, save only among the negroes of the South. Children may sometimes be happy elsewhere. Some peculiarly favored ones may be generally happy. I meet with not many, now, so peculiarly favored; and I remember few of the companions of my own childhood of that favored class. Very certain is it, that the children of the immense majority of the people of the North, find sorrow, and trouble, and misery enough, in and beyond, the first decade of their years.

I have seen little girls of five or six years, taking hard lessons in scrubbing, under a northern mistress of high, and allowed, pretensions to *benevolence.* It was her benevolence that put the little one so early to the scrubbing brush, that she might learn, with facility, to do the toilsome tasks to which she was born:—born among the benevolent, *par excellence.*

I have seen a little boy of like age, tied on a horse by his father, before sunrise, to guide his way among corn rows! Why was he *tied* on? That he might not fall asleep and tumble off, or be jerked off by a sudden stop of the plough against a stump or a stone. And was not that kind and fatherly? Certainly. If the poor little white boy must work hard at an age when all the little negroes of the South sleep or play, why then, to be sure they should be kindly bound with cords, to secure them from the danger of being maimed at their work.

"You have *seen* such things?"

"In abundance, my dear Doctor."

"And I too, have seen; and 'part of which I was.'—I have *felt* the sorrows of childhood."

"You have *felt* them, my friend?"

"Aye, sir, I have felt them. And the remembrance is still felt;—felt, sometimes, I fear, sinfully. May I be forgiven, if it be a sin to remember, that in my childhood, I felt that a good right was mine, to lament and sorrow over, if not—but not—to curse,—not the day, only, of my birth—all—almost all, the circumstances of my childhood!"

"My friend!—

"Allow me to proceed. To talk it over, may soften a little the miseries of memory.

"Late in the productive life of my parents, was my birth, in the rear of a host; and therefore very delicate and sensitive, was the organism of my nervous system. Almost every thing that moved not in harmony and love, and gentleness, grated upon, and rasped my sensibilities.

"My father was a generous and kind man to every body outside of his paternal household. To the poor, he was proverbially a father; though, as I remember, he sometimes frowned darkly on their improvidence and follies, at the moment of his supplying their physical necessities. His slaves,—for there were slaves then in Yankee-land—were his most interesting pets. His treatment and general bearing towards them, were well adapted to play the mischief with Dr. Paley's definition of slavery at the moment he was writing it; perhaps thinking of an English press-gang: 'An obligation to labor for the benefit of the master,' exclusively, 'without the consent of the servant.' This, I am quite sure, was never felt

by my father's slaves, even in Yankee-land; and not less sure am I that, in the generous South, it is very rarely so felt, but that they are laboring for the comfort of the household, of which they form a large and important portion.

"The word *household*, in the South, is used, as we know, in the Scripture sense; including slaves, but not *hirelings*. My father was kind to his hirelings too; some of whom he employed more for their sake, than his own."

"Kind to slaves and hirelings; and not to your childhood kind, Doctor, it seems passing strange."

"I hope, and suppose, indeed, that he never thought of excluding me from his kindness; but he seemed always to expect from me what, to me, was impossible. He often rebuked, and sometimes—not seldom—chastised me for not fulfilling his expectations. My childhood was infirm and feeble; and sensitive exceedingly. And, perhaps, from early caresses and other sorts of flatteries, I became vain, before I knew any thing of the meaning of that miserable vice, of every age. O what skill is required in the management of childhood!"

"If, at the same time, delicate and vain, from slight causes, your sufferings were not slight. A little harshness you felt as a great cruelty."

"Yes, I suppose the little negroes, who rarely, if ever, have to bear such hardships as fell to my lot, would have borne them better. So far back as memory reacheth, and no doubt beyond, I suffered so intensely from bodily and mental pains as to make life a burthen to me. I wished for death, but it came not. Awaked early to my little, but hard duties, I sighed, and sometimes wept, that I had not been allowed to sleep for ever! And yet,

"Not the least part of my early wretchedness was the horrid fear of death, which infernal nursery tales had scared and corrupted my soul with. I could tell of many circumstances of my early childhood, vividly remembered, in illustration of the misery I endured. Among persons who were kind to me, as I thought, most fresh in my memory are a slave and a poor hireling, who used to take me out with them for a rural ramble on Sunday mornings, and always spoke kindly to me.

"At twelve I was sent away to school, where I was one of an hundred and fifty boys; as well as I can remember, all unhappy! Think of such a number of unhappy boys in one house, and then think of all the thousands of young negroes, under twelve, that you have seen, and whether you can recollect one half of that number, that were less happy than the usual run of white children in the North."

"Doctor, the story of your own childhood is remarkable; and I trust not common. Yet I must confess, that, save among the Southern slaves, I have rarely found any thing like the general happiness and joy of life, which always ought to prevail among children.

"That pic-nic party, as you called it, of the little negroes of the Island, in the shade of a huge live oak surrounded with orange trees, and profusely decorated by a grape vine, you no doubt remember, Dr.?"

"Yes; and well too, how bitterly the joyous comfort of those little slaves, so called—wrongly, if Paley's definition be right—reminded me of my own joyless childhood."

"And you have not forgotten that vernal and verdant Sunday morning on the Island?"

"Nor our cheerful walk, before the Sunday services, through the beautiful village; every cabin—as they are called—every beautiful white cottage of the negroes, clean as cleanliness itself, surrounded with cheerful and beautiful shrubbery and flowers; and held rent free, and tax free, by happy tenants; many below, and some above, the age of labor; and all far more comfortable than the average of the whole free population of any country. Indeed, it is not so easy a matter to describe a more comfortable home than had those negroes. Well do I recollect the impression made on my mind, by the perfectly happy condition of the old people,—that they appeared to enjoy the rest of old age more completely than I had ever witnessed it, even by old people of considerable property and ample means."

"But, my dear Dr., you are aware, of course, that it is not deemed respectable to be happy in our present part of the country?

"'Our IDEAL of a highly respectable man,' says Governor Seymour, in his noble lecture in New York, 'is one who thinks only of his business and works himself to death.'"

"The Governor is right. And surely such an Ideal must exclude every rational notion of happiness. Thanks to his Excellency for a key to many a mystery of my life."

"Do you remember Old King, Dr.?"

"Old King!—a lord of the Isle—with the dignity of a retired field-marshal, and the authority of a patriarch? I shall not soon forget the good and happy old man!"

"And the spacious hospital;—on week days the playhouse and nursery for the children, and all days and nights the asylum for the sick; where ma'am Betsey presided with benignant cheerfulness and skill, and untiring assiduity?"

"She always appeared to be thinking of the southern side of every subject; and to wish to direct the thoughts of others to the sunny side of every thing. An excellent specimen of the nurse was ma'am Betsey."

"'*Every one born a slave in our country, has a moral and civil right, or legal birthright, not only to food, clothing, and shelter; but to care and support in childhood, in sickness, and in age.*' How fully and generously, under all these circumstances of childhood, sickness, and old age, was this rich birthright recognized, on that lovely Island!"

"But cruelly defrauded of it, by emancipation, have been hundreds of thousands, thrown off as discarded children, to suffer; while to the slave it is more secure and permanent than any birthright to property in our country."

This noble and benevolent feature of the system is kept out of sight by the abolitionists, even when they profess "to show it fairly in its best phases."

"In its best aspect," the model artist says, "she has perhaps been successful."

"That *perhaps*, Dr., is not badly put: and yet how certain is it, and how certainly she knew, that NOT, instead of *perhaps*, would have been the true word!"

"She cannot be ignorant, that thousands of old slaves, past labor,—and yet more able to work than are many poor men in the North, black and white, who are compelled to work or starve,—are living in perfect comfort on their birthright. Nor, in practice, is this peculiar to the born in the land. The privileges of birthright are extended to all alike. Old King was not born in the land; and though still, by name, a slave, he became, indeed, almost a Lord of the Isle.

"Now, Dr., please hear the story which I would submit to your criticism, of King's happy old age.

"Old King had been, for several years, exempted from labor, on account, not of infirmity—for he was a strong man—but of age; though it still sat upon him almost youthfully. In his active life of labor, he had been a sub-overseer;—*driver*, as technically, but wrongly called. They are no more *drivers*, than are the overseers of the laborers on the canals and railroads, or elsewhere.

"In his official capacity, many years before, King had brought into culture one of the large fields of the plantation. It was called after him, KING-FIELD. This field, of the size of an ordinary northern farm, was to be laid off in *tasks.* To do it with facility and well, requires experience and skill. These had old King, and the overseer, proposed to the proprietor to have King lay it off. By the field hands, who were acquainted with King's talent in that department, it had been suggested to the overseer, who was a new man on the place.

"King is applied to by the master. The manner and spirit of the application, and the result, it would be difficult, I suppose, for one of our unhypocritical abolitionists to make any thing out of, but a mystery; and as a myth, I suppose, they must consider this narrative, which, however, is neither mysterious nor mythical.

"Undramatically it cannot be represented with any thing like an approach to the true facts of the case. I shall be pardoned, therefore, for making a little drama of it.

"Time: a vernal sunsetting eventide. Scene: Old King standing six feet in his shoes, straight as a British grenadier on duty, in front of his neat white cottage surrounded with flowers and fruit-trees bursting into promise. His children, grand children, and perhaps, great grand children, in cheerful idleness about him, to make glad the heart of the happy old man. The master approaches with the usual evening salutation, which is respectfully reciprocated. All but the quite little ones retire.

### SCENE FIRST.

MASTER.—"King, I come to ask a favor of you."

KING.—"Well, Master Jacob, what have you come to ask? What can I do for you, Jacob?"

MASTER.—"I wish you to ride over to King-field in the morning, and help the overseer lay it off in tasks."

KING.—"Can't the overseer do it himself, Jacob?"

MASTER.—"I dare say he might, King; but he is a stranger, you know, on the plantation; and so can't know the field so well as you, who have so many times laid it off. It would save time and not give you much trouble, I should think, to ride over and show the overseer how to do it right."

KING.—"If the overseer don't know yet, he had better learn as soon as possible, how to lay off a field into tasks."

MASTER.—"Yes, King, that's true; and I came to ask you to give him a lesson in laying off King-field."

KING.—"I'll think about it, Jacob, and let you know in the morning."

MASTER.—"Very well, King, I hope you will conclude to oblige me in this matter."

"Oblige the overseer, I suppose you mean, Jacob;" said the old man, as he entered his cottage, with two of the little ones hanging to his long-tailed black coat; fine enough for a parson. King preferred a black coat; and on his Island home, he was not afraid to wear it from apprehension of being asked to preach as a strange clergyman.

"Night throws her sable mantle o'er the Earth,
And pins it with a star."

She passeth away; and morning comes; bearing on her silken Zephyrs the mingled fragrance of the orange flower, the multiflora, and the jessamine.

The master and the servant again meet on the green and spacious lawn, that surrounds both the modest mansion and the picturesque cottage of the respective parties. After the morning salutations, cordial on the part of the master, and on the other part respectful, with a dash of ominous dignity, pass they on to

## SCENE SECOND.

MASTER.—"Well, King, I have ordered your horse for you to ride to King-field this delightful morning."

King.—"I am sorry to disappoint you, Jacob; but I have concluded not to go to King-field this morning."

Master.—"Why, King, what's the matter? Are you not quite well this fine morning?"

King.—"Yes, Master Jacob, the morning is fine enough, and I am well enough, and the ride would be pleasant enough; but I have concluded not to go. If I lay out King-field for the overseer, there will be no end to his wants of King to help him. You remember the last overseer, Jacob. I'll not help to spoil this one."

Master. "Really, King, I thought certainly you would be more obliging."

The master turns away with a disappointed and not well pleased air. King calls after him:

"Master Jacob, send the overseer to my house with the Kingfield plot; and I will show him how it must be laid off in tasks."

Each goes his own way. At breakfast, the master tells the story of King's contumacy, in not the most agreeable humor. He is listened to with gravity; and not without interest in the result. It comes out, and a ringing laugh of delight from the mistress restores all hearts to harmony.

"King *is* a king," says one of the ladies.

"I wonder," says a guest from the north, "if our anti-slavery folks would believe this story if told them, with all the particulars?"

"But how comes it," says another guest, "that the old negro takes such airs upon himself, with his master?"

"Naturally enough. When a child, King used to carry me in his arms. As a boy, he seemed to think that I was somehow under his special guidance and protection. And now, I have no doubt, he considers me, rather than otherwise, an appendage to his dignity; and that the plantation is quite as much his, as mine."

"Yes, and as I have been amused to observe, the words

'my plantation,' come much more frequently and familiarly from the mouth of the man than of the master; and with evidently more satisfaction."

"And truly speaking, with good reason; for, without the care—often not the most agreeable—that falls to my share, King enjoys all the comfort it can afford to any one."

"May we all be as comfortable and happy in old age, should we need it, as that old slave!" ejaculated one present.

"Ah," sighed a grave guest, "few, very few persons find his solid happiness in old age; and I fear there may be little hope of it for any of us, in all respects! Few old people seem to have so little of the past to regret; with so much of the present to enjoy; and at the same time, a so perfectly satisfied confidence in the future, as that old slave has."

These remarks were kindly and soberly received; and in thoughtful silence, the breakfast party separated.

With what a discordant absurdity would have sounded in their ears, these maxims of abomination:—"ANY THING BUT SLAVERY."—"SLAVERY MAKES MAN A BRUTE!"

Old King is a remarkable man. I speak of him as yet alive; for I have not heard of his demise. If still alive he is not much above ninety;—no uncommon case of longevity with the race in his happy condition; nor might it be, perhaps, with ours, but for our "Ideal of Respectability;" and had we as comfortable, contented, and easy times and tranquil lives, as they have. For cases of even toilsome life, very great ages are sometimes known among us. Besides others, here old Cash of the Catskill Mountains, worked among the stones of his miserable farm, at a hundred years old, or more; and at a hundred and seven, I saw him in his almost utterly comfortless state, waiting for death to come to his relief. The poor old man! The little purse made up for him by our party may have afforded a few unwonted comforts to his miserable old days and sleepless nights!

There are enough of cases of longevity to show that white people as well as black, are generally "*well made for length of life*," as Oliver said, when he examined the dead body of Charles. And that there are many more instances of longevity among the slaves of the South, than among free whites any where, clearly proves to my mind, that they have easier, and on the whole, happier lives than we have; to say nothing of our "Ideal of Respectability."

KING came to this country, at mature age, a Mahomedan. His first great trials seem to have been his forced companionship with pagan negroes on his passage, and submission to "*Christian dogs*," to which his captivity had doomed him. But as a sensible man, and a fatalist withal by religion, King soon schooled himself to submit with a good grace.

By his first master and his family in the South, he was considerately and kindly treated; and his talents and his prejudices were respected. King soon learned the language and the religion of the country of his captivity; and not many years elapsed before King became happy;—a happy Christian servant. And, with the freedom indeed, of a free soul, he rendered a hearty, faithful, and willing, obedience to them, who, in the providence of God, had become his rulers.

His vernacular Arabic, King did not exchange for the *nigger* jargon. He always too much despised it to allow himself, like the whites, to be amused by it; but the "English undefiled" of his first friends in America, he adopted as his model. His Islamism he did not abandon for any other ism *called* Christianity; but yielded only to true and hearty instruction in the Gospel, which he came heartily to love, and obey, as doing service to Christ, and not to man, merely. In advanced age, however, King's early impressions and habits of mind seemed sometimes strangely to mingle with his later Christian faith and sentiment. There is still remembered and spoken of, an interesting exemplification of this of seventeen years since.

A daughter of a former master, was on a visit to her island relations, and became dangerously ill. In her childhood, she had been one of King's darlings. His frequent and fervent prayers were offered for her safety and restoration. In these loving prayers, when carried out of himself by his ardency, and by the anxiety of the occasion, he would sometimes mingle the language of his old and of his new faith; and call on 'Allah,' as well as on the Saviour, "to have mercy, and raise up and save, my dear young mistress!"

On one of these occasions, it was said that King's attitude, in relation to the sun, seemed to indicate a mixture of even Sabeanism in his absorbing devotions, as if in early life he had known about and reverenced that sublime, and almost half divine idolatry:—perhaps, quite as good a religion as that which in our own day, says, "Down with the Bible."

But, for the present, enough of this remarkable old African. The history of his whole life would doubtless be one of great interest. Should it however tell in favor of the anathematized system, which, under God, made him a happy Christian, but of which Stowe, Sumner, and the rest, say that nothing bad enough can be written, or sung, or said, it would not be popular. Little else in our day is popular, except violent and unmeasured abuse of existing institutions; or, at least, the greater part of them. Fanny Wright was popular, and so is Mrs. Stowe.

Indecency, abuse, scoffing on subjects dear and awful—appeals to the vanity, appetites, and malignant passions, of ignorant and incompetent judges—such, alas! are the popularities of our times! No wonder that a scoffer of the Bible, and a sneerer at the protestant clergy of our country, has become a literary titular saint in popish and profligate Italy.

"Well, Doctor, what of my old King?"

"It will do. I was thinking more of its revival of my recollections of an interesting and pleasant passage of my life, than of the composition as a work of art."

"It is scarcely, if any thing, more than a simple transcript of memory."

"It can hardly be to others, as pleasant a tale of truth and happiness as to me; but as an interesting record of real scenes, showing how happy good servants in the condition of slaves may be, under the rule and care of kind masters and mistresses; for the truth's sake, it ought to be prized by all who love the Truth."

"And let us hope that so it may be, and do a little of the good it is intended to do."

"So will we hope; and that your pictures of negro happiness may help somewhat to qualify our ideal of respectability."

# CHAPTER XIV.

## PREJUDICES OF EDUCATION, AN APOLOGY FOR ABOLITIONISTS.

"—— Warp'd the line of every other favor;
Scorn'd a fair color, or express'd it stolen;
Extended or contracted all proportions,
To a most hideous object."

AMONG conscientious abolitionists there are very many worthy persons, whom I hold in much esteem. I would not say one word to wound them, if it were possible to avoid that word, and, at the same time, to discharge faithfully the duty which I have taken upon myself *as* a duty to which I feel myself called. Such conscientious persons are misled, generally, no doubt, without fault of theirs. And even for many of their misleaders, whom they respect as wholesome teachers, I would urge the apology of their misfortune of early prejudice. To meet the case of each, this chapter is offered with an open hand, and a heart full of charity.

To all who may honestly disclaim political motives and consideration, the charitable hope may be extended, that the rancorous spirit, in which they indulge themselves in speaking and writing of Southern Slavery, was originally and principally, derived from the study of pagan authors about ancient slavery. Their erroneous notions, unreasonable prejudices, and violent resentments, may also have found nourishment in former abuses of the institution, which no longer exist; or, except, possibly, in very rare instances; as in a late case, in which a monument was erected to commemorate it, in the form of a gallows for the master, who suffered on it the extreme penalty of the laws, enacted for the protection of the slave; whom the abolitionist would have to be believed, is without rights, and without protection.

But chiefly, from ancient pagan literature, they have drawn their poisoned shafts, which in such clouds are sped,

> ——— "As the feath'ry snows
> Fall frequent, on some wintry day, when Jove
> Hath risen to shed them on the race of man
> And show his arrowy stores."

At "*slavery in the abstract,*"—"hated of gods and men,"—they thrust their sharpened weapons, so directed as to transfix real masters, over the heads of their imaginary men of fiction. In their classical reading, they learn, that the condition of the slave of heathen antiquity was as miserable as toil, and oppression, and cruelty, and degradation could make it; and, without farther investigation, they at once apply it to the slavery of the South; as though, in all ages and countries, the same word expressed the same character and condition;—knave and knight, to the contrary notwithstanding."

At fifteen, or before, they read in classic authors, that slaves have no rights; and, at fifty, Dr. Channing has it stereotyped for the use of the whole school; in every essay, and speech, and sermon, and poem, and romance, on Southern slavery. "*The slave has no rights;*" says Dr. Channing; and, at once, the school all respond, "The slave has no rights." "*Slavery makes man a brute,*" says the Doctor. "Slavery makes man a brute," echo all the disciples; with an inflation of enthusiasm that prepares them to embrace heartily, and vociferously, the doctor's mad maxim—"Any thing but slavery!"

They find the Roman law forbidding the marriage of slaves; and though against reason and authority, they seem not to doubt, for a moment, that such a law is existing in full force in our own South.

They read that once in Rome, the master possessed over his slaves, the uncontrolled power of life and death; and that he might torture, mutilate,—kill his slave, for any or no offence; and, though impossible, they seem to think the Southern master now clothed with such unlimited and despotic power.

The father had like power over the child, and the husband over the wife, for a long time in ancient pagan Rome; but no where now, I believe, are fathers permitted, in Christendom, to kill their children with impunity; or husbands allowed to kill their wives. They sometimes do it, and are hanged; oftener they are cleared, on a plea of insanity; oftener yet, still, they go unpunished, for lack of testimony; but the law condemns it, as it once did not, in ancient Rome. To judge soberly, by our daily papers,—scarcely one of which in a month, is not soiled horribly, by one account or more of detected *family* murders,—of all others the least difficult to conceal,—the very thought is most frightful, of how many such murders, in our practically, almost atheistic age and country, may be daily and nightly perpetrated! More, I much fear me, within a hundred miles of where I am now writing,—many more,—than of Southern slaves, murdered by their masters, in any whole year of the present century!

The laws of Rome recognized no obligation upon the master of a slave to furnish him with food and clothing; or to take care of him in sickness; yet most effectually is this obligation bound on the Southern master. Among free people, all over the wide world, thousands daily perish from destitution and neglect; but most rare are such cases among Southern slaves. By an authority to be relied on, it is declared that the offence, for which the unhappy culprit was executed a few weeks since in South Carolina, "consisted as much of the *neglect* of his duty as a master, as of any other ingredient." Will the North understand this? Or will people still give large pay, and fill the world with peans, to abolitionists, to write, and to preach, and to talk, as though it were not so? And still, will they affect to believe, that if masters so please, they may, unrebuked, and undisturbed, in their abominable heathen wickedness, allow their slaves to go naked and starve; or, in sickness, die, uncared for and neglected?

Many pagan masters of old time, acted upon the barbarous principle, that great severity towards their slaves was necessary to keep them in subjection. Abolitionists write—Lord Palmerston inclusive—and preach and talk, as though it were still so. There may still be such masters, occasionally found;—fathers there are more than occasionally:—but very different are the views and practices generally, among the Christian masters of the South; whatever may be the classical notions of our abolitionists to the contrary.

Of the Roman Hortensius, it is written that he cared so much less for the slaves of his household, than for his fish in his ponds, that with the former he was accustomed to feed the latter; and our abolition authors and orators seem anxious to inculcate the notion, upon their readers and hearers, that the South is principally populated with masters of this Roman type.

Cicero was a man of heart; though a Roman in its age of hardness; and aware that his sensibilities were not popular, he apologizes for the feeling of sorrow at the death of a domestic, as being greater than it ought to have been for a slave. What would the ancient Roman think of one of the bravest of the brave weeping over a dying friend, in the person of a slave? But such sights have been seen;

and that slave not a fair and accomplished Greek, as Cicero's probably was, but a jet black African!

For a long time, it was a practice common in Rome, to expose sick, helpless, decrepid, and aged slaves, on an island in the Tiber, in order to save their maintenance. But does, therefore, any one suppose that in the South there is any such practice? With great tenderness, and boundless generosity, as elsewhere shown, the sick and disabled slaves are most kindly cared for and gently nursed; and to such extent is this Christian kindness pursued, that the aged slave, when past labor, is often as comfortable as if independently rich and free.

According to the comic writers of the Roman Empire, instruments of slave chastisement seem to have formed, not only a part of the useful, but even of the ornamental furniture of the parlor, the drawing-room, and the ladies' toilet, that they might be always at hand, and ready for use.

In view of this fiction, probably, of the Roman satirists, the model anti-slavery author of the age, thinks it necessary, somehow, to match them in her romance, and so she imagines a modern pagan master boasting of a fist, hardened into something like a Roman "bull's hide," by knocking down negroes.

In Rome, it may not have been altogether uncommon, to chain the janitor, like a house-dog, to his post at the entrance-door;—but I beg of my abolition friends not to think me romancing, when in sober seriousness, I assure them, that such sights are by no means common in the South; for when there, I looked with no little diligence and curiosity, and looked in vain, for a single example of that renowned custom of classic antiquity.

Cato, the censor, may have been in the daily habit of going afield, at early dawn, with a gang of chained slaves, led by a strong team of bullocks; but such practice, or habit, belongs not to the southern planter; as also I beg of my friends to be persuaded to believe.

In fine, nothing can be truer, than that the slavery of the South is generally as unlike that of ancient Rome, as is the religion of the Gospel unlike the religion of ancient Rome. Nowhere now on earth, perhaps, is there found, on an extensive scale, any parallel to the ancient pagan slavery, but in Africa alone, where the life of the slave is apparently of no consideration; and where, by thousands in a day, tyrant savage masters sacrifice them, to give zest to a holiday sport, as did the pagans of two thousand years ago,

—— "to make a Roman holiday."

Not altogether from the classic sources of antiquity, have the abolitionists imbibed the bitter waters of their unhappy delusion. Partly, too, from what they have greedily read and heard of the abuses of the relation of master and servant. By closing their eyes, ears, and hearts, against every other abuse, they have been able to keep warm their violent feelings, and to kindle into frequent flames their passionate hate of an institution that has existed, through God's providence, from a period long anterior to the days of Abraham, "the friend of God," and an extensive slaveholder.

It would seem that, blinded by a most obstinate prejudice, while they can discern the progress of improvement in other relations of life, they can discover none in that of master and servant. In some other relations—as generally of master and apprentice, employer and employee—most decided deteriorations have befallen. These they cannot see. And so closely have they sealed their eyelids, that they cannot, because they will not, see and acknowledge the happy progress that has been made in the slaves' condition, by benevolent legal enactments for their protection and comfort, and by the diffusion of Christian knowledge and principles.

In the last century, the poor of New England were annually sold at auction to such men as could press the greatest amount of toil out of them, and sustain them at the cheapest rate. And they were treated most unfeelingly. It is not so now. This is seen and acknowledged. In the last century, many masters may have treated their slaves as badly as did the people of the North their poor neighbors and relations; and in some cases even worse,—if worse *can* be. It is not so now. But this is *not* seen and acknowledged, by even abolitionists who pretend, and perhaps intend to be candid.

From the early days of Wilberforce, to the present days of Palmerston, they are learned in all that has been said and written and sung of abominable abuses, and they affect to suppose, that, as Palmerston says, they are *necessary* concomitants of the relation, and peculiar to the connexion of master and slave; than which nothing more false or absurd could easily be said by the most rabid reformer of the most radical type. With the viscountess, does the viscount too, disclaim political motives?

The abolitionist goes back fifty or an hundred years, for instances of atheistic cruelty towards slaves in the West Indies, and elsewhere,—Algiers perhaps,—and he burnishes them up to apply to the present generation of Christian masters. Why not thus ignore the history of progress in other things? Because the infamous Jeffries was a murderous judge, why not insist that all British Judges are still murderous?

Henry Eighth certainly was a very decidedly bloody tyrant; and James Second was very little better; but the Charleses and Georges were not so bad; the Williams were still less bad. Of Mary and Elizabeth not much of good can be said; but VICTORIA is a little gem of a queen;

though still unable to keep any of the bad things belonging to slavery out of her dominions, save the *name* only. The character of the sovereigns of Great Britain has very decidedly improved, no doubt; and yet there are plenty of people, even there, ready to assert, in as bold language as Lord Palmerston's on slavery, that *sovereign power must necessarily be abused.** And thus apply it unhesitatingly to the British sovereign. The character of the slave master is quite as much improved, generally, though Lord Palmerston condescends to echo the absurd Stowe declaration of the inevitable necessity of the abuse of slavery and sends his wife to the Stafford house to add her name to the multitude of female endorsers.

* A little anachronism? "It's of no consequence."

# CHAPTER XV.

## LORD PALMERSTON AND HON. E. EVERETT.

"Pray, how came you to know that men were formerly fools? How did you find that they are now wise? Who made them fools? Who in Heaven's name made us wise? Who d'ye think are most, those that loved mankind foolish, or those that love it wise? How long has it been wise? How long otherwise? Why did the old folly end now and no later? Why did the modern wisdom begin now and no sooner? What were we the worse for the former folly? What the better for the succeeding wisdom?—Now answer me, an' t please you!"

FR. RABELAIS, *as quoted by Coleridge.*

THAT great men are not always great, and that the wise are sometimes otherwise, are true sayings which are seldom better exemplified, than has appeared quite recently that they have been on either side of the Atlantic, by Viscount Palmerston, and our own learned and estimable Secretary of State, who will pardon this ungenial and reluctant coupling and charge it solely to the account of chronology.

The former has so fairly exposed the designs of his government as to render them quite harmless. I will therefore propose a few simple questions to his lordship, and leave him in other hands.

My lord, has the experiment of emancipation in your own West Indian islands induced your belief, that it would be wise and humane to "render free the negro population of Cuba?" It might, indeed, "create a most powerful element of resistance to any scheme for annexing Cuba to the United States;" for soon would it reduce that noble island to the wretched, and all but uninhabitable, condition of your thrice miserable Jamaica,—every third man a pauper!

"With regard to the bearing which negro emancipation would have on the interests of the white proprietors, *it may safely be affirmed that free labor costs less than slave labor.*"

Yes; certainly; the history of England has made that so plain that it may indeed *be safely affirmed.* When the peasantry of England, in a *quasi*, if not real, slavery, had allowed claims on the proprietors of support, for themselves and families, their labor cost more to the proprietors, than now, when no such claims are recognized, and they are suffered to perish in multitudes. Is this your meaning, my lord?

You speak of "a free and contented peasantry as safer neighbors for the wealthy classes above them than ill-treated and resentful slaves." Has England a free and contented peasantry? Why then the frequent incendiarisms and alarms about chartism? Has Ireland a free and contented peasantry? Why then are they fleeing in droves from oppression, famine and pestilence?

Have your West Indian possessions contented peasantries? Why then the necessity of armed police corps, day and night under arms to secure their tranquillity by the point of the bayonet?

"Ill-treated and resentful slaves!" Is this indeed an authentic copy of a real public document, from the "FOREIGN OFFICE" of Great Britain, and signed "PALMERSTON?"

Is it not rather a hoax?—a trick of some wag; or of an enemy to his lordship, to make him appear contemptible?

Can it be, that a man who is *ever* wise, and not *always* otherwise, could write thus, on a grave and important occasion?—"That slaves *must*, from the nature of things, be more or less ill-treated, is a truth which belongs to the inherent principles of human nature, and is quite as inevitable as the resentment, however suppressed it may be, which is the consequence of ill-treatment." ! ! !

Is this man a miserably benighted atheist? Has he no belief in the influence of a divine Spirit on the human heart and human principles? The wisdom of his religious views has long been suspected, by good and wise men; but I am not aware that he has ever before officially declared his utter infidelity, and his total unbelief of the renovating principles of the Gospel! If this document be indeed authentic, I have no more to say to or of its author; but to such others as may be of a different character of faith, and who may be deluded by him into this gross error, I will say, in passing, that it is a profane absurdity, to say that slaves are *necessarily ill-treated.*

The good slave of a good master is no more, *necessarily*, subject to ill-treatment, than is the good child of good parents, or the good wife of a good husband. To Lord Palmerston, it may go for nothing; but with many of my readers, I trust it will not go for nothing; that hundreds of thousands of the slaves of our Southern States are fellow members of Christian churches with their masters; and with them and their families participate in Gospel privileges and ordinances. Are they *necessarily* ill-treated? No: in such relation, they are NECESSARILY well-treated.

> Then "stay, my Lord!
> And let your reason with your choler question
> What 'tis you go about."

The Hon. EDWARD EVERETT, at the late annual celebration of the American Colonization Society, made an eloquent and edifying speech, which was heard by a large and delighted audience of beauty and greatness; and it has been very extensively read with pleasure and approbation.

Among his introductory remarks, Mr. Everett says he

had been able to make "but the hastiest and most inadequate preparation." He regretted this; and so do I. He is a great man, of high reputation, and eminent station and authority; therefore, whatever he says as a fact, is supposed to be rightly said; and that not only all his positions, but his passing remarks, are to be relied on as verities. With great and sincere deference for the character of Mr. Everett, it is my purpose to call attention to a few things in his generally excellent address, which appear to me as not thus reliable. They do not however take every thing from its value, as an appeal, and a most forcible one, in behalf of the Colonization Society; and heartily do I wish, that, as it ought, it may do great and lasting good to that enlightened scheme of true philanthropy.

In speaking of the native races of Africa,—meaning of course the negro races, he has this passage: "It is said that they alone, of all the tribes of earth, have shown themselves incapable of improving their condition." Well, sir, who knows that? Of the early history of our race we know but little, in any part of the globe. A dark cloud hangs over it. "The whole of the North and West of Europe, till the Roman civilization shone in upon it, *was as benighted as Africa is now.*"

"The whole?" Is not the Hon. Secretary led into error by contemplating things too much in the gross? Would it not be difficult to find an authentic account of a great and powerful tribe of Europe before the Roman invasion, who, inhabiting an extensive and rich country abounding with noble rivers, and having and knowing of no better way to cross them than on a bullock's back, or hanging to his tail? But such was the great Zoolu tribe on the Eastern coast of Africa less than thirty years since, before they had seen the white race.

He says, "It is quite certain that, at a very early

period of the history of the world, some of the native races of Africa had attained a high degree of culture." The negroes? No; not the negroes; the Egyptians. But what has that trite schoolboy fact to do with the "improvability" of the negroes to be colonized?

"Races that emerged from barbarism *later than those of Africa have*, with fearful vicissitudes on the part of individual States, acquired and maintained a superiority over Africa, but I am not prepared to say, that it rests on natural causes of a final and abiding character. *We are led into error by contemplating things too much in the gross.*" Nothing may be more true or common than such leading into error; and the Secretary stands not alone as an illustrious exemplification.

What "races of Africa *have*" emerged from barbarism? There are doubtless some Mahomedan tribes of Africa, of a mingled breed, that have made some sort of advances towards civilization, but does it not still remain to be proved, that any purely negro race, uninfluenced from abroad, have improved at all since negro Africa was known to the civilized world?

That by the sacrifice of untold funds and lives they may improve in the lapse of several ages, under the persevering and Christian instruction and example of their self-sacrificing devoted friends, the missionary colonists, with the efficient and enlightened aid of a NATION of negroes already civilized and Christianized, in a Christian land, it would be shocking, if not absurd, to doubt. It must however be a slow business, as shown by all experiments yet made. Among the very last Reports from the Missionaries at Liberia,—the chiefs, with savage indignation, forbid all "*palaver about peace*" among the tribes, even in the very neighborhood of the colony.

"They are not savages;" says Mr. Everett. This can hardly, with strict propriety, be said to be a matter, or question, of *taste;* but it is certainly of definition. And as he has not informed us of any negro tribe which has not emerged from barbarism, or even from savagism, but by compulsion, or foreign aid; and as he allows that *some* of the tribes are "feeble hordes," and others "squalid and scarcely human," the definition of the word savage, is no great matter; and I will only remark, in passing, that the beaver, and many other animals, have "*a rude architecture;*" and many of them less rude far than that of the African savage.

Mr. E. speaks of slaves *collected from every portion of the interior of Africa.* There are still vast portions of Central and Eastern Africa, where the foreign slave trade has never penetrated, nor been heard of; and where prisoners of war are all butchered on the spot, saving only such as are selected and enslaved by the conquerors to be *sepoyed* for further conquests. And he speaks of re-captured slaves at Liberia *finding their way back to their native tribes;* as if such return, if possible, were always desired and desirable. Does Mr. E. really *believe* such to be the case? In this, then, at least, he believes too much, and inconsistently besides, as we shall see.

Of the Africans in the palmy days of the slave-trade, he says, "*it is not without example that these benighted beings*"—but they are not savages!—"*have delivered their wives and children to the slave dealer.*"

Would it be very desirable for these wives and children to find their way back to such husbands and fathers, to be again sold to the slave dealer? For Mr. E. says of the often so called *suppressed* slave trade, "It still exists to a frightful extent, and the more active the means used to suppress it by blockade and cruisers, the greater the cruelty incident to its practice." It would seem, then, as a pretty clear case, that it would not be a very desirable boon to enable the unhappy negroes to "find their way back to their native tribes."

There are several other things in this generally excellent speech for the occasion on which it was delivered, that might be named and noticed as not ill adapted to mislead careless readers, who *judge of things in the gross*, from selected specimens. From Mungo Park, who certainly describes the African condition, as in general, miserably savage, he takes his account of educated Mahomedan Africans so far advanced in civilization as "that lawsuits are argued with as much ability, fluency, and at as much length, as at Edinburgh." And this, many of his readers—all abolition readers—will take as undoubted example of the *improvability* of the African race generally; although the following sentence says, "I am certainly aware that the condition of the most advanced tribes of Central Africa is wretched, mainly in consequence of the slave-trade which exists among them in the most deplorable form."

What slave-trade, Mr. Everett—the foreign slave-trade? No, sir; but a domestic slave-trade, which has existed for thousands of years, and I fear, in spite of any foreign intervention to abolish it, will continue still to exist. Such too, was the well weighed, enlightened, and dear bought opinion of the lamented Mungo Park,—as elsewhere I have shown,—notwithstanding his discovery of a mixed breed of black Mahomedan Lawyers.

But I will not pursue this ungracious task. It is true, this speech of our admirable Secretary, before the American Colonization Society, not very pleasantly revives my recollection of a speech by a British Secretary of State, of some fifty years ago, before the House of Commons; in which, like ours, he compared ancient Savage Europe, with modern Savage Africa. It was "the Secretary who stood alone, and had no fellow." Pity it had not been so; for he was the great pauper-maker of England.

But with all our own Secretary's "hastiest and most inadequate preparation," which so unfortunately and fully he has shown, there is still more good and valuable sense in his speech, than can be found in the declamatory and adcaptandum speeches, on the negro subject, of Burke, Fox, and Pitt, in the British Parliament; and with all the essays of the smaller ones to boot. Therefore, the more to be regretted is it, that there should be aught else in it than the good, the sensible, and the truthful; and most sadly is it to be lamented, at this time, especially, that it should contain so many things—or any thing—to mislead the unwary, and to encourage the ignorant and the prejudiced, to be satisfied with their ignorance, and to cherish their prejudices.

## CHAPTER XVI.

### BRITISH SLAVERY.

THE Ladies and Nobles of England, zealous to do good, will pardon an old man, if he more distinctly indicate to them where work may be found to fill all their hearts, and to employ all their hands; with as many to help them as may be procured on both sides of the ocean.

You are all, no doubt, on the best and most cordial terms with Mr. D'Israeli, the late distinguished Chancellor of the Exchequer. He seems not to have been prepared to solve the problem of manning your war ships without the aid of the worst and cruelest system and acts of violence that ever yet marked any species of slavery. Safely, however, and without much inconvenience to him, he may be consulted on the more general and terrific national evils of poverty, destitution, depravity, criminality; of the most startling pictures of which he is already the accomplished and truthful author. He may point out to you a limitless scene of suffering and degradation, to employ all your great powers, and to keep in warmth and action all your deep sympathies, without exposing them to the dangers of a sea-voyage. He will show to you a great body of the ENGLISH people, compared with whose wretchedness and vileness our slaves, as a body, are not only clothed in purple and fine linnen, and fed sumptuously every day, but that they merit such distinction, from their superior intellectual and moral excellencies. Does this sound extravagant? Ask the Chancellor of the Exchequer.

Ask him concerning men, women, and children, without bread and without work. Ask him of their condition, and how they fell into it. He may discreetly pass over the origin of the evil; but he will tell you, that so long as the *miserables* retained any sense of moral responsibility, they begged of their fellow creatures for leave to *toil*, that they might live *honestly;* but so generally and so cruelly were they repulsed, that the generation of to-day, by hundreds of thousands, of both sexes, and of all ages, never apply for labor, and only prowl for prey! Men, women, and children,—without bread and without work! What a picture has he drawn with his truthful pencil, of revolting, loathesome vice, and of astounding and frightful crime!

Through a darkness that may indeed be felt, follow his guidance, and you may perceive with more than one sense, a lurid, ghastly, fetid flame, around which are grouped multitudes of squalid, desperate, ferocious human beings, standing in furious pride of strength, and brandishing their fists and their clubs, as if in defiance of both heaven and earth; over and among half bent cripples, lunatics, imbeciles, disgusting inebriates, and crying and starving children!

From their dog-like birth to their "burial as of an ass," such is their wretched life-long being, such their death—the only desirable event from their no-cradle to their no-grave!

And what says the ex-minister concerning the religious and moral education of these ENGLISH people? Ladies, he tells us, on the best authority—not as a fancy—not as a truthless fiction, nor a worthless romance,—but as a truthful and sustained representation—that among these native English people—these subjects of the British crown, there were numerous grown up men and women, who did not know of a God! Grown up men and women, who laughed at the idea of a Bible! Grown up men and women, who had never heard of a Saviour, sent to redeem the world!

Is there *one* such slave in all of our calumniated land? God be thanked, that I have so good reason to doubt it!

And what says the chancellor about the morality of those English *miserables?*

Morality? They had no conception of its meaning! What is the morality of atheistic desperadoes, struggling incessantly for food to allay hunger; for objects on which to gorge their beastly appetites; for victims of their wrathful indignation, that they are uncared for by their reckless betters? What is the morality of life-long and atheistic hunger?

"A large portion of the crimes punished by law," says the Abbe de la Mennais, "arise from hunger; they will disappear, when the men whom it now besets shall be beyond the reach of its fatal suggestions."

But the multitudes of English *miserables* are *never* beyond its reach, and never even hope to be; and, therefore, they say, practically:

——"Evil, be thou my good;"

and when, by cunning or violence, they have procured the license to add, "let us eat and drink, for to-morrow we die," they have declared their entire code of morals and of religion.

But, not too much to trouble the ex-Chancellor of the Exchequer, allow me, ladies,—having first recommended to your special perusal the writings of the Rev. author of Alton Locke,—especially his "YEAST A PROBLEM"—to refer you, for further information, for work to do, to your colonial secretary.

Ask him, if it be indeed true, that England has, at this day, hundreds of thousands of slaves in the most wretched condition, held by her subjects in her Eastern possessions;

and not by her subjects only, but even by herself, as a slaveholder! Ask him, "Is it indeed *true*, that BRITANNIA—that VICTORIA herself, even, is a *slaveholder?*"

As an honest man, he must answer you affirmatively.

And what does Victoria do with her slaves? For, by that *name*,

"Slaves cannot breathe in England."

She hires them out abroad, and receives pay for their toil!

Should not the colonial secretary be at leisure to explain all this to you, ladies, please send your own secretary's deputy's servant, to turn over the volumes of the ASIATIC JOURNAL, in search of a satisfactory and authoritative explanation. As he proceeds in his special pursuit, let him take notes of the character and condition of the miners, and pearl-fishers; palanquin-bearers, &c.; and of the sepoys; especially what amount they enjoy of the privilege conferred on the human race by "*God's own law,*" *instituted in the time of man's innocency.*

Or, if, without such investigation, you should desire an immediate explanation, look at once into the "Journal" for 1838, at page 221, and you will learn that slavery, in your own Indian colonies, is, indeed, the wretched thing that you have been wickedly deceived into supposing it to be in our country.

You will there learn, from the undoubted authority of an official work, published in your own metropolis, that, by your own Government, "hundreds of thousands of" your own "fellow creatures are fettered down for life to the degrading destiny of slavery." That they are not worse off than your own London chiffoniers and paupers, or millions of your laborers, and cutlers, and trampers, is not to the point. *They are slaves!*

"We KNOW," says this high official authority,—"we

know that these unfortunate beings are not, as is the case in other countries, serfs of the soil, and incapable of being transferred, at the pleasure of their owners, from one estate to another. No: they are daily sold, like cattle, by one proprietor to another; the husband is separated from the wife, and the parent from the child. They are loaded with every indignity; the utmost quantity of labor is exacted from them, and the most meagre fare that human nature can possibly subsist on, is doled out to support them."

Ladies of England; this is said truly, no doubt, of slavery in British India; but this language becomes a base calumny, when applied to the mild servitude of our Southern States. Oh, then, first make the wretched condition of your own Indian slaves, as comfortable as are our Southern negroes, and then intervene in favor of our slaves, to make them, if possible, still more comfortable; if, indeed, you can find nothing more pressing, nearer home, to employ your charity upon.

A word more from the Asiatic Journal, in explanation of the slaveholding position of your royal and excellent queen, well beloved of all and every where.

"Will it be believed, that the Government itself participates in this description of property; that it actually holds possession of slaves, and lets them out for hire to the cultivators of the country, the rent of a whole family being two panams, or half a rupee per annum?"

On these several very important points, ladies and nobles of England, in your commanding position,—whence you can more easily see across the Atlantic Ocean, than across a narrow court or lane in your own metropolis,—you may easily procure every desirable satisfaction. And when this you shall have done, please propound to the Colonial Secretary; or to some other noble friend, who may be able and willing to answer them,—these few simple questions; which, we think, in our simplicity, ought to interest the ladies and nobles of England, not less than the condition and circumstances of our happy Southern negroes:—

1. "Is it true, that the hundreds of thousands of slaves, spoken of in the Asiatic Journal, make but a small sample, comparatively, of the slavery of British India?"

2. "Is the whole of Hindostan, and all the adjacent possessions, in the East, virtually in fact one monster and magnificent national plantation; and worked by more than AN HUNDRED MILLION OF SLAVES?"

3. "Are all these human creatures under a despotism which is not responsible to British law?"

4. "And is it so, as said, written, and printed, and published;—or is it a calumny, as we wish we could hope,—that, of these same slaves, a very large army is organized and disciplined by British officers, to carry war into neighboring regions for the purpose of making *more slaves;* and of farther and farther extending the slave territory of the British nation?"

"For the payment of a claim of £990, is the whole of Burmah thus cruelly enslaved?"

5. "If such be indeed the truth of the case, abroad, how is the anomaly to be explained that,

"A slave cannot breathe in England?"

When these interesting inquiries shall be fairly disposed of, perhaps through the Colonial Secretary, or some other accredited avenue of high intelligence, you may derive some valuable information about the state of things in your West Indian Islands.

If you will enter upon it with the zealous devotion, which you have brought into the service of your present enterprise, you will certainly find it an exceedingly attractive subject of inquiry.

Some of your own noble lords at home, may be well able to tell you whether it was a good and wise measure, commercially, to add twenty millions to the national debt to hang on the already tired neck of British labor; and so to invest that large amount as to destroy the prosperity, and to blast the prospects of those fair islands of the sea. They may perhaps inform you, whether the measure were purely philanthropical, or partly commercial and avaricious. History says, that the people of England were principally moved by the *money argument;*—that in the reduction of the price of sugar, for their 20,000,000 they would get 100,000,000.

But wasted revenue, taxed labor, and multiplied pauperism and crime, in your own land,—though all but overwhelmed by them;—may be thought less worthy of your ladyships' attention, than the condition of foreign negroes. If so, then, let the negroes of your islands claim a portion of your thoughts.

"But they are not *slaves!*"

No: by *name*, they are not, as from your own island home, with great care, and expense of cash, credit and comfort, you have abolished the name. But is the thing too abolished? The shadow may be gone; but as a greatly increased evil, to both white and black, the substance remains, in its hardest form and character.

And now, since I have taken upon myself to indicate to your Ladyships, sources of information on other important matters, I will suggest to you a very agreeable method to obtain all required knowledge touching the West India negroes. With their former masters you need give yourselves no trouble. They are all ruined; and such, as have not fled or become victims, at home, are clerks, and very subordinate employees of Government, principally; and, of course, not worthy your Ladyships' attention. From them you may not look for reliable information.

Take this pleasanter course of investigation, into the condition and character of the negroes;—the only portion of the population at all worthy of your attention. By way of simplifying your study, let the Island of Jamaica be the limit of your research. And by the way of something like a "royal road" to the needful learning, cause a digest to be made for you, of colonial and parliamentary reports; and let them be collated with the missionary and ecclestical reports of the Island, and with the accredited accounts of impartial travellers. In this way you may learn the present condition and character of the independent negroes

Having thus made yourselves learned on the subject of the *present*, in Jamaica, please read the very pleasant book of a former member of Parliament,—the "Journal of a West India proprietor. By the late Hon. Matthew G. Lewis." In it you may find many pleasant things of the *past*, of Jamaica, while the negroes were happy in their only happy condition—under the protection of a superior race, who cared for them. This work was published in London, in 1833; many years after the decease of the author; and when the hard destiny of Jamaica had been decided.

In the same year, there was also published in London, Mrs. Carmichael's "Domestic Manners in the West Indies." From these, and like works, you may learn what were the condition, and character, and comforts of the negroes as slaves; and you may judge whether they are better off, and better, as they are now;—like your neighbors across the channel,—kept tranquil, at the point of the bayonet.

This chapter I will close in the weighty words of one of our late departed great Senators, the dead lion that abolitionism will never cease to kick. Speaking of England's boasted abolition of slavery in the West Indies, Mr. Calhoun says:

"What has she, in reality, done there but to break the comparative mild and guardian authorities of the master, and to substitute in its place, her own direct and unlimited power? What but to replace the overseer by the army, the sheriff, the constable, and the tax collector? Has she made her slaves free? Has she given them the right of self-government? Is it not mockery to call their present subject condition freedom? What would she call it, if it were hers,—if, by some calamity to her and the civilized world, she should fall under similar subjection to France, or some other power? Would she call that freedom, or the most galling and intolerable slavery?"

Ladies of England; please think soberly and sensibly, on the subjects and suggestions of this chapter, and then, as Christian women, in the fear of God, judge ye, whether your proper field of duty may not be found nearer home than, at the Stafford House, you seemed to suppose. And may you be greatly blessed in the charitable work of *neighbors* to the "wounded and half dead," and down-trodden at your very doors.

# CHAPTER XVII.

## THE EARL OF CARLISLE.

To this noble Lord; in various ways distinguished honorably;—at present most distinguished, as an editor of an infidel and seditious romance, by an American woman of the age,—it is hoped the only one of the age who could so have prostituted *her* mind,—there are a few questions, which may be, with more propriety than to the Ladies of England, directly addressed. For, it can hardly be supposed, that so illustrious a senator of England, has failed to acquaint himself with the real evils and sufferings and wrongs of his own country, before identifying himself in a wild crusade of intervention, to remove imaginary evils and sufferings and wrongs, in a foreign land; and, if it may be, to overthrow the institutions of that foreign land.

Of the noble Lord, then, I would ask respectfully;—and in consideration of the honors and courtesies so amply extended to him in my country, it is hoped and expected, that he will reply at his earliest convenience to these few simple enquiries:—

1. Is it true, the Irish "cabin" is demolished, and poor "Uncle Pat," with his wife and children turned out on the high roads to perish; as so often testified by witnesses accredited by the British Parliament as men of truth and veracity? In this condition, how many millions are there in Ireland?

But we must enlarge a little on this thrilling enquiry:

Is it still true, that, "in Ireland, the law which protects

every shred of *property,* stops short of protecting *life?*" Does it still recognise no right to the continuance of existence in those unhappy human beings whom accident, misfortune, or the cruelty of their superiors, may drive to destitution? In its zeal for protecting the right of originally ill-gotten territorial property, does it still give to every landlord a ready and cheap power of ejecting his pauper tenantry from their only means of existence? Has he still this summary power of deciding the fate, the life, or death of these miserable beings; to be exercised alone at the dictates of his caprice or his cruelty?

As by astounding facts in millions, and as tens of thousands of martyrs have testified with their dying breath all these questions must still be answered affirmatively! And what is the consequence? Compared with it, the very worst consequence of negro slavery, under the very worst and cruelest master, is comparative comfort. For bad as the master may be, and cruel towards others, fear of the law of the land,—to the Irish landlord unknown,—will prevent his savage nature trifling with the life of his slave.

What is the consequence? Let those speak who know. Cast your eyes over the "Report of the Evidence taken before the Committee on the State of the Poor in Ireland;" and printed by order of the House of Commons, July, 1830," almost before the extremity of Irish suffering had been dreamed of! Gentlemen of the highest respectability for truth and veracity are the witnesses.

JAMES B. BRYAN, Esq., to the question, "What resources at present has the ejected Irish tenant?" answers,—

"He can get into jail by the commission of some slight offence; but he cannot get into the hospital without he is contaminated with some disease. He becomes therefore an idle mendicant."

REV. M. O'SULLIVAN. "Do you know what becomes of the tenantry at present ejected from estates in Ireland?"

"*I fear very many of them perish.*"

And this was before the potato famine.

Can the condition of the slave be worse? In pagan Rome only may its parallel be found. But worse even than this comes out in this authentic and unquestioned testimony! Worse than to perish of hunger and cold in a ditch by the wayside? Aye, worse far is the perpetuation of wretchedness by successive production.

DR. DOYLE says, "It would be impossible for language to convey an idea of the state of distress to which the ejected tenantry have been reduced, or of the disease and misery, and every vice, which they have propagated;—but what is, perhaps, the most painful of all, *a vast number of them have perished from want!*"

Pardon me, Doctor, if I consider that your own testimony brings out something still *more painful.*

"I have known a lane, with a small district adjoining, in the town in which I live, to have been peopled by thirty or forty families, who came from the country; and *I think that in the course of twelve months, there were not ten families of the thirty surviving—the bulk of them had died!*"

But here comes out now, in the same evidence, whatever the good Dr. Doyle may think, what I think, and what I wish all my friends to think, worse far than even to die in a ditch; or, on "a little straw strewed at night on the floor," which the Doctor speaks of, as the *best* lodging of the poor ejected tenants. "*The children begotten in this state of society become of an inferior caste; the whole character of the people becomes gradually worse and worse; they diminish in stature, they are enervated in mind; the population is gradually deteriorated, till at length, you have the inhabitants of one of the finest coun-*

*tries in the world reduced to a state of effeminacy which makes them little better than the Lazzaroni of Naples, or the Hindoos on the coast of Malabar.*"

"We have, in short, a disorganized population becoming by their poverty more and more immoral, and less capable of providing for themselves; and we have, besides that the frightful, and awful and terrific exhibition of human life wasted with a rapidity, and to a degree, such as is not witnessed in any civilized country upon the face of the earth!"

With our aid, and from the filial munificence of her own sons and daugters in our country, it is hoped and believed, that the miserable condition of many of the Irish poor has been considerably ameliorated. For within the last three years, as officially reported, those sons and daughters have sent back to their kindred, to help them to bear the grievous wrongs of a cruel oppression, nearly FIFTEEN MILLIONS OF DOLLARS!

Very sad must have been their wretched condition if this great sum has not much relieved it. How terrible the thought, that so large an amount has been required to keep a portion of them from perishing! How shocking the reflection of what would have been, and what would now be, their unspeakably miserable condition, without such source of relief.

Our Secretary of State speaks of this great remittance of money, as a fact which would defy belief were it not the result of official inquiry. On the other hand, I think "official inquiry" has been able to find out only a portion —perhaps a large portion—of the money, that filial love and friendship have conveyed to unhappy Ireland to sustain and comfort her suffering poor. It must be within the knowledge of many others, as it is within my knowledge, that funds have been taken to Ireland from this country, which no official inquiry, with which we are acquainted, could have discovered. And if all had sent home to their suffering parents, in proportion to their means, as liberally as have our good girl of the kitchen, and her good sister, I think the aggregate amount would have been nearer *fifty*, than *fifteen* millions in three years.

Poor unhappy Ireland! O that thy oppressors, by whom thy wisest sons have been maddened, would withdraw their pseudo-sympathy from our happy negro slaves, and extend to thee a true and efficient Christian sympathy, that should elevate thy children to the condition of happy freemen!

A cotemporary in the Quarterly Review, thus comments on this Parliamentary evidence: "The evidence before the Committee is full of similar descriptions. Nor does there exist any restraint whatever on the clearing of estates by landlords, and the consequent production of a mass of misery horrible to consider—nothing, in fact, to prevent an individual, residing, perhaps, at a distance, out of sight and hearing of the agonies he may inflict, from passing a *sentence of death* upon hundreds who have been encouraged to breed and multiply upon his estate—up to the moment when he became aware, from the lessons of political economists, the change of general opinion, or caprice, that it was against his individual interest any longer to allow them to live there—nothing to hinder his turning them out of their homes on the wide world, to starve or die of fever, engendered by want, after infesting, and severely burthening the charity of the neighboring towns—nothing but the *chance of his having a human or inhuman heart in his bosom—the mere chance* of this! Yes, there is one other check—his *fears*. Yes! Whiteboyism and Captain Rock are near him. But, on the other hand, he has to support him, the law, and an army. Our law and our army to protect the Irish landlord in the exercise of his despotic power over the lives of hundreds of his fellow-creatures; and, indeed, this power has been armed with additional facilities for its exercise, within a very few years past."

Will the Earl of Carlisle tell us if the state of things is now better in Ireland? Is a human life now, in that wretched land of oppression, of more, or less, value in the eye of the law, than a "shred of property?" From the unscrupulous romancer, to whom he has been lending himself as editor and eulogist, he may have imbibed some bitter fancies about our Southern negro slavery; but how will the most acrid of her lying imaginations compare with the killing bitterness of those Irish facts authenticated before the British Parliament? Should a master of slaves in our country play the murderous tyrant thus, and turn off his unprofitable slaves to perish, he would find even an army an inadequate protection.

2. Is it true, that emigrants and paupers, from Great Britain and Ireland, have been packed in emigrant ships, somewhat after the manner of the African slaves; and that, in this way the ship fever was originated, which has destroyed them by tens of thousands, and very many physicians and others, on this side of the ocean, who risked and lost their lives, in ministering to the necessities of such as survived the cruel miseries of the voyage?

3. Is it all true, which has been so often told and solemnly testified, of the sufferings of women and children,—*little* children, years younger than the children of the southern slave are allowed to be put to work,—is it true that women and such children toil and suffer in the mines and factories of England, as so told and testified? England, on whose soil "slavery cannot exist?"

4. As told by the London Times, is it true, that in the "centre and core of British civilization," the city of Lon-

don, there are one hundred thousand human beings who, if allowed to sleep, awake every morning in the horrid condition of the misery of having no certainty of a meal through the day, "except from a passing job or crime;" nor of a place of rest on the following night?

5. Is it true, as has been often very confidently declared as indisputable, that *more* than one hundred thousand young people—English people—in your Great Metropolis, male and female, are enrolled pupils of crime and infamy?

If all, or but some of these things be true, my lord, you will please allow my republican simplicity to enquire without offence to your lordship, if a philanthropic British Statesman might not find more suitable employment than in the Editorship of such a mischievous fable as "Uncle Tom's Cabin?" This in passing, however, to my last enquiry of this sort for the present.

6. Are the laws of England *still* "so arranged"—to use a phrase to your editorship familiar—that any thing so horribly revolting, beyond any parallel even in your dear adopted romance, may still be enacted in England, like the case of Mason, the impressed seaman and his murdered wife, as told in the "EXPERIENCE OF A BARRISTER?"

That it *did* happen, there is no question. The honest sailor was kidnapped, according to law; and his wife, in consequence, murdered, according to law, on the "soil of England." There is no doubt about the truth as declared by the eminent barrister, and described in all its *apparent* horrors,—no pen could tell half its *real* ones,—but the important question is, ARE THE LAWS OF ENGLAND STILL "SO ARRANGED?"

A word more, my lord, about the arrangement of English law. I am happily aware that since the days of Blackstone, a healing hand has been laid on some of the sorest ulcers of the diseased body. I am happy to believe, that when a horse happens to be missing from the stable of one of England's sporting gentry, a poor man found with a halter in his hand cannot as readily, as in the last century, be hanged for it, "that horses may not be stolen;" and I believe that a poor man has more chances to escape transportation and exile for life, for having a very partridge-looking fowl in his pot, to make broth for his sick wife. But it would be gratifying to know how much and what improvement has been made in the Law of England, since the late Jeremy Bentham lifted, a little, the metallic slide of its dark lantern, and let some light in upon it.

"In the teeth of Magna Charta," in which King John says, "We will not deny justice, we will sell justice to no man," is it *still* "denied to ninety-nine men out of a hundred," and at a ruinous rate to the purchaser, sold to the hundredth?

Is English law "so arranged" and administered as to be a grossly demoralizing institution? Is truth still commanded or forbidden according as a man is plaintiff or defendant? While the defendant is punished for telling lies, does the plaintiff lose his cause if he will *not* tell lies? In some cases must you still confess yourself guilty of having laid a wager, before you can procure a question to be sent to a jury? Must you in some cases acknowledge your estate to belong to some body else, before you can be permitted to sell it?

If these legal-fictions still obtain, my lord, then is English jurisprudence still a demoralizing institution. Whether they do or do not continue sadly to mar your boasted Law; they had a long-enough reign to account for the present state of morals in England, where the most fabulous of fictionists finds friends among the proudest of her NOBLES.

In the charge of a British Judge of sixty years ago, there is found this declaration: "*The law of this country only lays such restraints on the actions of individuals as are necessary for the safety and good order of the community at large.*

On this declaration, Bentham thus comments:

"I sow corn: partridges eat it; and if I attempt to defend it against the partridges, I am fined or sent to jail; all this for fear a great man, who is above sowing corn, should be in want of partridges.

"The trade I was born to is overstocked: hands are wanting in another. If I offer to work at that other, I may be sent to jail for it. Why? Because I have not been working at it as an apprentice for seven years. What's the consequence? That as there is no work for me in my original trade, I must either come upon the parish, or starve.

"There is no employment for me in my own parish; there is abundance in the next. Yet if I offer to go there I am driven away. Why? Because I *might* become unable to work one of these days, and so I must not, while I *am* able. I am thrown upon one parish *now*, for fear I should fall upon another forty or fifty years hence. At this rate, how is work ever to get done? If a man is not poor he won't work; and if he is poor the laws won't let him. How then is it that so much is done as is done? As pockets are picked—by stealth, and because the law is so wicked that it is only here and there that a man can be found wicked enough to think of executing it.

"Pray, Mr. Justice, how is the community you speak of the better for any of these restraints? And where is the necessity of them? And how is *safety* strengthened, or *good order* benefited by them?"

This "Wicked" arrangement of the laws has received, I believe, some modifications. But by these very modifications, is it not, that they are "*so arranged*" as to separate families—mothers and children.

"At the cursed workhouse-door?"

The same Judge says, "*Happily for us, we are not bound by any laws but such as every man has the means of knowing.*"

Is this, my lord, what is termed, technically, a "legal fiction?" Certainly not, or it would not be found in the solemn charge of a venerable English Judge. But has every man in England the means of knowing all the laws he is bound by?

Bentham says, "Scarce *any man* has the means of knowing a twentieth part of the laws he is bound by. Both sorts of laws are kept most happily and carefully from the knowledge of the people; statute law by its shape and bulk; common law by its very essence. It is the Judges that make the common law. Do you know how they make it? Just as a man makes laws for his dog. When your dog does any thing you want to break him of, you wait till he does it, and then beat him for it. This is the way you make laws for your dog; and this is the way the Judges make law for you and me. They won't tell a man beforehand what it is he *should not do*—they won't so much as allow his being told: they lie by till he has done something which they say he should not *have done*, and then they hang him for it. What way, then, has any man of coming at this dog-law? Only by watching their proceedings; by observing in what *cases* they have hanged a man, in what *cases* they have sent him to jail, in what *cases* they have seized his goods, and so forth. These proceedings they won't publish themselves; and if any body else publishes them, it is what they call a contempt of court, and a man may be sent to jail for it."

Are the laws of England still "so arranged," my lord? Is your common law still what Bentham calls a dog-law; and which can only be known in short detached lessons disposed of by the courts at the various prices of life, liberty, property? Does the English lawyer still glut his mercenary cruelty on the child unborn; and so act the savage more ferociously than the cannibal African?

"Miserable," says Lord Coke, "miserable is the *slavery* of that people among whom the law is either unsettled or unknown."

But under its present existing institutions, the English law must ever remain "unsettled," *and* "unknown" by the people. What then follows according to this great jurist? "Miserable is the *slavery* of that people"—the people of England!

In the days of Lord Coke, the English were not so squeamish as now about the use of the term *slavery* and the name *slave*, but as applicable abroad only. His definition of the term is a great deal better than Paley's; and by the better definition, Bentham declares that *scarce any* of the people are free; and by Coke himself is it shown, that *all* are in a "*miserable slavery.*"

But it may be better now, than in Benthan's time; and we should like well to know *how much* better. We know that the great body of English sailors and watermen are still in that very worst condition of slavery, of being subject at any moment to be bound in chains and taken by violence on board of a war-ship;—a slavery compared with which the quasi slavery of our Southern negroes is the very largest liberty. Work enough, then, without meddling with miserable fictions about imaginary negroes, may the noble Earl of Carlisle find in the re-erection of Irish cabins, and in wresting the galling yoke of a "miserable slavery" from the bleeding necks of his own country.

## CHAPTER XVIII.

### ERRORS OF IGNORANCE AND ARROGANCE. THE BRITISH COURT PRESS.

"Think not to shroud yourselves securely among the thickets of ignorance."—ABP. LEIGHTON.

"O thou monster, Ignorance! how deformed dost thou look!—dull, unfeeling, short armed Ignorance—the cursed of God!"—SHAKESPEARE.

So long as even learned Englishmen shall remain in ignorance,—not of our general institutions only, but of even the geography of our country;—so long as our young men abroad are seriously inquired of in European colleges, if they left America from fear of the Indians; and, if the people of our country are not nearly all black, and colored people;—and if we have any churches and institutions of learning;—so long we ought not, perhaps, to be surprised at the gross ignorance, which prevails across the water, with regard to the character of the Southern institution of slavery in our country; and the condition of the people subject to it; in subordination, as it is, to the benign principles of an enlightened Christian jurisprudence.

May the reign of the deformed monster be shortened! We may hope, and shall not cease to pray, that under the soothing influence of melting charity, the class may increase, there and here, of honest and innocent men and women, who use no language of ferocity in speaking of negro slavery as a practical fact; who indulge in no insolent and vulgar exultation; and who belong not at all to the large class of professors of scurrility, sedition, blasphemy and treason,—

> "The scum of men;
> The ulcers of an honest state; spite-weavers,
> That live on poison only, like swol'n spiders."

Nor have we any doubt they will increase; but yet slow, exceedingly, will be the increase of the class of persons who shall understand well the practical questions connected with it, so as to judge, not ignorantly nor arrogantly, but well, wisely, and charitably.

Into these reflections, I have been drawn, partly by a current number of a religious quarterly, of considerable claims to be an authority in many matters, if not an unquestioned oracle, which reckons the slaves of the South as belonging to the "Legion of nine millions" of our republic, which "must be set down as believing and professing nothing at all;" and partly, by reading over afresh, the debates, controversies, and documents, in relation to the manumission of the British West Indian slaves; and comparing them with the current periodical British Court Press.

From all these sources, the inference seems to flow, naturally, that, both in New, and Old England, the grievously erroneous notion is the most common one, that slaves are considered by their masters merely as *property*, and in the same soulless sense, in which they look upon the teams used on their plantations.

In the debates in the British Parliament, on the West Indian Emancipation, there seems to have been no other consideration involved in the matter, save only that of property and profit.

What is the money value of the slave to the owner? Such seems to have been the whole of the matter; and such the only existing relation between them.

Now if such be indeed, the notion of the writer in the religious quarterly, which I have alluded to, it is no wonder that he is in contented ignorance of the very remarkable religious character and condition of the slaves in the South; and that so unqualifiedly he reckons them as among the Legion of benighted infidelity; though, while he was penning the article, there was a greater proportion of the slaves of the republic, who were "believing and professing" Christianity, than of the whole free population of the republic;—including, of course, our free blacks; out of, and in, asylums and penitentiaries.

If such be, indeed, the ignorant views of Lord Palmerston, and that, every where, the slave is held only in the light of a chattel, and not of a human being with senses and a soul; his unfortunate ignorance, acting upon a hard sceptical nature, may be some poor apology for his preposterous and infidel folly, in supposing ill treatment to be inseparable from the relation of the slave to the master. And if the noble and simple women of England had been so unfortunate as to imbibe such errors of opinon from their husbands and fathers, or otherwise, it should not be wondered at, that they were easily persuaded to turn away their eyes and hearts from all the multiplied miseries of their own country, to plunge into a Quixotic crusade against a foreign evil.

By their own literature,—religious, romantic, and political—and by their own political and religious teachers, they had been prepared to become the easy and willing victims of a renegade traitress, who from motives of money and malice, had concocted a bubble to cheat them into confirmed ignorance, of what she made them think she was the priestess—oracle of all knowledge; and when they beheld how she did

———"Untie the winds, and let them fight
Against the Churches;"

they had no longer any doubt of their mission in the crusade.

And if it be possible to suppose, that the Earl of Carlisle is so ignorant of the matter, as to believe there is no more sacred relation, recognized by the masters of slaves in our country, than that of the sordid one of property, it should surprise no one, that he, too, become a willing victim, and act on his ignorance, in blindly disgracing his name and blood, by editing a scurrilous romance, written for the purpose of countenancing and perpetuating such ignorance, lest, in the light of truth and knowledge, even geese might refuse to be plucked.

It requires but slight observation, in travelling through our Southern States, to be convinced, that the mere sordid relation of owner and property, is often one of the feeblest which connects the slave with the master and his family. Thousands are the instances in which the sale of an affectionate and faithful servant is as foreign a thought, as that of so disposing of a beloved child.

At the breaking out of the Florida war, several planters were driven by the Indians, from their plantations into the forts, and the garrisoned towns. Some of them, with their families and servants, having been compelled to abandon their crops and stores of provisions, found themselves destitute of means of support, and applied for aid to the Government; as they had a good right to do. A certain member of Congress with the English notion—but unhappily not to England confined—that slaves were mere chattels, proposed to deny the application, on the ground that if they had slaves, they might sell some of them, to feed the rest. That member would certainly have been surprised; and if not quite heartless, he must have been grieved, to witness the effect of his reported proposition on some of the masters; and more especially, on the females and children of their families, when they learned that possibly it might prevail, and compel them to the hard necessity of separation from their humble friends.

Said one of those unfortunate masters,—a good old man, now no more,—and who had never sold a slave during a long life of mastership;—"How little those people seem to know of our sentiments towards our servants. I never any more thought of selling one of them, than of selling one of my own children; and may heaven's mercy avert the cruel necessity from my old age." And it was averted; and the kind old man and his amiable and excellent family were happy again.

A glance now at the British newspaper press. It is enough. A wistful search is not needed for the purpose of learning that mostly, if not all—certainly not all—the English newspapers under court patronage, are of the very rabidest class of abolition prints; and rarely less ignorant or arrogant, than even Palmerston could reasonably desire. Among these mendacious prints, there has been a long and agonizing struggle for preeminence, in the great and thrifty arts of fuss, fawning, and falsehood; and quite recently the redoubtable "Morning Advertiser" has exhibited itself a head and shoulders above all competitors; by a series of long and windy articles, which not only echo the wicked and absurd nonsense of the "FOREIGN OFFICE," and eulogise the Stowe; but actually urge the Nation to consummate its reckless folly, by a *national monument* to express the nation's approbation of the great talents and *self-sacrificing* philanthropy of the compiler of a romance from anti-slavery newspapers and other kindred sources.

Henceforth the "Morning Advertiser" can surely have no fellow in the craft, and may hold its lofty head above all pretension to rivalship. The lucky editor has certainly now caught a strange fish, even in English waters, that can hardly fail to make a man of him. "Any strange beast there makes a man. When they will not give a doit to relieve

15

a lame beggar, they will lay out ten to see a dead Indian." Munificently, and three-fold, shall he find himself paid—if so great a man can be paid—and besides, he shall have a niche for his own statue in the monument. Happy man!

The ten doit fees of the people, the guineas of the many thousands of the "women of England" in the lead of the Duchess of Sutherland, with the sure and rich patronage of the Court, may enable him to erect the monument at his own expense, and even make a duke of him to boot! Among editors, he is already a duke, of course.

Apropos. That final phrase, *of course*, brings to my recollection another celebrity among the editorial corps of England:—THE LONDON NEWS. This court paper says, "The press of Great Britain is the refuge of American honor and honesty." And the very chit and marrow of his argument to prove it, is this handy phrase,—'of course.' It is of wonderful and diverse power and use in the London News. It is declaration, evidence, argument, rhetoric, logic, law;—and I know not what all!

It is every where a standard abolition argument; yet rarely is it found to play so many important parts, and with such ease and grace, as in an anti-American article in a London News some weeks ago. Of our Southern States it speaks thus: "The Electors return a number of representatives as the representatives of slaves—a fiction *of course*. Three fifths of the slaves count as whites, without having, *of course*, any rights." How very like "Sir Oracle," is it not?

What means the London News, "by rights?" Does he mean that one of them is the right to vote for representatives? The great body of the people in Great Britain and Ireland have this right, of course; and they exercise it of course; do they not? or is it a fiction? Of course it is.

Is it a fiction, that the people of Great Britain and Ireland are represented at all? It certainly is, if *our* slaves are not represented. If only one in about thirty, or more, of the people, elect members of Parliament, is it a fiction *of course*, that they go there as representatives of any others than such as have the right of suffrage? Does the British Parliament represent the nation of twenty-five millions, or only the fraction of it, who vote? If only the latter, then the rest "have no rights," *of course.*

Are there not laws passed in the British Parliament, in reference to the support of your millions of poor? Of course there are. But what acknowledged rights have they, compared with the clearly and legally defined rights of our slaves? Next to none, *of course.* Yes, indeed; the legislation of your Parliament has often enough, and unmistakably enough, decided, that the people's rights are the merest fiction!

"We in England," says the News, "have made some sacrifices for the abolition of slavery." Of course you have; very great sacrifices;—sacrifices that would ruin a nation not accustomed to such sacrifices—sacrifices of principle—as yours undeniably are! You have sacrificed good faith and good sense, on the altar of a reckless caprice. Towards both masters and slaves you have been faithless, in the withdrawal of protection from both, and allowed both to suffer. Yes, you have sacrificed the property and comforts of the white population of the West Indies, and the lives even of the blacks. Of both robbery and homicide you are guilty towards them, beyond all dispute! "Some sacrifices," indeed! What greater sacrifices *could* you have made?

But that is not what you *mean* by "some sacrifices?" I am quite aware of that. You mean the TWENTY MILLIONS. Yes; and that was not far less cruel than the other. With a stroke of a pen you added twenty millions to your national debt, which will never be paid; and charged the same amount to your half-starved operatives, who are to pay the interest on it, for ever, out of their scanty earnings! What! do you frown, and say *of course*, it is not so? How else, than by *labor alone*, can revenue be raised? Let only the hammer and the loom stop, and who is to pay the interest on the national debt? Should the Court, the Press, and the "Women of England," succeed in the object of their crusade, the answer to this question may involve a difficulty of solution to gravel even the London News.

In addition to the "some sacrifices," of which you are so *justly* proud, of course, as you think in your folly, how much more have you sacrificed in kidnapping our slaves to starve and freeze in Canada? You find it more expensive, do you not, than to kidnap men at home for your navy?

Speaking of Mr. Benton's St. Louis speech, the News says—"it is a welcome statement to us, for we knew before its shameful truths; we felt the necessity that the world should know them; and we are only too happy to be able to tell them in American words." Of course, "too happy." Yes; and you are pursuing a course to learn too soon, that you *were* too happy, in the anticipation of a ruin that inevitably involves your own. If capable of it—think of this.

"Henceforth," says this demented thing,—"henceforth, if charged with severity in imputing to the American nation the disgraces of slavery, we have only to refer the objector to Mr. Benton's speech to the citizens of St. Louis."

> "This is mere madness:
> And thus *awhile* the fit will work on him."

In Mr. Benton's speech, he learns that our Constitution has been respected by the representatives of the nation, while the British Magna Charta has been trampled on in scorn of its wise provisions in favor of the people, by the so-called representatives of the people; and he thinks, of course, that our old-fashioned faith is too anti-progressive and superstitious for this enlightened nineteenth century!

"The disgraces of slavery!" And this from an oracle of Britain; an organ of British abolitionism, which is the merest of all fictions of abstractionism,—vain words to disguise real meanings: for, in a worse than the worst kind of African slavery,—out of Africa herself,—the British Queen is now waving her sceptre over many millions, at home and abroad, of the most miserable slaves that the sun shines upon. It is no matter, of course, how many *real* slaves a nation, or an individual may have, "by any other name;" or how wretched soever they may be;—but the *name*—ah! in that lies the "disgrace!"

"American honor and integrity are not safe in the hands of American representatives."—"The press of Great Britain is the refuge of American honor and honesty." And is not such madness,

"A sight most pitiful in the meanest wretch?"

So much for the London News. It is a darling, of course, with the women of the Stafford-house convention; and with the male, as well as female, Sutherlands, Palmerstons, Carlisles, Trevallians, and all the like-minded.

A glimpse at "The London Shipping Gazette," and we have done with these mouth-pieces of British arrogance, ignorance and prejudice. This respectable print—respectable, save when it becomes dogmatical about American affairs—is very naturally, and yet very foolishly, fussy about the Monroe doctrine. Had not England been acting on the very same principle, time out of mind, the Gazette could scarcely be more dogmatical on the subject of what it presumes to call "American Piracy." It even speaks of the "disregard and contempt," which our policy, of justice and caution, against the evil of bad neighbors, "merits;" and it tells us that "the Spaniards, the Portuguese, and the English, have much older claims to the American continent, than we possibly can have;" that we had no right, but to the Old Thirteen States; and if England had chosen to do so, she might justly have interposed to limit our territory, and prevent its extension; but that "it did not suit her views or policy to interfere."

How very happy, for both parties, and for all concerned, that it did not suit her views or policy to interfere in our affairs, to the extent of saying to us, that we must carefully confine ourselves within such limits as she might choose to prescribe for us! Sad will be the day for the world's peace and comfort, when England, or any other foreign power, shall so interfere with American measures! May they never be such as to provoke or to invite such interference!

I might aptly enough close this short chapter, by a brief call of attention to the gross ignorance and arrogant assumption of a learned and accredited cotemporary English historian; who, with apparent disregard of truth and fairness, charges "the principal States of this Union" with fraudulent insolvency; charges the general Government by overreaching duplicity, of defrauding the British Government in the matter of the North-eastern boundary; and of plotting against the supremacy of that Government over a neighboring colony. But I may well trust, as it is supposed, that quite enough has been done in this way, to make very plain and undeniable the proposition, that the people of England,—titled and untitled,—male and female, are altogether too ignorant of our institutions and character, and too blindly prejudiced against us, to deal fairly by us on any question. May the healing spirit lead to better things and better times. In the meanwhile let us be patient, and wait, until they have rung out all the changes on the *simple laws of Nature.* But how long? It took a very long time for them to learn that slavery was a violation of the simple laws of Nature; and now they are clamorous for free-trade, as required by the simple laws of Nature. What next? Coercive Intervention?

# CHAPTER XIX.

RESPECTFULLY DEDICATED TO THE QUAKERS OF PHILADELPHIA.

——— "Will not God impart His light
To them that ask it?—Freely—'tis his joy,
His glory, and his nature to impart.
But to the proud, uncandid, insincere,
Or negligent enquirer, not a spark."

---

"Knowing the heart of men is set to be
The centre of this world, about the which
Those revolutions of disturbances
Still roll; where all the aspects of misery
Predominate: whose strong effects are such
As he must bear, being powerless to redress;
And that unless above himself he can
Erect himself, how poor a thing is man."

---

"——————— his country's name,
Her equal rights, her churches and her schools—
What have they done for him?"

---

"Farewell, farewell! but this I tell
To thee, thou wedding guest!
He prayeth well, who loveth well
Both man, and bird, and beast.

He prayeth best, who loveth best
All things; both great and small;
For the dear God, who loveth us,
He made and loveth all."

THAN among the Friends, or Quakers,—as it is believed they are not offended to be called,—I have not found personal friends, towards whom I have been more strongly attracted by their amiable and excellent qualities; and for the body of the Friends, as such, I have much esteem and affection. If, therefore, in this chapter to them addressed, there should occur any thing not agreeable to them, it is desired that it be referred to any thing, rather than a want of respectful consideration.

Their fundamental principle of religion, as I believe, calls on them, as Friends of Light—the Light of Life—to become pattern men and women; and to rear up their children to become so. And many of them have, no doubt, succeeded excellently well, in obedience to the call of the Spirit to become pattern people, according to their ideal.

THE PATTERN MAN, however, never became weary in well doing; but "went about doing good," wherever good was to be done; always doing that first which was nearest to Him, though often urged from this course by the more zealous than wise. And without respect of persons, he fed the hungry, and clothed the naked, and healed the sick, and gave comfort and consolation to publicans and sinners; and delivering them from rulers that had no pity, told them to go in peace, and sin no more.

From French and English literature, and from police and Parliamentary revelations, long have we known that in Paris and London, there were extended quarters of squalid wretchedness and beastly vice, of the most frightful character. Of them, the literature of those two great cities, has given us descriptions of facts, with such graphic truthfulness, as carried conviction with them through a conscious feeling that no fancy could have invented them. And if any could doubt their truthfulness, their doubts were removed by legal and legislative testimony, that they were rather under, than overdrawn.

Repeatedly has the present writer endured the all but killing mortification and disgust, of a personal survey of the horrors of the too celebrated Five Points in New York, in order to be able to speak from knowledge of the miseries and morals of the poor, to the rich, and to the respectable and Christian portion of the city, in the hope of helping to arouse them to think soberly of the evil thing in the very heart of their city; and in mercy to the suffering, and the inevitably vicious; and in the prudence, demanded by home and personal considerations; to put forth their energies for good, in removal of the cancerous nuisance which was diffusing moral and physical disease and death through the whole body.

Long and well has it been known, that to the great injury of the welfare and reputation of other large cities, poverty, and suffering, and vice, had been allowed to increase until the evil became unmanageable, and so appalling, that even the devotedly benevolent fled,—not from the contact only, but from the attempt of removing it!—in horror, in despair, and in tears, fled from the city itself, as if it were all, and every where, infected by the impracticable, revolting, and fearful evil.

Until lately,—quite lately,—it had been hoped that the city of *brotherly love*,—the city of Friends,—the Quaker City,—in whose shop windows may be seen fancy pieces, of human degradation and misery, inscribed with the pathetic appeal *"Am I not a man and a brother?"*—in this beloved and loving city, it had been hoped, that no such plague spots,—no such masses of misery and vice, could be found, as in others, less favored in their foundation—less favored iu their superstructure; and less honored and distinguished in their history.

Strange, and, I will not say what more than strange:—

strange to say, Philadelphians themselves were so entirely ignorant of the sad and something else truth of their having among them a " *La cite,*"—a "Saint Giles,"—a " Five Points," that but a few months since, a most excellent, intelligent, and benevolent lady of Chestnut street, and to the manor born, and always active in good works,—in reply to a remark of my own, that cities were all and always remiss—sinfully and imprudently remiss, in their care for the poor,—with no slight appearance of triumph and self-gratulation, remarked that " she thought Philadelphia an exception." " I fear not," was the rejoinder; " for already has my short visit here been long enough to discover many indications of distress and vice, as the offspring of the tyrant poverty, under the countenance of the merciless despot, public contempt."

"Well, at any rate," said my lady friend, with a not unbecoming spirit perhaps, and with a manifest and undoubting perfect confidence,—" Well, at any rate, we have no 'Five Points' in our city."

" I hope not," I said; and then it was as confidently presumed, there was solid ground for such hope to stand upon. But what turns out to be the amazing and astounding *truth*, to the contrary? What are the terrific facts, which are authenticated by the high judicial authority of a Grand Inquest of the city and county of Philadelphia?

So to speak, accidentally came to my ears and knowledge, the awfully fearful discovery, that, in our wide Republic, Philadelphia is probably preeminent in this unhappy distinction. Thus it befel a short time since:

Among some dozen or more of detained passengers in the Ladies' room of the Bordentown Depot, there was a Quaker gentleman of seeming general intelligence, who introduced the *handy* subject of conversation in the North—southern slavery. He was evidently well informed—as the students of ignorance on the subject usually are—on whatever had been said against it; and he agreed with Mrs. Stowe, that nothing bad enough *could* be said in condemnation of it, as the monster sin and evil of the age; and, indeed, the principal source of human suffering and degradation in our country. He showed himself quite familiar with the *cabin* romance; though novel reading is one of the anathematized abominations of the Quakers, for which I respect and honor them; not less than I regret, that they, and many others, have been cruelly cheated into the wicked notion, that the strangely popular Stowe, and Beecher, and Garrison, and Greely, and Parker, and Douglas romance is not a novel.

As if to occupy a little space of a pause in the fluent Quaker's talk, a taciturn gentleman, who had before made no remark, interposed these few words:

"Friend, I have travelled pretty extensively in the South and Southwest, in all the slave States. I know a good deal about the condition of the negroes and their treatment; and if thee will go with me when we get to Philadelphia, within one hour's time, and within a space of four blocks of the city, I will show thee more of human suffering, and degradation, than can be found in a whole year in all the slave States."

The Friend seemed indisposed to a reply; and I said to the taciturn man, "Is it possible that you are in earnest in your challenge? I am quite aware, from personal knowledge, that there is less suffering from poverty and want in the South among the negroes, than I have ever found in any country among other people; but I was not prepared to hear the city of Brotherly Love so represented. Has it, too, its Five Points?" He sorrowfully replied—

"And worse, if worse *can* be. Nor Paris, nor London can supply any sight or scene of more squalid poverty, and destitution—of more mental and atheistic brutality, or of more degrading vice and ferocious criminality. People may write about it; and they may talk about it; but no adequate conception can be conveyed to any human mind—

even the most imaginative—that has not contemplated it with the open eyes of all the senses.

I could only exclaim, "Is it possible," and begged the taciturn man, no longer taciturn, to give me a little account of some of the more prominent features of the social abomination he had thus spoken of. With apparent reluctance, he seemed for some minutes, to be arranging his recollections. At length, he thus addressed himself to the ungrateful subject, and to me:

"What number of promiscuous human beings have you ever known to be lodged in a single room of ordinary size?"

"In the sad winter for the poor, of 1816–'17,—alas! what northern winter is not sad for the poor?—a committee of a benevolent society in New York, employed in exploring the regions of want and destitution, in one room of twenty feet square, found four families, each occupying a separate corner! In astonishment, they enquired of one of the miserable women, how they could possibly live so; and she answered rather indignantly, 'We *done* well enough till that woman in that corner there took boarders.' That, said I, is the hardest case of the kind that I was ever acquainted with."

"O, they probably lived in decent luxury, compared with cases which I have seen by scores in the Baker-street district of Philadelphia; men, women and children, black and white, in such numbers in a room as scarcely to allow them space to lie down, though unincumbered by any piece of furniture of any kind!"

"But that is not their *home?*"

"It is all the home they have. In the day, their time is passed in roaming about, begging and stealing; and at night, they huddle in there to pass it, or some portion of it, and pay a cent or two each for their lodging."

"Pray, who is the provider of such lodgings?"

"Their landlord is usually one of themselves; some

poor creature of the same class, who has rented the room at a shilling a day, always in advance. He gets twenty or thirty night lodgers, and the operation gives him a clear income that will supply garbage and whiskey for his wretched wife and children; or, at least, make up any deficiency in the avails of their own beggings and stealings."

"Can it be that there is any great number in this wretched condition?"

"If the number were not great, they would be relieved and taken care of; but with such masses of moral and material filth, such persons as would gladly do what they could for them, know not what to do; and so they stand appalled and do nothing; allowing the evil to go on and increase. And, unless the wealth and power of the city put forth their mightiest energies to remove it, there is no imagining what it may come to. I suppose there are thousands of those miserable beings, who go forth from such lodgings every morning; and from such as are even more undesirable, without hope of food for the day of any kind, or lodging of any sort for the following night, but as the wages of beggary or theft, or of something even worse. Beggars they claim to be, and thieves they prove to be, whenever any thing falls in their way, which they can pilfer. And they seem to think they have a perfect right so to do."

"Poor creatures! and who can say that theft, in their wretched condition, morally and physically, is more criminal, as seen by the Omniscient, than is the sinfulness of the community, which has suffered them to fall into such condition of depravity and wretchedness?"

"True enough. The thought is most awful! And suppose such a true charge of intensified cruelty towards their negroes, could be made against the slaveholders of the South, what then would be the just, but unmeasured indignation of the good people of the Quaker City of Brotherly Love?"

Here comes the train which is to take us to that Quaker City of Brotherly Love.

Arrived there, I introduced this subject to a citizen by adoption,—a good man, always busy, to the full limit of his moderate means, in doing good to men's souls and bodies too. I told him what I had heard. He replied that no description of the wretchedness in question could possibly be overdrawn, as regarded its quality, and that its quantity was too appalling to attempt to estimate. And he put into my hands a newspaper, remarking at the same time: "In that paper, you may find an article on the subject, which may be relied on so far as it goes:—

'Inspired beyond the guess of folly;'

but no words, written or spoken, can convey a really truthful picture of the deep degradation and intense sufferings of the miserable human beings of which it treats."

The article I have read, and re-read, with a shocked and shocking interest. With painful mortification, I am reminded by it of the pleasurable delusion I was under, when I read the graphic accounts of D'Israeli and Dickens, of the miserable state of the London poor, and reflected gratefully, that, *in our far more favored country such things could never be.* Alas, what a delusion! and how rudely and recklessly has the mask been torn away!

FAMINE.

"I heard a groan and a peevish squall,
And through the chink of a *hovel* wall—
Can you guess what I saw there?"

FIRE AND SLAUGHTER.

"Whisper it, Sister! in our ear."

FAMINE.

"A baby beat its dying mother:
I had starved the one, and was starving the other!"

"The Mysteries and Miseries of Philadelphia." Such is the very appropriate title of the article alluded to; and it may be found in "Cummings's Evening Bulletin," of Jan. 29, 1853.

It fully confirms all that was told me by the taciturn man in the depot, and illustrates his positions by details of the most dreadful character. It says: "Within a few squares of our most fashionable thoroughfares, there is, we honestly believe, quite as much misery, degradation and crime, in proportion to the size of the city which contains the plague-spot, as in the most squalid scenes"—in London and Paris—"described so graphically by Dickens, Ainsworth and Sue.—The majority of our citizens are aware that we have a Baker street and a Small street in Philadelphia, and the local columns of the newspapers occasionally contain paragraphs headed significantly, '*Death from Want*'—'The result of Intemperance'—'Murder in Moyamensing'—and even, at times, the terrible words, '*Death from Starvation!*' The scenes which furnish the material for these paragraphs are laid in this wretched neighborhood, but our citizens are not much startled by the shocking facts disclosed, and they are too prone to console themselves with the reflection, that such things are not of very frequent occurrence; that the suffering wretches are but few in number, and that the quarter infested by them is not of wide extent. How sad a mistake!"

Death from want! Death from starvation! When we hear, or read, of such things as overtaking the wanderers through the wilderness, on their perilous route to California, our hearts sink within us, that no human being was near to save the hapless wanderers from death by starvation; not dreaming of the possibility of such calamities within the reach of civilized—nay, of savage man!

> ——— "A thousand ways frail mortals lead
> To the cold tomb, and dreadful all to tread;
> But dreadful most, when by a slow decay,
> Pale hunger wastes the manly strength away!"

And can it be that this most dreadful way to the cold tomb is trodden, not only by wanderers far away from the haunts and habitations of civilized men; but even too in the very midst of our most wealthy and prosperous cities?—saddest of all, and sorest of all, in the city of Friends? the city of Brotherly Love? the city which has been supposed generally to have a fair right to self-felicitation, if not to boast that it was a city of benevolence, and of unbounded philanthropy?

Alas! its benevolence and its philanthropy, have been too much employed abroad and far away from home, in the unprofitable work of sympathy for the negroes of the South, who need none of their sympathy, to allow them time, and means, and heart, to intervene between their own poor neighbors and citizens, and death by starvation! The

> "Pale hunger that wastes the manly strength away,"

in the very midst of abundance of food, where the Father of all has opened his bountiful hand to fill all things living with plenteousness; but where His creature man has closed both his hand and his heart against his starving brother and sister, and their little ones!

And if such things can be, can it be, also, that He who careth for the poor will so protect such wealthy and prosperous cities as to preserve them in wealth and prosperity? Will He who commands, "*thou shalt open thy hand wide to thy poor, nor shut thine hand from thy poor brother*"—will He continue to shower His blessings on such as have no pity, and care not for the poor; but allow them at their very door to die of *want* and *starvation?* "He that hath ears to hear let him hear:" and let him also see to it that he have a heart to understand,—a heart of flesh, and not of stone; for "the expectation of the poor shall not perish."

Look we again at this fruitful article. "There are in Philadelphia *thousands*—absolutely *thousands*, who rise in the morning without knowing where they are to obtain a mouthful of food, or where their wretched heads are to rest at night."

This is a parallel of a part of D'Israeli's picture of London misery, that very few of us ever feared to behold in one of our cities, and, certainly, least of all in Philadelphia!

"These creatures prowl about during the day, on the look-out for what they may pilfer while begging or gathering refuse for an ostensible employment, but depending mainly upon the pickings, in the way of plunder, which may fall in their way."

And can no better employment be found for these poor Philadelphians, which even they might like better, as more surely supplying them with sustenance and with the comfortable hope against "Death from starvation?"

"At night, they gather into their appropriate quarter, and squander away their earnings or stealings by indulging in the most vile and brutish appetites."

Have they been taught better? Have their souls been cared for? Have they had line upon line, and precept upon precept, to teach them that the way they have taken is the way of Death? Or have they fallen into it because other and better ways are closed against them?

"When nature requires rest, the poor wretches swarm into houses which are not fit to be the abiding places of swine, and there lie upon the filthy floors of cellars and rooms which are mere dens, and scarcely fit for the abiding places of the vilest beasts."

What an outcry would go forth from this Head-Quarters of abolitionism, could any large number of slaves be found so lodged!

"We have visited many of these dens of misery in company with a competent guide, and we have had opportunities afforded us of seeing their inmates in their haunts, in the enjoyment of their peculiar pleasures, and in the every-day routine of their terrible lives." Hence the writer goes on to describe what he calls very properly the *infected district*, with its hovels and habits. To give a notion of the magnitude of the district he gives a list of FIFTEEN streets, courts and alleys, "all of which are crowded with wretched dens of misery." "In these squalid lanes and thoroughfares, there are immense numbers of low groggeries." He gives the names of TEN taverns as mere specimens of their high sounding, and their fanciful titles; among which are the "Astor House,"—"the Girard House,"—"the Moonlight House,"—"the Haven of Rest,"—and "the Weary Traveller's Home." To describe one of these dens is to describe them all. We visited several of them and explored them from the cellar to the loft, and found them alike in all essential particulars.—They are in reality lodging houses;—ostensibly designed for the rest and entertainment of human beings.—We declare, without the slightest exaggeration or distortion of the naked truth, that in scores of lodging rooms which we visited, there was not a single article of furniture, neither bed nor bedding—not a crazy table, nor even a rickety stool. The walls and floors were invariably bare of every thing but filth and a few dirty rags."

Is it possible to imagine any thing worse than this? But in such places in the beautiful and rich city of Phila delphia, *thousands* of "human beings are nightly gathered in clusters."

"Foreign writers, in describing similar scenes in Europe, usually speak of mean furniture of some description, with which their dens are furnished. From this fact we infer that the denizens of the wretched locality we are attempting to picture, are even worse off than the same class in Europe." This is mortifying enough, after all our loud talking about the contrasted conditions of European wealth and poverty.

"When we visited the squalid neighborhood the weather was intensely cold, and had the wretches been deprived of almost any article they possessed, even to a single shred of their filthy rags, they must inevitably have frozen to death, so near were they to that point of utter destitution, at which nature gives up the struggle in despair, and the creature dies!"

This needs no comment. It needs however to be soberly thought upon by such, as within striking distance, indulge in sumptuous and extravagant luxuries; and by such, especially, as send far from home their sympathies on romantic crusades.

The writer describes one of the hovel taverns and its location, and gives the name of the *hideous looking* being who keeps it. It is a small two story frame, divided into ten by twelve rooms, with a bar room on the ground floor, the only room in the house which contained any article of furniture "except some damaged furnaces and miserable stoves;—*as wretchedly uncomfortable as it is possible to conceive.* Yet in every one of these apartments, including the cellar and the loft, men and women—blacks and whites by dozens—were huddled together promiscuously, squatting or lying upon the bare floors, and keeping themselves from freezing by covering their bodies with such filthy rags as chance threw in their way."

The description of the bar room, its presiding genius—a subject that Salvator Rosa would have prized as a sitter for a deformed bandit—and the bar room company of all colors, smoking rotten tobacco and swilling so called rum at a cent a glass, we will omit, as too finely graphic to be here appropriated; and especially as we are now about to say to the editor of the Bulletin what is hoped may not be said in vain: viz., Give to your readers that article every week, with such alterations and additions as may be desirable until the subject shall belong, not to the character, but to the history of Philadelphia.

"The cellar of this den is nightly filled with lodgers who lie upon the bare floor. We descended into it, determined to see and judge for ourselves. It contained a cluster of male and female whites and negroes. The steps leading to this under-ground abode were so broken that but a single step was left in a space of about six feet; yet down this dilapidated passage the debased occupants were compelled to pass to reach their quarters."

Has any Philadelphian ever seen negro slaves so wretchedly quartered? But the Bulletin says, concerning the accommodation of these "*thousands*" of human beings in this philanthropic city, "The description we have given of this 'crib' will answer for all the others—all are conducted on the same principle, and all are of the same standard in respect to character."

The Astor House, in Duffy's Arcade, which "seems to be an experiment as to how much misery a human being can bear without yielding up the ghost,"—One of the hundreds of these nuisances having become too confident of impunity in vice and crime, has been abated by the Grand Jury. The "Hoodle," or negro den, is more cautious, though the known "resort of the abandoned of all colors and sexes."

"In our explorations we witnessed many shocking

scenes. We saw men and women lying on the bare ground in cellars, suffering with fevers and destitute of fire, food, drink or medicine. The poor wretches were covered with any bit of carpet or canvass they could procure. One man who appeared to be dying of the prison fever, had no bed but the bare floor, no covering but a Manilla coffee-bag, and no fire, food, or attendance whatever. We saw little children, pale, sickly and emaciated, crouching in rags around a smouldering fire, while their parents lay drunk upon the ground." Has the Earl of Carlisle found any picture of wretchedness horrible as this, with which to commemorate his editorship?

Here is another. "A filthy cellar." No article of furniture save only a stove filled with glowing anthracite; some dozen, male and female, blacks and whites, *as usual*, huddled around it, making themselves *comfortable* for the night. One man has taken down the stove pipe for a pillow, allowing the coal gas to fill the den and the lungs of the lodgers. But the writer says "stoves and furnaces without pipes are very usual."

Another, of another sort, but probably not uncommon. The surveyors are induced, by loud cries from a house in Baker street, to venture in. "A young man weltering in gore and writhing in pain." A bloody knife on the floor, "just drawn from its human sheath." Police officers,—the murderess, with the other inmates of the room taken off to prison. A surgeon probes the wound and declares it fatal, and the victim is carried to his father's hovel, *hard by*, "and we left the dreadful scene."

"Is that a DEATH, and are these two?'
"Is DEATH that woman's mate?"

The cellar-den of "Crazy Nancy," the astrologer, who "reads the stars" and performs charms *a la Afrique*, is distinguished as having, besides the stove, "a rickety bedstead" and "a dirty straw mattress, but not a shred of clothing upon it." Still another article of property,—"a tin coffee pot, with the astrologer's supper simmering in it, with *her tallow dip stuck in the spout.*" The damp gathers on the walls, and trickling down forms puddles on the floor.—Wrapped up in an old piece of carpet, a sick man lies on the floor; for "Crazy Nancy takes in lodgers besides reading the planets."——

From this well authenticated work of truth and charity, other scenes of equal interest may be drawn; but we forbear. Enough are here presented to demonstrate that nothing of a more revolting character can be found of the like kind in either London or Paris. In those great cities of Europe, one of the most revolting sights is that of the sickly baby in the arms of the squalid beggar—not the mother, but a wretched impostor who has hired it of its miserable mother to excite sympathy. But what says this heroic surveyor of poverty and infamy; destitution, suffering and crime, in the loved and loving city of Philadelphia?

"*Babies are hired for begging purposes, and sickly infants are at a premium.* The mother is always entitled to one half of the proceeds.——"

Had this "Bulletin" revelation of "The Mysteries and Miseries of Philadelphia" been made but a few weeks earlier, I could hardly have been able to make up my mind and pen, to remind the women of England of the pictures drawn by D'Israeli, Dickens and others, of the destitutions and miseries of the poor of their own Metropolis; for, though, perhaps, slightly more picturesque, the London scenes of poverty, infamy and crime, are certainly not more revolting with loathsomeness and horror than are these home scenes, almost within the reach of my own senses!

But they all tell a plain and forcible tale, in favor of an institution that saves millions of human beings from such miseries of destitution, and from such infamy and crime, as these FOUR OR FIVE THOUSANDS" of Philadelphians are found fallen into and overwhelmed!

"But they are not *slaves!*" O, that terrible word, which reconciles otherwise sensible people with absurdity; and shuts up the hearts of the otherwise charitable against every real call of practicable charity, and so turns them into hearts of stone! O, that odious title, in which even the apostles gloried as their most honorable distinction, and for which their authority is, perhaps, repudiated by thousands who would be much offended not to be thought among the best of Christians! O, that word of offence to so many who are so unhappy as to think the Bible can not be God's Word, because that odious word *slave* is in it! O, let them not deceive their own hearts with the vain notion, that in this alone they find the Bible obnoxious to their objections.

It is very true that personal slavery is spoken of throughout the Scriptures, and that not one text can be adduced in which its existence as an institution is condemned. It is twice solemnly recognized in the decalogue, though disguised in the English translation by an intended euphamism. It is true, that the Bible tells us, with no word of disapprobation, that Joshua, the chosen of God, as the successor of His slave Moses, reduced the inhabitants of the promised land to the condition of personal slavery. It is also true, that the Roman Empire was crowded, so to speak, with slaves in the time of the apostles, many of whom became disciples; and that not one word is said by them against the relation of master and slave, but many rules are given by them to regulate, and so, of course to sanction it. On the masters they enjoined justice, mercy and kindness; and on the slaves, submission, faithfulness, and affection. It is true, that not one instance of emancipation is recorded in the New Testament; though an instance of the remanding of a fugitive slave is the subject of an apostolic Epistle.

If it were not so, and the Bible were in all other respects as it is, there would still be found plenty of abusers of it; as there were before the Anti-Slavery army was arrayed against it. "Down with the Bible!" was the shout of the infidel host, long before the days of Friend John Woolman, when among the Friends there was many a happy Quaker slave, some of whose descendants are now, most certainly, among the wretched beings in the Baker street district.

It is a common, and often expressed, notion of abolitionists, that the surest way to drive, or lead people, to reject the Bible, is to teach them that it sanctions the institution of slavery. So said the Friend at the Depot.

But there is another class of skeptics, who say, there can be no God that judgeth the earth, or that He cannot be a good Being, or there would not be allowed such inequalities in men's fortunes, nor such partiality in the bestowment of His gifts and favors. Such skeptics, after contrasting the luxurious enjoyments of Chestnut street, and other fashionable parts of the city, with the terrific destitutions and sufferings of the Baker street district, would find a much stronger argument to support their theory,—and that of the fool's heart,—that there is no God, or an unjust and merciless one, than the institution of slavery, as sanctioned by Scripture, can possibly supply to abolitionism against the Bible as a revelation from God. For, surely, no condition of the most miserable slave can be more miserable than that of these poor unfortunates!

But they are not slaves; and therefore, after awhile, by some means yet untried, some of them may reform their lives and become respectable, and have property of their own.

A terrible problem! What portion of the *Four or Five Thousands* of all ages, colors and sexes, will be likely to arrive at such distinction? Some of them have property of their own now. Some of them own the hovels in which they live. Some of them have *push-carts*, with which they gather rags, and bones, and cinders; and carry their pickings and stealings to their dens. Even "Crazy Nancy" has property, and is making more by fortune-telling, and other such respectable occupations.

This notion of the illustrious immunity of *property*, and that the slave is not allowed to have property—which is a great mistake, as elsewhere shown—is one of the hugest stumbling blocks in the way of the abolitionists coming to their senses on the subject of slavery. If with food and raiment we should therewith be content; and if these, and other comforts of life, be secured to us with reasonable certainty; then little, if any thing, short of the sin of covetousness, "which is idolatry," can be anxious for more. But all these belong to the Southern slaves; and they are secured to them by the laws of the land in perpetuity.

Such,—besides his many visible things and comforts of possession, and scarcely ever without money in his pocket, and out of it too,—is the slave's property. It is an investment made for him by legal authority; and it secures to him a comfortable support in sickness, debility, and age; and to his little ones, it insures protection and nursing care, of a character for generous and affectionate kindness, such as comparatively few little ones in the North are blessed with, even though elevated in condition several degrees above that of the Baker street children who are let out for hire while yet in arms!

This property of the Southern slave is made as secure to him as the law can make it; or as the law can secure any other species of property. Indeed, in our own happy land, there are an hundred times as many destitute people who were born to ample inheritances, now in the asylums for the poor, or suffering in poverty out of them, as there are of slaves in the South, who are not living comfortably on *their inheritance.* And is this nothing in favor of the institution so abhorred? Make a visit to Baker street; and then answer me:—Then tell me, if it be nothing.

In conclusion,—to the Friends of Philadelphia, I will offer an apology for the dedication of this chapter to them, and for the matter and manner of it, which I trust, will be as kindly accepted as in kindness it is offered.

It is not to condemn the Quaker principle, but to remind them, that in consequence of their neglect of it, this evil has come upon their beautiful and beloved city. Other bodies of believers may do well to take the same friendly hint. But as the Friends are generally held as eminently responsible,—so far as they may make their great means and influence to be felt,—for the character of their own city, it seemed to me good and right to call on them specially, to limit for a while, their sympathies and charities to their own household.

To correct the evils of slavery, whatever they may be, they cannot possibly suppose themselves so stringently responsible, as they certainly are to tread back their steps to the exercise of "their fundamental principle," which, Friend Gurney says, "lies at the root of all their particular views and practices—the perceptible influence and guidance of the Spirit of Truth." And of which the greater William Penn says, "they were directed to the Light of Jesus Christ within them as the seed and leaven of the kingdom of God; near all, because in all; and God's talent to all. A faithful and true witness and just monitor in every bosom, the gift and grace of God to life and salvation, that appears to all, though few regard it.—The Light of Christ within as God's gift.——"

"Brother," said George Fox,—"Brother, there *is* a light within thee: resist it, and thou art miserable; follow it, and thou art happy."

Surely, Friends, the Spirit of Truth, which is also the Spirit of Love, and which says "OUR FATHER," and so recognizeth the human race as a *brotherhood*, must be a too watchful Spirit, to allow "death by starvation" within the length of its arm! Dives resisted it. O, so may not henceforth the Friends of Philadelphia!

The Spirit of Truth and Love in a human soul could surely never rest in satisfied peace while *thousands* of neighboring souls were sinking uncared for into the embraces of the spirit of evil—the spirit of falsehood and hatred. It would seem then that it has become the hard and heart-aching duty of the Quakers of Philadelphia, to acknowledge, with the celebrated English penitent Friend, of the seventeenth century—James Naylor, that they "have been deceived by a false spirit, or by the fleshly workings of their own minds."

If, with the contrite Naylor, they will "look upon their errors as the consequence of a departure from the Spirit of Truth—the faithful and true witness and just monitor,"—they *will* doubtless tread back their steps, and do their first works at any and every cost, that they may follow the light of life and be happy; and diffuse comfort and light, and happiness among the comfortless, the benighted, and the miserable. They will then rejoice in opening the warm bosom of love and light to the poor wandering children of ignorance, poverty and sin, and lure them back from the precipice adown which they are daily and nightly falling into the dark abyss below. And if this poor, imperfect essay to do good shall have, but in the very smallest degree, accelerated their speed in the good work, in their heart of hearts they will thank me, though I may never know it in the life that now is.

"BROTHER, THERE IS A LIGHT WITHIN THEE, FOLLOW IT AND BE HAPPY."

# CHAPTER XX.

## EMANCIPATION.

"Alas, it was a piteous deed!"

WHO are the man-slayers? Abolitionists say, the slaveholders are the man-slayers. Suppose the charge retorted; and the question tried; how would it be settled? What is the history of the emancipations which have been effected by their efforts? What is the present condition of the emancipated; and of the fugitives which they have forwarded to Canada,—what is it? This subject may be well enough and fitly introduced by

### A SADLY TRUE STORY.

"It was in the chill and gloomy month of November." May such another never again visit our great Metropolis, threatening the lives of thousands.

Two students of Theology were taking their evening walk, in what then was the suburban portion of the city of New York. A part of their object was needful exercise of body, and an even more excellent part, to seek out proper objects on which to exercise their charity, by ministering to the wants of the ignorant and the afflicted. It was in the early twilight; and the coming night was threatening discomfort to the destitute poor. One of the young men was from the South. He is now, I believe, a devoted and laborious, and loving minister of Christ, to both white and black, in his native State.

As they were passing along their thoughtful way, they observed themselves looked at by a couple of very miserable looking black men, as if hoping for an alms. The Southern student said to the other; "Those poor fellows are from the South, and they seem to discern in me a southern man, and to expect my sympathy for them in their evident distress. Poor fellows; I must enquire into their troubles."

The students stopped and looked towards them, as an encouragement for them to approach. They did approach; and were thus interrogated:

"From the South, boys?"

"Yes, Mas'r," in a very sorrowful tone, somewhat peculiar to the negro in great distress.

"Ran away from your Master; did you?"

"O, no, Mas'r; no runaway."

"How then, were you free men in the South?"

"No, Mas'r; not till old Mas'r die, an' lef us free."

"From what State do you come?"

"Ole Virginny, Mas'r."

"So I supposed. Virginia is becoming somewhat famous for deathbed philanthropy; as they call freeing negroes to freeze and starve."

"But did your Master make no provision for you in his will? Did he leave you nothing to start with in the world, as free men?"

"O, yes, Mas'r. He tell Dr.——, his *Zeceter*, he must take us to free State, an' give us all money. Ebery man to have 50 dollar, ebery woman 30 dollar, an' ebery chile 10 dollar."

"Well, that was not so bad. But what have you done with your money?"

"Money all gone, Mas'r; an' we almost starve an' freeze;" said the poor fellow, in tears, and in a tone of deep distress. They had not yet become hardened beggars. The other than the interlocutor seemed unmanned entirely by grief and alarm. They both shivered in the northern cold; and seemed fearful lest the increase of its strength would be quite too much for their weakness.

They had been landed in the city in the spring, and now it was in advanced November.

"Men, women and children, eh! well, where are they?"

"Will Mas'r please go see? Not much far."

So the two students walked with the two negroes. On the way to their wretched abode, they got out of them that when the money was gone, which they seemed to have thought would last forever; but lasted only through the working season, when they ought to have been earning instead of spending; they made some movement towards getting work, and failed. Neither man nor woman knew how to do any thing, that in the city, was wanted to be done. The students arrived at their hired home; a large rickety hovel of a building, standing by itself, above the then built up city. What a scene presented itself, of loathsome destitution; made more glaring by means of tattered, and torn, and broken finery.

They had sold, since the cold began to find its way through the thin walls and broken windows of the great shell, all the furniture they could sell at any price; but there was remaining, plain indications of what had been done with a good deal of their wasted cash, of the value of which they were as ignorant as children. Scattered about, here and there, sprawling on the floor, or seated on bunks and boxes, and damaged chairs, telling of the life they had been leading, were 'twixt 40 and 50, half clad, filthy, and diseased blacks—men, women, and children! It was a most sorry sight. And yet many a set of white teeth grinned through the grime of their stupid and haggard faces.

In consternation and disgust, the kind-hearted students gazed at each other; and in saddened tones, exclaimed;—"what rude and frightful wretchedness! What a loathsome mass of misery! Poor creatures! What *can* be done for them!"

Their immediate necessities were not very great; but it could not be long before they would overwhelm them. The students gave them needful aid and counsel, with the promise to see what, if any thing, could be done for them on the morrow.

With a rapidly falling snow, and chill November's wintry blast upon its wings, the morrow comes! The whole city stands aghast! There is a general dreadful apprehension, that winter has really come to shut up the great city within barricades of ice, more than a month earlier than usual; and with no supply of fuel at all adequate to the shortest and mildest winter. All that was to be had was at once monopolized by men of means, and the poor generally left destitute! After much of real and apprehended suffering, the scene changes; the sun comes forth, radiant and warm; Indian Summer, dressed in parti-colored robes of state, rules in place of the late cold and cruel usurper; the rivers flow, and bear on their tide the needful preparatives for a coming Winter, on his easy way;—and to many of the poor is given "leave to toil." Men and women smile again, and again children laugh and sing.

But what of our poor negroes? How do they get through the short reign of terror? Freezingly and starvingly? Aye, with the best aid the good students can procure for them, at such a time of frozen selfishness, freezingly and starvingly, indeed!

Calamities, and strong apprehensions of personal suffering, freeze up the even kind hearts, with all their usually warm streams of charity, of all, but the highest order of Christian humanity. It is an order of God's nobility; but, alas! nowhere a numerous order.

Of this class are these Gospel students. As the day dawns, they arise from their knees of supplication for mercy, and for "daily bread," for all the sinful race of man, and go forth into the pelting storm to show mercy; and, if possible, to secure bread and warmth to the poor and unprotected and uncared-for negroes, whom a mock and mad philanthropy had thrown on a pitiless world. They go at once to their wretched abode. Howlings and screams of suffering meet their ears, even at a distance, and sink sorrowfully into their hearts. They find them in all but an utter state of despair. The unlooked-for storm appals them with horror. Some few who have heard not in vain of the mercy of Him who careth for the poor, in their crude way are crying for that mercy; some are profanely execrating their late master's cruelty, in dooming them to such misery; some are grovelling, in stupid and stubborn silence, on the floor, wrapping their rags about them; and the poor children, shivering with cold in their filthy straw, are screaming and sobbing distressfully. The good students, as if good angels, soon succeed in securing quiet, by imparting consolation and hope. They direct the poor creatures to be patient and trustful; and having supplied immediate means of an apology for comfort, they go on their mission of mercy in behalf of the sufferers. They are directed—perhaps by some heartless and wicked wag—to apply for aid and guidance to the ANTI-SLAVERY SOCIETY. They make the application. They tell the sad tale of sorrow and of suffering. The great Philanthropist, who manages the financial department of the Anti-Slavery Society, hears the tale with an apparently stolid indifference; and as with

> ——— "unfeeling heart of stone,
> That never dreamed of sorrows but its own."

The interview terminates with the important intelligence to the students, that "the Anti-Slavery Society has nothing whatsoever to do with such cases." Its work is already done, when the negro is either emancipated; or, as a fugitive, placed beyond the reach of pursuit. It can do nothing for free negroes. Had the students' proteges run away from their master, they would have been entitled to the protection and care of the Anti-Slavery Society. But they are free;—free to perish of hunger and cold, for aught that the Anti-Slavery Society will do for them.

The young men retire from the office; one of them, chagrined and disappointed; the other, satisfied with his former conceptions of the Anti-Slavery Society, as not a philanthropic institution, in any true sense; but as a sedition club,—heartlessly unfeeling and malignly fanatical.

"What now shall we do? Where now shall we go in quest of aid for those poor creatures, whom the Providence of God has so strangely thrown upon us to care for?"

"Whatever we do, or wherever we go, to aid them, let it be in faith, that it is a summons to an act of love; such as the Priest and the Levite of the parable had served upon them, and would not obey it. Let us obey it, so far as we may be able, as did the hated, but good Samaritan; and we may be sure of help that will not fail us."

"Certainly,—and, by the way, that is a very fair specimen of preaching for a student in his second year, and on a stormy day, at that. But, while you were preaching so well, I was thinking, wisely, I have no doubt, of our next step. We will go at once to Peter Williams, and lay the case before him."

"Very wise, unquestionably. I agree with you fully. Peter is a discreet and a kind man. By the way, has not our respect for that worthy black priest, something to do with our solicitude for these black paupers?"

"Very likely, indeed; and so we have a valid claim on his sable reverence, since he, perhaps, though unconsciously, has involved us in this business."

"But let us not, even to ourselves, seem to treat the

matter with any thing like levity. The Rev. Peter has been made the instrument of leading many before in the way of Gospel love and Christian duty."

"A noble fellow,—pardon me, a good and sensible man, is the Rev. Peter Williams. Do you know his father?"

"The venerable old Tobacconist? Yes indeed, quite well. And I have often found myself speculating in the company of the father and his reverend son, on the providence, that, from a savage African, brought forth a son of the third generation, to become so excellent a minister of the Gospel as Peter Williams. His grandfather was a slave all his life. His father, a slave to a good natured tobacconist, who taught him his business, and set him up in it, as a freeman in middle life, with thrifty habits, and with good religious and honest principles.

"Had his grandfather been a free negro of the class of the present generation, is it probable, that we should find such a clergyman in his grandson?"

"Alas, no; it is not at all probable."

And by this time the young men are at the door of Peter's study. He receives them with respectful cordiality. They state their errand with simple eloquence, and with deference to the judgment of the colored gentleman. Such was Rev. Peter Williams. He goes with them on the errand of mercy.

Arrived at the scene of woe, he carefully, and anxiously examines into the hard case. The poor creatures had belonged to a man who had lived a godless life. His servants, he had excluded from all the opportunities of religious or moral improvement, that had been repeatedly offered. He had fed and clothed them comfortably, and worked them moderately. But, on his isolated tobacco farm, he had afforded them no means of knowing any thing of either earth or heaven, beyond the lines of his plantation, and the aerial canopy above them. On his deathbed, his long-banished conscience forced its way back into his bosom, and stung him into remorse. It was too late to study what was *best;* and in a horrid anxiety to do *something* to relieve a long neglected and insulted conscience, he was left to do the worst and most cruel thing he could have done.

The man of God, to his great grief, and with indignation and pity towards him who had died, laying the delusive unction to his soul that he was their friend and benefactor, found the poor creatures generally in utter ignorance of the meaning of either religious or moral obligation; and living together more like beasts than human beings. What could he do? With food, fuel, and blankets, *they* would have been content. Not so their new friend. But what could he do? As a Christian minister, and as a man, this is what he *did* do,—alas to little apparent purpose:—God knoweth. He did what he could to make the wretched beings to understand and feel the loathsome, beastly, depravity, into which they had fallen; and that there was an awful call upon them to arouse themselves from their moral torpor, and to strive manfully and obediently to become *free indeed,* in the faithful service of a better master than he who had suffered them to fall into the slavery of Satan, and then mocked them with the pretence of a worse than worthless freedom.

Difficult was the task; but with admirable tact and ability, he made them understand,—so far as human power could do it,—the meaning of Christian repentance and faith; and how they require obedience, in order to make them available and acceptable. From some penitent eyes, tears found their way, and seemed to cry out, "What shall we do?"

Among other things done for them, they were paired off as they declared their partialities, and solemnly united in holy matrimony; and charged, on the peril of their souls, to be faithful to each other, and to their unfortunate children. For several of them, employment was found among the pitying and the kind, and they were made as decent and comfortable as their wretchedness would permit. But they were generally so incompetent, as not long to retain their places; and a great expense of charity was required to keep them through the long winter. Mr. Williams took the special pastoral charge of them, and made great efforts in their favor. No other man, perhaps, could have done so much. He soon relieved the good students from their cares concerning them, that they might have their hearts and hands free for other work in the service of their Master. They were slaves of Christ.

Some four or five years after, Mr. Williams was enquired of by one of them, how had prospered that portion of his spiritual charge; when he answered, with a sorrowful look and voice, that all had died, excepting about a tenth of their number, and those, children, nearly all in the almshouse.

Such is the murderous philanthropy of abolitionism. By wholesale have the poor blacks been immolated by cruel and false friends, who have made political and fanatical capital out of them, by coining their blood. The masses of the party, in unfortunate ignorance of the true state of the question, know not what they are doing; and so are rather to be compassionated than blamed. But not so of the political demagogues; and the pursuers of popularity and wealth, through the lecture-room, the pulpit, and the press. They well know what they are doing, and careless of consequences to the poor negroes, they are urged on by ambition, vanity, and avarice.

## NORTHERN EMANCIPATION.

### "WHO ARE THE MAN-SLAYERS?"

From want of experience, in the Northern States, their Legislatures may have acted in good faith, and with benevolent intentions: therefore, the almost extinction of the old race of negroes whom they emancipated, without making any provision for their support and improvement, was an involuntary homicide. It was, however, a homicide, on a large scale, and of a most revolting and horrible character. The Spanish Inquisition can scarcely boast of any thing to compare with it!

Does any one pronounce this an extravagant assertion? Let him examine statistics. Let him ask of the old people who remember what was the condition of the negroes when slaves; and let him see for himself, what now it is in their miserable homes, or none! And then let him visit the penitentiaries; the insane and lunatic asylums; and the public workhouses, and almshouses! Then let him inquire whether the old stock of negroes, emancipated by Legislative enactments, have decreased or multiplied. If all this, he will do, candidly and faithfully, it may safely be left to his conscience to declare whether I am extravagant in pronouncing the emancipation of the slaves, by the Northern Legislatures, equivalent to a sentence of death on the race! It has been executed already, on the most of them; and a large portion of the residue are agonizing in the process of extinction from the face of the earth.

In one of these States, which I could name, an application was made to an ecclesiastical body, for a certain immunity to be granted to the free blacks connected with it by membership. A majority of the body was strongly opposed to it. But kindly they gave way, when shown by figures that could not lie, that in no long time the race would be extinct. "Poor fellows," said a kind hearted man of great influence, "then let them be indulged while they remain with us."

## SOUTHERN MANUMISSION.

I have before me a document, by a reverend gentleman of eminence and excellence—a southern man in the North—who, to conciliate, towards the southern, the northern abolition branch of his communion, claims that about 250,000 slaves have been emancipated by the South, at the real personal sacrifice of far more than the British Government, *nominally*, paid to emancipate the West Indian slaves. He says of it: "It gives me pleasure to remind you."—He speaks of it with high praise and approbation; and demands the same of others. If I have been rightly informed, himself is one of the number for whom the praise is demanded. He is, I have no doubt, a good, able, and amiable man, and well worthy of praise for many good works and good intentions; but he will please allow me to withhold my unqualified praise for other than good intentions from the manumitters of 250,000 negro slaves, until well assured that it was a "greatest happiness" measure; and not, in general, a cruel abandonment of sacred duties towards helpless incompetency.

Where now are those 250,000 manumitted negroes? To write the question makes me shiver! Where are they now? Are they better off than they would have been in a mild servitude to benevolent masters, capable of making such sacrifices? Or have they mostly perished—fallen into profligacy, and perished,—like one of the Virginia gangs, already noticed, which formed a part of the 250,000?

The late very worthy and much lamented Dr. Parrish was exceedingly happy, that one of his southern patients, on his death-bed, manumitted all his slaves. They formed another item of the 250,000. Could the good Doctor have seen a few years into the future, would the prospect have increased his happiness? Indeed, the good man lived long enough to know—perhaps, to his sorrow did know—what Ohio thought of such accessions to her population; and how there it had fared with the poor negroes, whom he so feelingly congratulated on their manumission.

In the document above alluded to, is found this proposition, of a most important character:

"*The men who dwell south of Mason and Dixon's line have done more to convert the heathen, than the whole world beside.*"

And this is proved most conclusively, by reference to authentic documentary evidence. But, to me, it does indeed seem unaccountable, that a clear-headed and good-hearted man of God, can dwell, as he does, on the superior religious privileges of the slaves of the South; enumerating Rev. presidents and professors of colleges, devoting their lives to the care of their souls; and knowing, too, the wretched character and condition of the free negroes of the North, and yet manifest so profound a respect, and so ardent a sympathy, for the cause of abolitionism; whose partizans he so anxiously labors to conciliate! He is one of the good men of "dignified moderation," of whom it is said by the Rev. Dr. Thornwell, they "never venture upon a plea of justification in our defence. . . They curse us in their sympathies."

V. his sermon—"THE RIGHTS AND THE DUTIES OF MASTERS. At the dedication of a Church, erected in Charleston, S. C., for the benefit and instruction of the colored population."

## CHAPTER XXI.

### THE SLAVERY OF THE POOR ABOLISHED ONLY IN THE SOUTH.

I WISH they could somehow be reached—the tens of thousands of candid, and honest, and good abolitionists, who are such only because they honestly think that Southern slavery is the horrible thing that they have heard it represented to be. If they could be reached, and made to know what it really is, and not what it had seemed to them through a dark glass of imposition, which had been practised upon them, they would see that the horrors of slavery, which had so excited their hatred and sympathy, is abolished already in our country; and that nothing is left but gratuitous mischief for the agitators to do.

That slavery, of which it is said, *the man works for nothing*, is utterly excluded from the slaves of the South; and it is found in the North only. Here, indeed, it is too sadly true, that among the millions of working people, the number is but small—miserably small, in proportion to the whole, who get for their labor more than necessary food, clothing and shelter, for themselves and families; and innumerable is the host that fall very far short of the commonest needful comforts of life. Alas, indeed, and in truth, beyond a question, with the single exception of the Southern negroes, in a condition—allowing the abolition definition—*falsely* called slavery—all over the world, a very large majority of the people who depend on their daily labor for their daily bread, are always, and at this moment, suffering from want of sufficiency of that daily bread, and are frequently met by all the horrors of destitution and famine; and are hurrying on that awful way to the grave—*death by starvation.*

While the strong voice of the LAW, imperiously forbids the negro slave to be in want of the needful comforts of life; and the kind and gentle voice of true benevolence says to him, in the words of a prophet,—"Go your way, eat the fat and drink the sweet, and send portions to them for whom nothing is prepared;—and they go their way to eat and to drink and to make great mirth."—What a graphic picture from an inspired pencil of the happy life of the Southern slave of our day—in all parts of the earth besides is found the reverse of this picture,—the poor for very want, "hanging down their heads, with their faces to the ground, and mourning and weeping," that the most awful of all the miseries of humanity has overtaken them and their helpless children in the haggard and frightful form of a famine of bread. To the poor laborer for daily food, often is it famine in the midst of plenty all around their cabins of destitution, and less frequently, a more general and sweeping evil.

And in view of such facts, is it nothing that the poor in the South are not only a well fed race in general, but that by law, their acknowledged right to plenty of wholesome food is watchfully protected? Whoever thinks it nothing, or of no value as a compensation for any presumed evil of their condition, would do well and wisely to visit the abodes of poverty in our own great cities and overpeopled towns and rural villages, and to pass a few sober hours in reading about famines and their effects. Read in our own newspapers of a few months past, republished accounts of the fearful distresses of the poor, in various parts of Europe, from famine producing disease, desperation, insanity and death; and then, say, if you can, that, when

"God openeth His hand and filleth all things living with plenteousness," He does not dispense the greatest of earthly blessings.

Let your mind's eye fall on large and populous districts of people, "deprived alike of the productions of nature and the fruits of industry;" and, to consummate wretchedness and despair, "whole herds of cattle and sheep killed by disease!" Look at this picture of "the condition of the peasantry in many parts of Germany," as drawn by an excellent Lutheran clergyman, and try to reckon truly the blessedness of abundance of food.

"All feelings of human nature begin to be more and more convulsed. The most loathsome food, meat infected by murrain,—is eagerly sought after: in some instances dogs have been slaughtered and ravenously devoured by a famishing population.

"In one case in Wurtemberg, a dog buried for some days, has been dug up, and what will scarcely appear credible, the flesh in its advanced state of decomposition has actually been made use of as food! To satisfy the cravings of hunger, the last miserable remnant of furniture is not unfrequently disposed of. And what kind is it, which to sustain their mere life and unenviable existence, these wretched people are forced to, and too glad to procure? Wholesome meat is out of the question. Bread made of bran must supply its place. And bran soaked in water in which salt has been dissolved to give it a taste, and the skins of potatoes, and coffee boiled over and over again to extract the last remaining particle of nourishment. * * * Hunger knows of no ties of patriotism, and *sauve qui peut!* is alas! the anxious cry repeated from village to village by hundreds and thousands in many districts of my native land, and driving them recklessly and helplessly, away from their peaceful home in search of another in foreign and distant countries."

Such is a truthful European picture of actual starvation and despair. It is a single figure of a multitudinous group, compared with which the Laocoon is almost beautiful. Nor is this picture at all too highly colored to represent the sufferings from like cause in parts of Ireland and Scotland; nay of proud England herself. And think you that destitution is unknown among the poor of our own prosperous and happy land of freedom? Think you that none suffer and die of want in our land of plenty?

Ask the self-sacrificing city missionaries of New York, Philadelphia, and of other cities, about the wretched scenes of destitution which they often discover;—sometimes where from outward appearances they are entirely unlooked for; —scenes that sink their hearts, and in such numbers, especially in winter, as to defy all the means of remedy within their reach in this cold unloving world that, for the most part, has "no pity."

Examine what has been written, on the single subject of the destitutions and sufferings of *one* class of the poor of our cities,—the laborious sewing women, by the venerable Matthew Carey, and by others, since his philanthropic efforts for their relief, and then declare it to be a small matter, that a distinct class of millions of the poor of our country, men, women and children,—the infirm, the aged, and the infant,—have neither experience nor apprehension of such sufferings from destitution as you find there described.

Is there any way to the knowledge of the number of free blacks--so called--that have perished from destitution in the single city of New York, since the reign of pseudo-philanthropy directed all its energies to the especial case of the miseries of *slavery*--so called--where destitution is unknown?

Whoever remembers the particulars to some extent, of the sufferings of the poor of that city in the winter of 1816, 17—the winter of soup-house memory,—when thousands of the lives of the starving poor were saved by the distribution of poor soup—may recollect that in one house on one morning, there were found the dead bodies of five black persons and children, who had perished from hunger and cold!

Indescribable were that winter's sufferings among the poor, and especially the African poor. They perished by scores;—hundreds, perhaps;—and when there was a small number there compared with the present. And since that sad time too, they have increased in idleness and vice, as well as in numbers. By immigration only, has been their increase.

The next year after that frightful season, "The Society for the Prevention of Pauperism in the city of New York" was formed, and proceeded to the discharge of their important duties under the management of about 40 gentlemen of the highest character for talents, integrity, and benevolence.

Gen. Matthew Clarkson, the first President, was aided by six vice presidents, of whom were Brockholst Livingston, and Nicholas Fish; and John Griscom, Secretary.

The rest, with thirty managers, were men of similar mark. By means of vigilant and active committees, the haunts of vice and crime, and the abodes of poverty and wretchedness were explored, and the loathsome and revolting and heart-rending details were spread before the Society: Having enumerated TEN sources of Pauperism, in their first Annual Report; The following paragraph reads thus:

"Such are the causes which are considered as the more prominent and operative in producing that amount of indigence and suffering, which awakens the charity of this city, and which has occasioned the erection of buildings for eleemosynary purposes, at an expense of half a million of dollars, and which calls for the annual distribution of 90,000 dollars more. But, if the payment of this sum were the only inconvenience to be endured,—trifling, indeed, in comparison, would be the evils which claim our attention. Of the *mass* of *affliction* and *wretchedness* actually sustained, how *small* a portion is thus relieved! Of the quantity of misery and vice which the causes we have enumerated, with others we have not named, bring upon the city, how *trifling* the portion actually removed by public or by private benevolence! *Nor* do we conceive it *possible* to remove this load of distress, by all the alms-doing of which the city is capable, while the causes remain in full and active operation."

So spake those great and good men more than 34 years ago, when New York was a village, compared with itself now; and all the causes they then enumerated still "remain in full and active operation;" and several more, not less potent, have since been added. And if then, such men talked of a "mass of affliction, and wretchedness," and of a "load of distress," which they could not "conceive it possible to remove," what now may be supposed the amount of misery and suffering among the free, unknown to the people of the South, technically called *slaves?*

When will honest and quiet people learn any thing of the true merits of the question, and be able to judge righteous judgment? Surely not so long as by their pastors and teachers, and great Ecclesiastical bodies they are in effect falsely taught, that it is better to die of starvation under the name of freedom, than to live in comfort, and fearless of want, and be called a slave.

A few years since, one of the most numerous and respectable bodies of Christians in our land, through their highest constituted tribunal, so represented the system of southern slavery, as to receive from a like body in Great Britain the highest expression of approbation in these pregnant words: "Ardently do we desire your encouragement in your praiseworthy career; most sincerely do we appreciate your Christian testimony to the *essential sinfulness of slaveholding.*—We beseech you, dear brethren, to persevere in your righteous agitation, till the object be achieved. Cease not to expose the enormity of the crime of buying and selling a fellow creature; of reducing a human being endowed with an immortal soul to the level of an ox or an ass. Stand fast by that clause of your declaration which asserts that American slavery is intrinsically an unrighteous and oppressive system, opposed to the prescriptions of the law of God, to the spirit and precepts of the gospel, and to the best interests of humanity."

Who would be able to believe, beforehand, that such greetings and congratulations, and announcements of theological belief and Christian morals, could possibly be addressed to one great body of Bible-believing Christians, from a like body in another land of Bibles? The *essential sinfulness of slaveholding,* proclaimed by people who insist on the supreme authority of the Bible as the Word of God, in which a great slaveholder is called the FRIEND OF GOD, in the Old Testament, and in the New Testament, an Apostle sends an Epistle by a *fugitive slave* to his master, to solicit and plead for pardon for the returning runaway!

Alas! to what does all this contempt for the authority of the Word of God tend and point? Are those great Christian bodies about to deny the faith utterly, and become infidel? With them, too, is Christianity to become a "failure?" May Heaven forbid, and avert the seemingly real impending danger, and bring them back to their old and honest rule of faith—"the Bible, the whole Bible, and nothing but the Bible."

"Intrinsically an unrighteous and oppressive system." And these are words of Englishmen!—English Christians! Have they been so long, and so familiarly, acquainted with the very cruelest oppression of the poor in their own land, as to become callous in their sympathies with realities, and only able to feel for fictions? Can it be that they know of the British Parliamentary confessions of oppressions? And do they know nothing of the slaying of women and children to make room for sheep? "Opposed to the prescriptions of the law of God!" Their own oppressive and brutalizing pauper system is not—is it?—opposed to the prescriptions of the law of God. How a beam in an eye of one effectually hides a mote in that of another! "To the spirit and precepts of the Gospel;" and yet, the spirit and precepts of the Gospel are better observed by masters, giving "that which is just and equal" to their servants, than they are towards poor hirelings in any country under heaven, not to say in England, where they are confessedly under the most grinding and starving oppression; to the dwarfing, even, of thousands, and so creating, by cruelty, an inferior caste!

"To the best interests of humanity." Our Southern system of Slavery opposed to the best interests of humanity! What are those best interests of humanity? Are they paganism, savagism, vice, crime, and starvation? If so, then, indeed, is this system opposed to the best interests of humanity; for, with the most remarkable blessings of Heaven upon it, it has done, in successful opposition against them, what no other means or agents have ever done.

In opposition to Paganism, the forces of the Christian world have been combined, impliedly and actually, for many centuries; and there have been expended millions of means, heedless of the cries of the poor at home, and careless of the condition of the worse than pagans at their own doors; and yet this world-wide combination has not effected the tithe of the spiritual conquests over Paganism, that have been quietly effected by this blindly and blasphemously anathematized system of "American Slavery."

"Opposed" to savagism; it has civilized and Christianized a large portion of the number of savages than have been exterminated, by other and very different means, from the face of the earth. Let a candid and discerning mind compare the savage character of the African race, in their native land, with the Christian condition of a very large majority of the negroes of the South—among whom are a greater proportion of devout and enlightened worshippers of the True God, than among the population of either London or Philadelphia—and such candid and discerning mind may be able, in a good measure, to appreciate to what purpose this system is opposed to the dominion of Satan over the black race of Ham.

"Opposed" to vice and crime; it has shown, in the most satisfactory manner, to all candid persons who love the truth and are willing to know it well, that they may love it better: that the social Christian virtues are found prevalent among the negroes of the South, as they are nowhere else found with their fellow-Africans; and very rarely elsewhere.

But all the slaves of the South were not originally either pagans or savages? No, a slight scattering of them were Mahomedans. And is it opposed to the best interests of humanity to Christianize Mahomedans? Of this interesting class of Africans—a race apparently distinct from the general negro type—there are some still living in various parts of the South, and they are mostly, if not all, good and happy Christians, such as I have elsewhere described one of them—Old King.

I have before me a letter from the South, which gives an account of one of these African Mahomedans, and that seems very clearly to suggest the interesting supposition, that those of them who came as captive slaves to this country—as others doubtless to other countries—were banished into slavery by the rulers of their tribes for political offences:—a long-standing Mahomedan custom.

The letter referred to was received two days since, by a reverend neighbor and courteous friend, who had seen and conversed with the old man, and listened to his reading his Arabic Bible, and to his very poetic translation of the 23d Psalm. It was procured at my request; and, by withholding names—for which I can see no other very good reason than custom, which is certainly often "more honored in the breach than the observance"—I trust no confidence will be considered as violated by the use here made of it, to show that the *best interests of humanity* were not opposed by the purchase of this Mahomedan captive and retaining him in captivity, unless the best interests of humanity are promoted better by Islamism than by Christianity.

## THE LETTER.

————— "N. C., Feb. 4th.

"Dear Sir,—I cannot give you very definite answers to your queries concerning "Uncle Moreau," as the old gentleman is rather averse to talking about his early life.

"Uncle Moreau" was born on the banks of the Senegal River, and belonged to the tribe of the Foulahs, a Mohammedan tribe of Africans. His father appears, from his statement to have been a man of wealth and standing among his people. According to Moreau's statements, he was the owner of seventy slaves; and was a candidate for election as chief ruler of the tribe—in which he was defeated. (This is Moreau's statement. I had always thought that this office among these tribes was hereditary.) Slavery was a very mild thing in that country in some respects, as the slaves work but half the day. After his father died, he lived with his uncle at Footah. His uncle was principal officer of state to the ruler of Footah. His elder brother married his uncle's daughter, his first cousin. This brother educated Moreau—their education consisting in learning to read the Koran, and to write in Arabic. Uncle Moreau, when his education was finished, became a teacher, and taught for ten years. Then he became a trader—trading principally in salt.

"He was two years a trader, and then, by some means, was made a slave. He is very dark upon this subject, and averse to speaking upon it; though he intimates it was by a fault of his own—perhaps a misdemeanor or crime. ("Old Satan make me do bad," were his words to me.) He arrived in Charleston with only two of his countrymen with him, though the vessel was crowded with captives. He was sold to a planter near Charleston, who treated him harshly, and from whom he soon ran away. He was taken up and put in jail at Fayetteville, N. C., where he was brought to the notice of General ———, of this place, his present master. When he came to General ——— he was still a strict Mohammedan. The first year he was with him, he observed very strictly the fast of Rhamadan. Some friends brought him a copy of the Koran, which has since been destroyed in the burning of Gen. ———'s residence. His master and mistress read the Bible to him often, and talked freely with him about Christ. Seven years after he was purchased by the General, he says he began to soften. He felt that he was lost—gave up Mohammed, and sought peace in the cross of Christ. He was baptized and admitted to the church in Fayetteville.

"Uncle Moreau says, it was good for him to come to this country—all good—'Master *very* good,' (meaning thereby his Saviour!) 'MASTER *very* good.'

"He is now between 83 and 84 years of age—very devout in all his habits, and patiently waiting for the coming of his MASTER.

"I do not know whether I have answered all your

questions—but I have given you the substance of all the old man said to me—in reply to my queries. He has written an account of his early life in Arabic, which he has given to Mrs. ———, after exacting the promise that it should not be translated during his life.

"When General ——— returns from Alabama, where he is at present, it is my intention to prepare an extended account of Uncle Moreau for some of our periodicals.

"Sincerely your brother in Christ.

—————."

With many thanks and grateful considerations for the writer, and for my friend, his correspondent on the Upper Delaware, I shall look with much interest for the fulfilment of this promise; well assured of its supplying a thrilling and valid testimony that Southern slavery is not always opposed to "the best interests of humanity."—*Uncle Moreau says it was good for him to come to this country: "all good—*MASTER *very good."* And so have said, and still say, thousands of Christianized Africans.

Now, if we are not much mistaken, candid people,—not lashed to parties and prejudices,—will agree to say, that we have given some strong enough proofs to convince *them* that "American slavery," which feeds the hungry, and clothes the naked; instructs the ignorant; reclaims the savage; converts the idolatrous pagan, and the beleaguered Mohammedan, is not opposed "to the spirit and precepts of the Gospel, and to the best interests of humanity;" but that they are the opposers of these interests who allow their own hungry neighbors to go unfed, and to *die of starvation;* and who suffer them to go unclothed and to freeze to death; and to remain in uninstructed ignorance from generation to generation until they become savages; as found by thousands in Philadelphia, and by tens of thousands in London,—the favored abodes of these Chris tian correspondents, whose pious sympathy seems of the very peculiar cast of not being able to find any thing to exercise itself upon but at a very great distance. In their denunciatory anxiety for the negroes of the South, who are in no need of their aid or interference,—they altogether forget, and lose sight of the real and killing evils at their very doors. Elevated above all considerations of home duty and mercy;—from their balloon of self-righteousness, they can see no Saint Giles; no Baker street; and indeed nothing short of a Southern plantation, and that through a false medium.

The South very meekly complains of the hard words of their Northern Christian Brethren, and a Northern organ and oracle says, "The question is thus pressed to an issue, now whether the great body of Christians at the North sanction the violent measures and vituperative denunciations of a few, who are represented as saying, '*We have exhausted the argument with the slave-holder and must now try the virtue of cold steel.*'" On this point there can be no mistake. Our Southern brethren must know that the great mass of Christians in the non-slaveholding States give no countenance to the mad projects of a few who would "call down fire from Heaven" upon those who will not submit to their dictation. But the mass of Northern Christians—there is not the slightest doubt—and it is but kindness and honesty to our Southern brethren explicitly to say so, they will never say less than that American slavery is opposed to the prescription of the law of God, to the spirit and precepts of the Gospel, and to the best interests of humanity." This is the lesson sent by the British abolition brethren to the "*Northern Christians*"—how very modest, and meek exceedingly—and they learn the lesson by heart, and pour it into the ears of the "Southern brethren," and in "kindness and honesty" explicitly assure them that they shall abide by this teaching of the British abolitionists!

These Northern Christians, who send forth from Philadelphia this hostile missive to the South to be defiantly hurled in the teeth of their Southern *brethren*, disclaim all connection with the *cold steel* party. They give no countenance to their mad projects! By no manner of means. Certainly not. Were not this subject so awfully serious, I should be tempted to quote here a thought or two from Coleridge's "Mad Ox." It is commended to this disciple of British abolitionism.

"Apart"—how far apart we shall see—"apart from the raving of mad fanatics, there is a deep and growing conviction"—it grows just in proportion to the growth of irreverence for the WORD OF GOD, and disloyalty to the Constitution of the Union. "There is a deep and growing conviction of the unutterable abomination of slavery, and an increasing determination not to rest until this foul blot is wiped away from the Church, and a jubilee is proclaimed throughout the land." Of course, in these meek and modest words, no countenance is given to *vituperative denunciations!*—no invitation to the fanatical use of *cold steel.* By no sort of means! O no! But we will proceed with our extract from this gentle Northern Christian—this *kind* and *honest,* and most magnanimous philanthropist, whose charity is so far from beginning at home as to forget that it has one, and goes to England for lessons in the art of economising a distant crusade; and in the somewhat more practical and available art of modern fuss-making.

"These are the views, the feelings, and the purposes of a great majority of the wisest and best men in the non-slaveholding States. Our brethren at the South ought to be apprised of this *as settled, unchanging truth.*" The statistics are his own.

As one of the *wisest* and *best* of men, he condescends—

as due to the Southern brethren—to tell them this *settled, unchanging truth.* His condescension is scarcely inferior to his marked and very remarkable modesty. There can be no doubt that this man is a distinguished member of that very polite and courteous class, who take off the hat when speaking of themselves in profound reverence for the subject.

Were I a Southern man, it seems to me that I should feel in no little degree obliged to this modest gentleman—not merely for his very amusing arrogance and presumption, but for his frank manner in removing the curtain to expose the doings of the independent conclave—independent of the *cold steel* party, I mean—of conspirators against the liberties and immunities of the South. Some irritable people may be not a little nettled by his assuming, that his party comprise "the mass of Northern Christians;" but surely it is not worth while. History supplies abundance of examples of even cliques and cabals indulging in this sort of amusing self-complacency.

Such as this interesting specimen of arrogance—this phenomenon of stupid vanity—have often appeared for a little while above the horizon, presuming that in earth and heaven there remains nothing for them to learn. That there is any thing not known—to say nothing of dreamed of—in their philosophy, never enters even the abode of their imagination. That to reform, according to their notion, some particular branch of moral science, founded on a basis of everlasting truth, might involve the derangement of the universal system of morals, never enters the three by four apartment of their puny intellects; and that any interference devised by them, to improve the scheme of Providence, might turn out to be no better than "a rude jog from the clumsy fist of a clown, who knew nothing of the component parts of the machine;" they are not able even to dream of. It is not given to such to see, that "the wisest are but as fools when measuring themselves against Him whose ways are past finding out, and who oft, amidst

> "Thick clouds and dark
> Chooses to dwell, his glory unobscured,
> And with the majesty of darkness round
> Circles his throne."

To attempt any thing like a sober discussion of such people's crotchets—to break a lance with such champions of impracticableness, in sober earnest—would be the veriest quixotism imaginable, if not a culpable waste of time in air-beating. But there is something due to the busy, and to the young; who have not time to explore their hollowness, and to measure their shallows; or whose experience is too short to have reached the standard by which to measure their magnitude—or rather—what? Why, in the world, has not Dr. Noah Webster given us *minitude*, as well as magnitude?

But this little gentleman is a scribe—a sort of amanuensis of his party—as such, what he tells us is to be heeded as such. I don't mean as the sentiments of the "mass of Northern Christians," but of the pretty numerous party—exclusive of the *cold steel party*—whom he considers to be the mass of Northern Christians. And when he speaks falsely, and in the very teeth of general experience, of "The working of the system," as "proved by an experience of more than half a century, to be fraught with the most disastrous consequences—socially, politically and morally—that it is a deadly Upas tree, sending forth putrid and poisonous exhalations in every direction;—that all good men ought to unite in "hewing down and casting it into the fire;"—when thus he proffers the strong hand and the heart of fire to the cold steel party, in the name of his own party, which he dignifies as the mass of Northern Christians—then it is not good sense to smile upon as amusing; but to look gravely on him as the representative and mouth piece of his party, by which the South is thus denounced.

But what is to be done? Let the South, and the friends of the South, learn to distinguish—not between the cold steel party and this party which denounces it while it sustains it, but—between their true friends and such as call them *our dear Southern brethren*, "curse them in their sympathies,"—are very sorry that they are under the *stupefying influence upon the conscience of slaveholders*, and fear much that they may have, at last, to give up their dear Southern brethren to the *cold steel*.

"All good men ought to unite in "hewing it down and casting it into the fire!" But this comes from the sympathising party of dear brethren who disclaim the use of vituperative language and Billingsgate denunciation. It is the party whose deliberate, *settled*, *unchanging* determination it is to subvert;—as soon as possible to subvert the Southern system of servitude, and so add a few millions to our free black population.

Is it desirable? Is such "a consummation devoutly to be wished?" Would it be a doubtless good for the blacks? Would they continue for any great length of time, as now they are, to be better off; and in all things better, than the free negroes of the North?—The denizens of Anthony street, the Five Points, the Penitentiary, the Lunatic Asylum, in New York? and of Baker street, Moyamensing, the Penitentiary, the Asylum, in Philadelphia? How long would they continue better, and better off, than are those hungry, naked, vicious, miserable beings, with no more care for either their souls or their bodies, than these have had extended to them? With such neglect of the white race they would dwindle away towards extermination.

But elsewhere I have intended, at least, to show the cruelties, and some of the "frightful results" of premature and promiscuous manumissions. As said by Dr. Johnson, that nothing is easier than to ridicule the Bible, so nothing is easier than for shallow recklessness to talk loud and learnedly about the evils of slavery, until every other evil in the human condition is forgotten or lost sight of. When all other evils are removed or remedied, there will remain no longer any difficulty in the removal of this. But so long as the poor are suffered to die of starvation in the midst of plenty, I am not for a war against the smaller evil of negro slavery.

## CHAPTER XXII.

### NEW ENGLAND.

In either history or experience, scarcely any thing can be found so strangely anomalous, as the prevalence of the abolition spirit in New England. By thousands of unimpeachable witnesses, it has been unmistakably declared to be an evil and wicked spirit; and yet it has multitudes of devoted followers. As a cruel and implacable spirit, it has inflicted on its victims, calamities and sufferings of the most lamentable character; and still it is lauded and worshipped; and high honors are conferred upon it by principalities and powers.

In Massachusetts, as a living power, this evil spirit has established his head-quarters; and thence sends forth his desolating hosts, blighting and blasting every thing that falls in their way of destruction. To the wise and the good, it is a great grief and mortification; but they have learned to bear the evil as best they may, with the comfort, that the sappers and miners of the Bible and the constitution, may not be able to destroy her well earned and fair fame, until the OLD SOUTH, and FANEUIL HALL, and her BUNKER HILL monument be all devoured by the tooth of Time, and that then their occupation will be gone.

Sustained in comfort and countenance by her history, and by her enduring monuments and noble institutions, she may calmly, though blushing, bear to be also distinguished as the head-quarters of the abolition faction;

as at this time she indisputably is, and apparently as the result of her people's choice.

For a goodly period already Massachusetts has had acknowledged claims—scarcely second to any—to be the principal rendezvous of abolitionism; and at length, she has fairly established them, and caused them to be nationally allowed. To this end, she has sent to the support of her abolition corps in the House of Representatives, an uncompromising and revolutionary member of the faction to the Senate of the Union, pledged to all possible efforts to destroy the Union, if he cannot subvert the system of Southern servitude.

In her high places of Church and State, for many years past, this has been a darling subject,—a topic scarcely inferior in interest to the Sea Serpent in its highest credit, or another—a contemporary—that I will not name.

A vast deal of verbal, learned, and ardent sympathy, has been manifested for the negro race, from the palmy days of Dr. Channing's visit to the West Indies, down to the senatorial days of Mr. Sumner. The literature, the logic, and the laudation of the Rev. Doctor, were bestowed on the negroes; and the only great effort of eloquence made by the senator was thrown into the same scale in favor—as intended—of their sable darlings;—"one of the best races of the human family," says the doctor, "singularly susceptible of improvement;"—and with "a gracefulness and dignity of form and motion, rare in my own native New England." "Their improvability is not to be questioned;" says an Honorable disciple of Dr. Channing.

How very happy for the good and singularly improvable race to have such champions, advocates and teachers, at home as well as abroad:—distinguished doctors of divinity,—members of both Houses of Congress,—of the British Parliament;—authors of eminence in prose and poetry, male and female, in numbers numberless. And now, last, not least, the female nobility and gentry of England have added their efficient and powerful aid still more to improve this happy people.

With such vantage ground to stand upon, and with such aids, surely, by this time, the negroes of New England, and of Massachusetts in particular, should be all highly polished images of God in ebony! Adorned with every virtue and every grace, they ought to be found first among the foremost, in the practice of all that is honest and honorable; and in the merited enjoyment of every sort of human comfort and happiness. As they are described by reverend doctors and honorable cabinet ministers and senators, as *singularly improvable,* we seem to have a fair right to expect to find their character justifying their teachers and advocates in their laudatory descriptions.

But is it so? Are the free negroes of New England thus found to justify such praise? With such powerful, learned, and benevolent friends; and with half a century of negro freedom, how have they demonstrated their *unquestioned improvability,* and that they are *one of the best races of the human family?* How have these proud claims been supported?

By even anti-slavery accounts, they are represented as being not better, nor better off, than their less favored brethren of the race elsewhere. Nay, wonderful, as it must, and ought to appear, the free negroes of Massachusetts are both worse in character, and worse off in condition, than are the free negroes out of New England by a large difference, and even than in most of the other New England States, in which they are less favored at home, and less honorably and ably represented in the national legislature.

According to a former Report of the "Prison Discipline Society," this best of the races of the human family had more than fourteen times as many convicts in the Massachusetts Penitentiary as had the white population in proportion to their numbers. One negro in every one hundred and forty was in the prison, and, only one in two thousand of the whites. In Connecticut—far less favored with abolition teachers—there was little more than half that proportion in the penitentiary;—about nine times the proportion of the whites. In New York and Pennsylvania less than in Connecticut.

Very strange, is it not? But the Report from which this statement is drawn was made in 1826. The free blacks of New England may have improved since; and particularly in Massachusetts. I have not so heard; and the Report itself, with the name of one of the most celebrated anti-slavery authors and teachers—the Rev. FRANCIS WAYLAND, as one of the managers of the Society, expressed a serious doubt of the *possibility* of their improvement *where they are;* Dr. Channing's and Mr. Everett's authority to the contrary notwithstanding.

By the recent census, it must be inferred that they have been allowed to sink deeper and deeper in vice, criminality, degradation and wretchedness; or that vain efforts made to elevate them had precipitated them into idiocy and insanity. Poor unhappy creatures! in either alternative how are they to be pitied!

While in Pennsylvania and New York, there is but one of the demented classes in more than two hundred and fifty; in Massachusetts there is ONE IN FORTY-THREE! Is it not wonderful as well as lamentable? My dear doctor, please lend me your aid. What think you of this?

"It does not at all surprise me. I am very sorry for the poor negroes. But to my mind, there is nothing strange in their dementation, and especially in Massachusetts.

"The Abolition atmosphere there, fully enough accounts

for it. It crazes the poor creatures. Look at the effect of it beyond the boundaries of Massachusetts; and you cannot fail to infer that there is the principal fountain of the dementing gas. Its poison is spread by every wind that blows. It is carried into Connecticut, and there largely increases the proportion of insanity and idiocy above that of New York. In Maine, where it seems concentrated in the alembic of fanaticism, every fourteenth negro is either an idiot or a lunatic! While among slaves there is not one in a thousand."

"But, Dr., the Hon. Horace Greely, the great socialistic philosopher, has condescended to tell us that 'all that is proved by the fact that the proportion of insane and idiotic among slaves is very much smaller than among the free negroes, is, that slaves are in a lower and more brutal state.'"

"Does that kind of reasoning unravel all the difficulties of the case? Are the negroes of Maine so highly elevated above those of the other Northern States?"

"But, seriously, doctor, what think you of this notion of Greely?"

"If it *were* his notion—as it is not—I should reply to you, that I think quite as well of it as of a number of his other notions."

"But why do you think him not sincere, Dr.?"

"I think him not sincere, because I think him not a fool—in the usual sense of the word."

"But why should he say so, and not think so?"

'He is one of the disciples of Dr. Channing, and must uphold his theory at any cost. And he knew well enough it would satisfy his party, the most of whom are aware that very stupid animals—the oyster, for example—is rarely, if ever crazy; and that therefore it is a plain case enough, that slaves are not crazy, whom their great Doctor has declared to be brutalized by their condition. The doctor himself seems never to have discovered that he had demolished his own theory of the brutalizing effects of slavery, by representing the West India negroes, reared in that brutalizing condition, as being more polished than most of New Englanders. And what Dr. Channing did not perceive of this contradiction of words and confusion of ideas, Greely had no fear that modern abolitionists would detect; save only the few of the class, whose talents are devoted to the wicked work of confounding confusion and blinding the blind, and hardening the stony heart."

"Yet some slaves *do* become crazy, my good doctor."

"O yes, but no more than barely exceptions enough to establish the general rule. In Louisiana and South Carolina, one in several thousands become idiotic or lunatic. Very low in the scale of being the negroes in these States must be when compared with the Massachusetts blacks, where one in forty-three is either a maniac or an idiot; and one in a hundred and forty, in the State's prison:—very low indeed—mere brutes! And yet, strange to say, in these two slave States, there are thousands of slaves who are accomplished clerks and mechanics; and tens of thousands who are trusted with responsibilities which their masters would be slow to transfer to a white man, in case of need, unless he came strongly fortified with well known vouchers of his ability and uprightness."

"But in sober seriousness, doctor, how would you account for the strange fact, that so few slaves become lunatic, or idiotic, and so many free blacks?"

"Well, in the first place, I do not think it a strange fact at all. Among healthy and virtuous slaves, under proper treatment; and steady, firm, gentle discipline—necessary to every body—well supplied with wholesome food, and not exposed to dangers and alarms, more than slaves usually are—less than any other people in our country, far—and so, of course, free from the goadings of care and anxiety, which drives so many others into madness; under these favorable circumstances, in which the good slave of a good master is always found, and you would not find one in one hundred thousand, either lunatic or idiotic.

"Disease, intemperance, vice, depravity, anxiety, hunger and hardship—sufferings of one kind or another, produce all the lunacics and idiocies which are found among people of all colors; and of these maddening evils, the slaves of the South have probably a smaller proportion than any other people on earth."

"But, Dr., insanity, lunacy, idiocy, are sometimes found in healthy and virtuous families."

"So, unquestionably, is the gout, scrofula, and other transmissive diseases; but health, happiness and virtue, never originated any one of them. When gout seizes with its vengeful fangs, a man who had always been temperate, it is—as a hard necessity belonging to the system of high law which governs the race of men—to illustrate for our benefit, the fearful truth, that the sins of the fathers are visited upon the children, even to the third and fourth generation! And so is it in the diseases of the brain, when they are visited on the healthy, the happy and the virtuous."

"In passing, doctor, what do you think of that high law of the human condition which thus entails punishments? I ask you, because a certain friend of yours says he don't believe in it at all."

"He does though; unless himself be either a madman or an idiot, whoever he may be, friend or foe."

"Why, with such confidence, do you think so, Dr.?"

"Simply because he *cannot* help himself. But to answer your first question—what I *think* of it—this is it:—I think mankind could not do without it. I think it a rod of rigid justice, not less necessary to our well-being, than the staff of mercy and melting charity! I think a single century of its suspension would hurry civilization back into savagism; and then reduce the savage to a brute."

"No doubt you are, at least partly, right, my good Doctor; but to return to our main subject; of the exemption of the Southern slave from the awful calamity of madness——".

"'O let me not be mad, not mad, sweet Heaven!
Keep me in temper; I would not be mad!'

"Few will be deceived by the unserious theory of Mr. Greely, save only such as love to have it so, and are therefore always ready and waiting to be deceived by any sophistry which any 'putter-on' may use to bolster up their spite and folly.

"From very early days, it has been the fashion to talk of the brutalizing effects of slavery. And where it is a real down-treading and irresponsible system, as was that of much of the slavery of pagan antiquity; and as is very much of the white slavery of Europe and of our own country; and of the slavery of the British East India Company;—and indeed, of the slavery of tyrannous sin, every where; its effects *are* brutalizing. But when we find that the slaves of the South are less brutal, and more civilized, than are the free blacks of the North, together with a very large and fearful number of the free whites also, as our own eyes, and ears, and newspapers, are constantly—daily and hourly—testifying, we are as certain as any thing can make us, that the mild system of our Southern slavery is quite the reverse of brutalizing."

"That the slaves of the South are less brutal than the classes you have referred to, Doctor, the records and reports of crime, North and South, bear ample testimony; but how do you make them out to be more civilized?"

"They are more faithful to their obligations. They are more submissive to the laws under which they live. They are more sober and temperate. They are every way more regular in their lives. They are more loyal and loving; and, generally, incomparably more religious. And now if all this is not to be more civilized, I would be very glad to know what is?"

"Mr. Greely would require to know that they should also be more enlightened with knowledge."

"Well, even *that,* I might also have added. For, of the best and most useful knowledge;—of knowledge that purifies the heart and expands the mind healthily, they have a much larger amount than the generality of the free negroes of the North; to say nothing of the millions of whites, in our own, as well as in other countries, scarcely removed from utter darkness of mind and heart, and sunken in the abyss of corruption, and steeped to the very lips in the most loathsome and brutal viciousness and criminality. LA CITE, ST. GILES', FIVE POINTS, BAKER STREET, supply only museum-specimens of this class of wretched monsters, which, to see, might frighten a Southern slave into derangement of intellect, if any sight could do it!"

"Some, besides Mr. Greely and other abolitionists, Doctor, may deem your account of the superiority of the Southern slave, extravagant and altogether apocryphal."

"No doubt; but it is not so, though For, among them there is a greater proportions who understand the obligations of religion and its true principles; and a greater proportion who understand the practical business of life than there are among the free blacks of the North."

"There is not, perhaps, so great a proportion of them who can read, however?"

"No. A comparatively few of them can read. There may not indeed be a much greater proportion of them who can read, than there may have been of the British nation in the twelfth century: somewhat greater, I should think, however. But of what great service is the ability to read a little—which is all that is *generally* possessed by the free negroes, notwithstanding their 'unquestioned improvability,'—if it do little in keeping them out of penitentiaries and lunatic asylums?

"Of good readers—readers to profit—there may be at least as many among the Southern, as among the Northern negroes. Many of them read their Bibles well, and sensibly. And of the arts of life, on which much of the superior comforts of civilization depend, they are happily far from ignorant. Of this kind of valuable knowledge, they have a greater share than was possessed but by a few of the people of Europe, only a few centuries ago.

"There is many a Southern slave whose valuable knowledge would have made an Englishman famous in the reign of the eighth Henry of unblessed memory. But their good learning does not lead to lunacy, as free-negro 'improvability' does in the Northern States."

"You do not think, Doctor, that their learning leads the free blacks into lunacy?"

"Yes; what they learn from antislavery lectures and sermons; newspapers, and other such literature, which they are so liberally supplied with in Massachusetts, makes them discontented with their degraded condition; and discontent makes them vicious and criminal; and their vices and crimes destroy the health of both their minds and bodies; and these scourges, acting upon their excited brains,—which have quite enough to do, even while in their best health, to contrive ways and means of living, drive them to distraction, and make of a fearful number of them lunatics and idiots."

"But, Doctor, do you not think the climate may have

something to do as an exciting cause of the Northern negroes' infirmities ?"

"Possibly; in a direct way; and certainly, in the way of making it more difficult for them to obtain the means of comfort."

"Their nature seems not congenial with a high latitude. They suffer from the cold more than white people; and their suffering from cold may well be supposed to act harshly on their mental and physical health."

"There may be something in that. Not much though, I think. For, as I remember the negroes in the days of my childhood, in New England, and in the very cold parts of the State of New York, in, and East and West of Albany, they were as healthy in body and mind as their masters. But that was before the days of abolition fanaticism. Therefore, there is no doubt in my mind, that it is to the hot blasts of that mad fanaticism, and not to the cold blasts of the Northern winter, that the evil is to be traced. Yes, sir; that is it, which is filling the Northern States with vicious, criminal, debauched, deaf, dumb, blind, insane, idiotic, sorrowing, and suffering negroes! And maddening even some white men who take copious drafts of this fanatical atmosphere.

"Poor, unhappy creatures! My heart bleeds at the thought, that, dreadful as the condition is of the poor free negroes of this country, it seems daily to be growing worse and more pitious; while that of their brethren in the South is gradually, but steadily, becoming better and better; notwithstanding the evil influence of the Northern fanaticism, the head-quarters of which is Massachusetts."

"As it was once the head-quarters of what now belongs only to history—the most heinous bigotry, persecution, and oppression, that our sun ever shone on! Where else, on this continent, save in New England,—in Massachusetts especially,—has a Protestant Government ever been found to 'chase, and scourge, and burn, and sell their fellow creatures and countrymen, into slavery?" But this was done by the General Court of Boston.'

Thus reads the record of one example of Puritan intolerance. "Two young persons, son and daughter of Lawrence Southwick of Salem, who had himself been imprisoned and deprived of all his property, for having entertained two Quakers at his house, were fined ten pounds each for non-attendance at the meeting, which they were unable to pay. The case being represented to the General Court at Boston that body issued an order which may still be seen on the Court records, bearing the signature of Edward Rawson, Secretary, by which the Treasurer of the County was '*fully empowered to* SELL *the said persons to any of the English nation at Virginia or Barbadoes to answer said fines.*' "

"No wonder the Quakers learned after a while to dislike slavery, having had so early a taste of it; and no wonder the Massachusetts men entered with so strong a relish into the slave trade, having been thus nurtured from their infancy in its principles, as sanctioned,—and as they were taught to understand, *sanctified*—by the saints of Plymouth Rock, in General Court assembled at Boston. As well as I can recollect, however, the order to sell the young Quakers into slavery was not carried into effect?"

No thanks to the General Court, for the failure, though. Among the English shipmasters, not a Puritan could be found, and of course not one that would take them on board his vessel to carry them into captivity. The order was never revoked. According to the Quaker poet, Whittier, —who tells us nothing of the young man—to the first application to the captains to take the condemned *maid* on board,

"No voice or sign replied."

Then to the stout sea captains, the Sheriff turning said
"Which of ye worthy seamen will take this Quaker maid?

In the Isle of fair Barbadoes, or on Virginia's shore,
You may hold her at a higher price than Indian girl or Moor.

Grim and silent stood the captains; and when again he cried,
"Speak out my worthy seamen!" no voice nor sign replied:
But I felt a hand press my own, and kind words met my ear;—
"God help thee and preserve thee, my gentle girl and dear!"

A weight seemed lifted off my heart—a pitying friend was nigh,
I felt it in his hard rough hand, I saw it in his eye;
And when again the Sheriff spake, that voice so kind to me,
Growled back its stormy answer like the roaring of the sea;—

"Pile my ship with bars of silver—pack with coins of Spanish gold,
From keel-piece up to deck-plank, the roomage of her hold,
By the living God that made me! I would sooner in yon bay
Sink ship and crew and cargo, than bear this child away!"

And so the maid was allowed to return to her desolated home. The cavalier captains shamed the puritans into a spasm of forbearance. But neither the chronicler nor the poet tells us what became of the male youth; and they leave us to suppose that he was actually sold as a slave.

The prose and the poetry I have quoted from Miss Mitford's delightful book—"Recollections of a Literary Life." She claims credit for the English nation that the English captains refused to take part in the Puritan persecution! Were not the persecutors themselves Englishmen? And were the same class of Englishmen at home guiltless of persecution?

Miss Mitford quotes from another of Whittier's poems, "Massachusetts to Virginia," full of fury, fight and falsehood, on a matter about a fugitive slave. In bepraising both poems, the dear, good old lady seems to lose sight of the glaring fact, that in the former the poet execrates puritanism, and in the latter lauds it.

"Thank God! not quite so vilely can Massachusetts bow,
*The spirit of her early time is with her even now.*"

Could he have been thinking of the spirit that condemned the two young quakers to be sold into slavery? The next line is a gem:

> "Dream not because her pilgrim blood moves slow and calm and cool."

Think of that:—the *cool and calm blood* of the puritans who more than once *St. Bartholomewed* the poor Indians; and, according to Miss Mitford, *scourged, imprisoned, burned, and sold their fellow creatures into slavery.* Calm and cool, indeed!

In this unhappily suggestive poem, Virginia is represented as being the author of her own slave institution. It is a false representation. This in passing. But it would be pleasant to know how many of the present race of Virginia negroes are indebted to Massachusetts for their greatly superior condition over that of their unhappy race in the wilds of Africa,—the most degraded and bloodiest of savages?

Perhaps Friend Whittier, or some other Massachusetts abolitionist will tell us whether Bristol in England, or Salem in Massachusetts. is entitled to precedence in the history of the slave-trade.

"You somewhere made a passing allusion, doctor, to the maddening effects of the abolition spirit on the mind of some white men as well as black. Will you be so good as to explain it?"

"Certainly. It has made monomaniacs of thousands, of the otherwise excellent, and highly accomplished, and respectable portion of the land, and driven many into raving madness."

"To whom of the latter class do you refer, doctor, that is still out of the Asylum?"

"I refer to the speakers generally, who so eloquently address the anti-slavery societies, as I have heard them, and as they are reported by the newspapers; and in particular, to such persons as we often meet in travelling, who are sometimes found even to froth like a mad boar, while pressing their abolition doctrines, and denouncing with furious execrations, the Southern system of negro slavery; which, by the way, would seem to be an altogether better school than they had been educated in."

"Yes; true enough; the accounts of the late anti-slavery society in Boston and Manchester do supply a large body of evidence of the manners of the members, and especially the principal orators."

"Until some three years ago, most of the Boston abolitionists preserved something like a decent control of themselves with regard to things most sacred; but at length they broke out, and broke over all the usual barriers, as by common consent erected, between them and the assaults of men in their senses, however impious in principle, and profligate in habit and conduct. At the meeting of the society in the spring of 1850, a man of learning and eloquence—and until then supposed, I believe, to be an altogether decent man, at least—in the course of his declamation, broke out in these awful and mad denunciations: "Down with your Bible!—Down with your political parties!—Down with your God that sanctions slavery! The God of Moses Stuart—the Andover God—the God of Wm. H. Rogers, which is worshipped in the Winter street Church, is a monster, composed of oppression, fraud, injustice, pollution, and every crime in the shape of slavery! To such a God I am an atheist!"

"Can any thing be more horrible? Can any thing better or more definitely indicate insanity than such sentiments publicly announced and promulgated in a Christian land?"

"I should think not, doctor. Scarcely any thing can be imagined more shockingly blasphemous!"

"And yet, at some of their later meetings, they have spoken—which is still more shocking—*deliberately;* and with an apparent determined coolness, of the necessity of destroying the Bible and the churches, in order to give the people some chance of coming to the truth on the subject of their duties towards the negroes; and as though there were nothing *due*, as duty, or forbearance, to any body else than the negroes and the abolitionists."

"But what wonder is it, that it has come to this, with the really fanatical, when such men as Channing, Wayland, Barnes, and others of like mark, have supplied them with weapons against the Bible and the Federal Constitution, and, indeed, against the sobrieties and amenities of every species of truth, righteousness and charity?"

"True enough, what wonder, that in a path in which those men walked proudly, in their denunciations, such persons as Garrison and Wright, Phillips, Foss and Foster, Theodore Parker, and the Abbys and Nabbys, and Harriets, should walk more proudly and recklessly, and denounce more loudly, and with bitterer execrations?"

"I hope their conviction of the Hon. Wm. King, of '*lying, theft, robbery and murder,*' will not act unfavorably on his supposed convalescence."

"I trust it may not. But was any thing ever heard of more absurd, than the serious pretensions of some abolitionists—themselves yet not quite distraught—that the actors in the late New Hampshire Anti-slavery meeting were neither mad nor fanatical?"

"Doctor, are there not to be found among the writings of the celebrated men already named, some very distinct indications of the fanatical spirit?"

"Plenty of them. What can better indicate that destructive spirit, than what is said by Wayland and repeated by Barnes—both claiming to reverence and defer to the Scriptures—declaring the principle, that if the Bible sanctions the institution of slavery, it is not to be believed; and if believed, it is one of the greatest curses that ever befel the human race?"

"Does their exact language, Dr., warrant you in so representing those eminently popular and celebrated men?"

"I have no doubt of it; or I would by no means say so. These are Barnes' own words, and they are recognized as true by all abolitionists—believers and infidels:

"'If the Bible could be shown to defend and countenance slavery, it would make thousands of infidels; for there are multitudes of minds that will see more clearly, that slavery is against all the laws which God has written on the human soul, than they would see, that a book sanctifying such a system had evidence of Divine origin.'"

"And that passage, all the abolitionists,—who yet seem to wish not to make entire shipwreck of the little faith they yet have in the Bible,—have carefully committed to memory. Even many of the good and peaceable Quakers, though not in general very fond of Dr. Barnes, have that celebrated passage at their tongue's end, and always ready for use, in every discussion in which they are asked to defer to the Bible. Very solemnly, and in a kind manner, they adduce or allude to it, and then, with still deeper and alarmed solemnity, they most kindly caution their opponent not to involve the Bible in the slavery controversy, lest he may encourage, and even force people—and the very best of people too—to become infidels!"

"It would be pleasant,—would it not,—to be able to ask Dr. Barnes, face to face, if it be quite *clear* that slavery is *more* against all the laws which God has written on the human soul, than to suffer men to *die of starvation* within arm's length; and from year to year to allow thousands of human beings to be constantly exposed to that most horrible of calamities?"

"It would indeed be pleasant enough, if only for the

purpose of learning how such men dispose of such home subjects in the North, while their warmest sympathies are sent off on a Southern crusade. But, doctor, what is the other passage that you alluded to?"

"It is an endorsement, by Barnes of Wayland, in this wise: 'Well may we ask, in the words of Dr. Wayland, whether there was ever such a moral superstructure raised on such a foundation? The doctrine of Purgatory from a verse in Maccabees; the doctrine of Papacy from the saying of Christ to Peter; the establishment of the Inquisition from the obligation to extend the knowledge of religious truth, all seem nothing to it. If the religion of Christ allows such a license from such precepts as these, the New Testament would be the greatest curse that ever was inflicted on our race.' "

"Now if such men have the hardihood so to speak of God's Holy Word, why should we wonder, that such as Garrison, Douglass, Theodore Parker and the rest of the great army of fanaticism, cry out with a voice that drowns the storm, and shocks every soul that has yet any reverence for sacred things and subjects—any belief, or fear, or love of God—any religious decency, even,—'Down with the Bible!—Down with the churches!—Down with God!!!—I am an atheist!' But such are the leaders of abolitionism in our day! May God in His great mercy give them repentance and a better mind."

"Doctor, you are moved. It would be strange if you were not. I could not envy the man, nor wish him for a friend, that such things could not move. But let us leave, for a little, the abolition divines, for the abolition politicians. Fancy yourself in the lobby, and disposed to be amused by a poppinjay or a butcher bird, and that you see one of them arising from his Congressional Chair of State, and look as if saying,

'I am Sir Oracle; and when I speak,
Let no dog bark.'

And then,—hear,—hear,—'Sir, I must express the most energetic dissent from those who would justify slavery from the Levitical Law. My reason and conscience revolt from those interpretations which

Torture the hallowed pages of the Bible,
To sanction crime and robbery and blood,
And in Oppression's hateful service, libel
Both man and God!'

Think of that, doctor, and laugh, if you can; for there is certainly no good reason to be otherwise than amused by such flippant fustian, from a foppish pretender to a deep knowledge of both politics and divinity, and to history and philosophy to boot."

## CHAPTER XXIII.

"DESPERATE ROW."
*All the newspapers.*

"The prosperity of fools shall destroy them."
"Rebuke a wise son and he will love thee."

ABOLITIONISTS speak often and self-complacently of the local insurrections which they have sometimes been able to ferment into bloody results in the South; and of their successful seditions in the North, they boast triumphantly; and very confidently they talk and write of greater things to come of the same sort. Would it not be as wise, and quite as Christian-like, to exchange their complaisance and confidence for lamentation for the *desperate rows* that are daily coming off in every part of the North?

Would not serious apprehensions, that such outrages of law and humanity, may grow into a general insurrection, to the overturning of the present order of things, here, be at least as reasonable as the hope of overturning order in the South?

When a Northern minister of religion, in his pulpit boasts of having supplied arms for resistance of law, there would seem quite as much danger of a revolt in the North, as of a servile war in the South. As even sanctioned by laws here, there is none of that *oppression* in the South, which is said in Scripture to *make a wise man* MAD!

There is none of that "life-long want that makes men beasts and devils!—the oppression that goes on all the year round,—the want that goes on all the year round,—and the filth, and the lying, and the swearing, and the profligacy,—that go on all the year round,—and the sickening weight of debt, and the miserable grinding anxiety from rent-day to rent-day, and Saturday night to Saturday night, that crushes a man's soul down, and drives every thought out of his head but how he is to fill his stomach and warm his back, and keep a roof over his head, till he daren't for his life take his thoughts one moment off the meat that perisheth."

In our own North, as well as in Europe—in England—proud abolition England—that sat to one of her own loyal sons for the picture—there are countless multitudes, "who feel this and feel nothing else."

In the South there is none of this depraving and maddening want and oppression. But to the North—it should be said—kindly but plainly—unless you will dare to despise the cries of the poor and downtrodden,—unless you will close your ears that you may not hear them, and shut your eyes that you may not see their loathsome wretchedness;—unless you will thus act the part of the accursed of God,—where can you betake yourself, but to the wilderness, to be spared the sounds and sights of misery, intensified by profligacy?

And think you, from this true state of things, there is no danger? Think you there is no call on the people of the North to attend to their own affairs better, and better to mind their own business?

You may have done well, perhaps, to put your foot on the neck of some old feudal oppressions, though it extinguish certain legal obligations recognized as such for a century, and more. But why did you this illegal thing? "Aye, there 's the rub." Was it done as an act of voluntary justice, or as a compulsory act of prudence?—an expedient—a *choice of evils?*

You have done well, no doubt, in the enlargement of your hospitals to prevent the effects of brotherhood conveying the infection of disease from the kennel to the kitchen, and thence to your bedrooms and parlors.

Well have you done, and well are you doing, in extending the dimensions of your lunatic asylums. For your artificial stimulants to avarice and ambition, and your prevailing spirit of contempt for, not only the dependent poor, but for the contentment of all who are not making haste to be rich, or great, is rapidly producing a state of things which will require far more space than you have yet provided for the demented classes, to which your evil spirit is daily and hourly adding.

## CHAPTER XXIV.

### SPIRITUAL FREEDOM &c.

Is it merely, that I am growing older, that my spirit of forebearance is growing stronger? Or is it, that as I grow older my wisdom is increasing with age? May the latter be the true state of the case. This, however, is undoubted: though

> "Knowledge and wisdom, though far from being one,
> Have ofttimes no connection;"—

yet, sometimes, little scraps of knowledge—a little fact, conveyed in few words in season—may give an impulse to the mind in search after wisdom of surprising force.

I am just now feeling so much of kindly forbearance towards the ignorance of the anti-slavery folks, who are such altogether, or principally, because they think the slaves of the South are in a state of heathen infidelity, and are denied the blessings of Christian privileges, as to induce something like regret, that I had not extended to them in the foregoing pages a larger allowance of forbearance.

This feeling I owe, through grace, to one of the smallest of letters, which came to me through the storm to-day, from one of the best of men—a good specimen of the true salt of the earth. Very *naively*, he tells me of an interesting fact concerning negro slavery, as if not only interesting, but strange and peculiar. Whereas, it is neither strange nor peculiar.

This is it:—" Mr.——, says he had two hundred slaves,

and not a vicious one among them; and that he often walked by their cabins in the night, unknown to them, and listened to their praying within, "for Mas'r, and little Mas'r, and Missus, &c.'"—"It is a pretty thought," says my beloved correspondent, "and ought to choke our abolitionists dead."

Bless me, my friend; if hundreds of such authenticated facts would effect for them such a metaphorical disability for hot soup, I would give neither sleep to my eyes nor slumber to my senses, until setting about in strong earnest, to supply them. Is not the delightful circumstance known to thee, my good sir, that some of the eminent men of the South have been induced, by the piety of their own slaves, to examine the claims of our holy faith in Christ and to admit those claims to their souls' health and happiness? It is even so. But the general rule is otherwise. The servants are led to the fountain by the master, as was the case I believe, with your excellent friend. And partly, hence, perhaps, the form of gratitude taken by their simple and fervent piety.

But, within a comparatively few years past, many others than your pious friend, from inferior, perhaps, yet commendable motives, have founded home churches for their slaves, and employed godly and efficient ministers to instruct and bring them to the happy fold of the living faith of the Gospel. And they have uniformly found it to conduce not to their quiet and comfort only, but also to their pecuniary profit.

And now, that spiritual freedom, which is superinduced through the Divine blessing upon religious instruction and worship, is not only as much within the reach, but really as much in possession of the South, as of any other people in our country, or, as I suppose, any other. Religious immunities are quite as well, perhaps in general better, secured to them than to the general free population of the

North. The full enjoyment of the Sabbath is secured to them by law and custom, and the privilege to attend religious worship and instruction;—a privilege which they far less generally neglect than do the people of the North—so far as I am authorised to say—without distinction of condition.

By tens of thousands, the children are carefully bred in the knowledge of Christianity, and thus grow up to prize their religious privileges above all price. By hundreds of thousands, these descendants generally, from a wretched stock of heathens, in the utter darkness of a loathsome pagan idolatry;—unmitigated and bloody savages—by hundreds of thousands these highly favored descendants are enrolled among the happiest of the happy in the fold of the Redeemer.

Happily, even the less spiritually free masters have learned, that it is for their interest that their slaves should be religiously instructed. Learning to know their duty, they do it faithfully as unto the Lord. Experience, and the examples of Christian masters, have demonstrated what should not have required demonstration, that religion secures the honesty and faithfulness of the slave. Some twenty years ago, a rich Southern planter, of great intelligence and goodness of heart and character, erected and endowed a spacious and noble Church, principally for the use and benefit of his negroes; called to it an accomplished, learned and laborious clergyman; and with his happy negroes the happy master and family, worshiped, received the same instruction, and ate of the same bread, and drank from the same cup.

Can even New England piety present a lovelier or a holier scene?

From the success of such experiments,—as this was called, and a bold and even prodigal one—many planters are doing likewise. I will glance at one more particular instance that came to my knowledge and interested me greatly. May it enough interest such as may profit by it, to secure their doing so.

To an excellent young man of the South there was left an extensive plantation and numerous slaves. While he was receiving his education abroad they were neglected, and probably otherwise ill treated. Absenteeism works badly every where. He came into possession. Little or no profit for years had accrued to the proprietor. The lands had been badly taken care of, and the people not better. They were vicious, insubordinate, and, of course, inefficient. His friends counselled him by all means to dispose of his inheritance for any thing he could get. Into this measure they tried to persuade, and they tried to frighten him. He was not to be moved. He felt a heavy weight of responsibility upon him. He would not throw it off, but strive faithfully to fulfill the duty, hard as it might be, that had devolved upon him by this apparently unfortunate inheritance. The first thing, and the great one, to be done was to reclaim the vicious, and of course miserable slaves.

He set about the task, which so few else would ever have attempted, with a sincere determination of patient endurance. With a good and honest heart, and with a well furnished mind, he became their loving and laborious teacher. So soon as he became satisfied that the object was not an impracticable one, he sought and found a like-minded helper—a help meet for him. The labor was sore, and for a long time yielded little fruit. They were not rich enough to procure efficient and steady assistance. Occasionally their task was lightened and furthered by some kind messenger of good tidings. The negroes, who had almost relapsed into savagism, were slowly but surely becoming civil and Christian. A few years of untiring labor and love passed away, and the great work was done;

and now, the model master and mistress, and their happy children and happy servants, all work, and worship God together, in their own comely church, and are all rejoicing in modest and generous prosperity.

Would it have been better for those negroes to be emancipated?

Very far gone in a furious and a foolish fanaticism must he be who would answer Yes. He is the slave. They the freemen. Folly and Fanaticism are hard taskmasters.

The spiritual capabilities—so to speak—of the good and honest-hearted negro, when the Gospel is first proposed to him;—the readiness with which he enters the vineyard to labor at the first call, without stopping to chaffer about wages, as if perfectly confident that whatsoever is right the Lord of the vineyard will award to him,—has sometimes induced persons of other types of soul, either to question his sincerity, or his knowledge of what he is about. So perhaps did the laborers in the vineyard, who would not enter it until they were certified of what they were to *have* for their work, judge concerning their fellow laborer who had made no bargain.

And the apparent naturalness, and of course manner, with which uncorrupted negro children take religious instruction, has often led to carping and faithless doubts of their capacities to improve by instruction. It is a very unhappy circumstance—a sad and sorrowful fact—that many persons of worth and piety, who have had hard struggles in their conflicts with worldly-mindedness and sceptical difficulties, seem thereby to have become incapable of understanding the nature and character of that better and simpler faith which takes God at His word, and asks not, "what shall we *have?*" but, "what shall we *do?*"

By the way, on reading over this passage on the honest-hearted negro's spiritual capabilities, doctor, it strikes me as something like *preaching*. Well it was not intended, and must be, therefore, forgiven; unless, indeed, it be foolish preaching, instead of what the apostle meant by "the foolishness of preaching." If it be, let no quarter be allowed. For of all the foolish things in the world, there is very little question, that foolish preaching is the very last of them that should be encouraged.

I have elsewhere alluded to the docility in Sunday schools of the negro children. And in this connection, to show something of their ready acceptance of religious instruction, there shall be noted a circumstance, that much pleased and interested several persons besides myself. To our Sunday School, there was an accession of a boy apparently of about ten years. His reputation had been damaged by detection in pilfering. For his special edification, but without any special allusion, there was given an extra, short, and simple exposition of the eighth commandment, as the words of God to such as He wishes to be good and happy.

Our new scholar was particularly attentive, and at times, evidently moved. After church, on his way home, the clergyman dropped accidentally his pocket handkerchief. This boy found it under circumstances in which he might have concealed it effectually. Instead of which, to the surprise of some who had known his character, he ran with it to the owner as quite a matter of course.

"Poor Jim," said one who had been often annoyed by Jim's pilfering propensities,—"Poor Jim; the seed of the word has already begun to bear fruit; he would not have done that yesterday." "Good Jim, hereafter it may be hoped," said the clergyman. So he was; and so far as I know never pilfered more.

What an encouragement to engaging and persevering in the onerous work of Sunday Schools, should one such case be, and especially for negroes, in the condition of slavery.

In their condition of freedom,—with sorrow be it said,—it is very difficult to induce them to attend,—so far as my experience can testify—and not less difficult to secure their attention, sufficiently to be of much use to them.

In nothing does a master show more lamentable ignorance of negro nature and of his own duty and interest, than in neglecting the religious instruction of his slaves. Happily, very many are the masters, who have discovered the error, to regret, and to do what they can to repair the evil. With the continuance of Heaven's blessing—in a comparatively few years—there is very strong reason for the hope, that a much larger proportion of the negro slaves of the South will be sincere and honest Christians, than now of any people under the sun. And then the abolition propaganda may be turned in among them without fear.

Within a short time since, there died in the South, a saint of a female slave, who had often accompanied her master's family in various parts of the North, where all sorts of schemes and measures were devised and tried in vain, to induce her to abandon her comforts and duties for the name of freedom. At the request of her colored minister, she was buried by the bishop of the diocese in which she had always lived. And her remains were followed to the grave by a procession which very clearly showed that her memory was sincerely and affectionately respected, as it would be not less impossible than absurd, to respect one who had been *brutalized* by slavery; as abolitionism insists that *all* in that condition are, *necessarily!*

Pardon and patience for a word more of this departed saint;—the early and long faithful friend of the "*wife*" and the "*sister*" of the writer. She visited them a few months ago, and a more cordial reunion may not easily be imagined. Tears were not witheld; and the ardently affectionate southern lady on the neck of the faithful and loving sable friend and servant;—and the mutual felicitations; —all these combined to produce a scene of much interest; and certainly one peculiarly well calculated to damage exceedingly, many a fine theory of the abolitionist. Degradation indeed! Sublime features marked the character of that jet black Christian woman's mind and heart. Let them be gratefully remembered for the good edification of her survivors.

It is doubtless too seldom considered, as it ought to be. what great spiritual advantages the slave has in the pursuit of heavenly mindedness, in being so completely relieved by his condition, from the vexings and irritations, and other temptations of worldly care. It places him on a vantage ground which very few of us are able to estimate the value of; and which so often many of us yearn for, that as we grow in age, we more surely may grow in grace. In seeking for the heavenly things of the kingdom of God, and of His righteousness, he has not to take thought for what he shall eat or what he shall drink, or wherewithal he shall be clothed.

In seeking for the better things of the soul, undisturbed by these common and corroding cares, the Christian servant will either find all desirable things for the body added, or the infinitely more valuable gifts of grace, that shall enable him to overcome the world, and so to be indifferent to them.

The true slave of Christ,—in Him free indeed—may care very little what shall come to him from an earthly master. Should even martyrdom come to him, it has come to many of whom the world was not more worthy, than able to comprehend their spiritual, sublime, and happy elevation above it.

To add to the value of this chapter, if it have any of its own; or if not, to make it of great value, by appending to it a combined lesson of two great men, the liberty is taken with Dr. Thornwell—before introduced—of adopting a passage from him, including some "thoughts that breathe, and words that burn," of the seraphic Robert Hall's "*Advantages of Knowledge to the Lower Classes.*"

"One of the highest and most solemn obligations which rests upon the masters of the South, is to give to their servants, to the utmost extent of their ability, free access to the instructions and institutions of the Gospel. The injustice of denying to them food and raiment, and shelter against which the law effectually guards, is nothing to the injustice of defrauding them of that bread which cometh down from Heaven. Their labor is ours. From infancy to age, they attend on us—they greet our introduction into the world with smiles of joy, and lament our departure with heartfelt sorrow; and every motive of humanity and religion exacts from us, that we should remunerate their services by putting within their reach the means of securing a blessed immortality. The church contemplates them only as sinners. She sees them as the poor of the land, under the lawful dominion of their masters; and she says to these masters, in the name and by the authority of God, give them what justice, benevolence, humanity would demand even for a stranger, an enemy, a persecutor—give them the Gospel without which life will be a curse. Sweeten their toil—sanctify their lives—hallow their deaths. We have begun a good work, and God grant that it may never cease until every slave in the land is brought under the tuition of Jesus of Nazareth. None need be afraid of his lessons. He was no stirrer up of strife, nor mover of sedition. His "religion on the other hand, is the pillar of society, the safeguard of nations, the parent of social order, which alone has power to curb the fury of the passions, and secure to every one his rights." Insurrection, anarchy and bloodshed—revolt against masters or treason against States, were never learned in the school of Him, whose Apostles enjoined subjection to the magistrate, and obedience to all lawful authority, as characteristic duties of the faithful. Is any thing to be apprehended from the instructions of Him, in whose text-book it is recorded: "Let as many servants as are under the yoke, count their masters as worthy of all honor?" Christian knowledge inculcates contentment with our lot; and in bringing before us the tremendous realities of eternity, renders comparatively indifferent to the inconveniences and hardships of time. It subdues those passions and prejudices, from which all danger to the social economy springs. "Some have objected," says a splendid writer, "to the instruction of the lower classes, from an apprehension that it would lift them above their sphere, make them disatisfied with their station in life, and by impairing the habits of subordination, endanger the tranquility of the State; an objection devoid surely of all force and validity. It is not easy to conceive in what manner instructing men in their duties can prompt them to neglect those duties, or how that enlargement of reason, which enables them to comprehend the true grounds of authority and the obligation to obedience, should indispose them to obey. The admirable mechanism of society, together with that subordination of ranks which is essential to its subsistence, is surely not an elaborate imposture, which the exercise of reason will detect and expose. The objection we have stated, implies a reflection on the social order, equally impolitic, invidious, and unjust. Nothing in reality renders legitimate governments so insecure as extreme ignorance of the people. It is this which yields them an easy prey to seduction—makes the victims of prejudice and false alarms, and so ferocious withal, that their interference in time of public commotion is more to be dreaded than the eruption of a volcano."

"Brutal ignorance is indeed to be dreaded—the only security against it, is physical force—it is the parent of ferocity, of rashness, and of desperate enterprizes. But Christian knowledge softens and subdues. Christ Jesus in binding His subjects to God, binds them more closely to each other in the ties of confidence, fidelity and love. We should say, then, to all our brethren of the South, go on in your present undertaking; and though our common enemies may continue to revile, you will be consolidating the elements of your social fabric, so firmly and compactly, that it shall defy the storms of fanaticism, while the spectacle you will exhibit of Union, sympathy and confidence among the different orders of the community, will be a standing refutation of all their accusations against us. Go on in this noble enterprise, until every slave in our borders shall know of Jesus and the Resurrection; and the blessing of God will attend you—and turn back the tide of indignation which the public opinion of the world is endeavoring to roll upon you."

The truly "*noble enterprise*" alluded to had just erected an additional church in Charleston, for the religious training of her slaves at an expense of nearly eight thousand dollars; connected with which is a Sunday school of about two hundred scholars, who are taught by the Minister and some twenty or thirty ladies and gentlemen.

"Masters, give unto your servants that which is just and equal; knowing that ye also have a Master in Heaven."

# CHAPTER XXIV.

## A CHAPTER OF LACONICS.

### SUGGESTIVE HISTORY.

"The Greeks and Romans, descended from Japheth, conquered Canaan, and whatever relics there were of them any where; for instance, at Tyre, built by the Sidonians; and Thebes, by Cadmus; at Carthage, by Dido;—they were all cut off by the Greeks and Romans. It is observed by Campanell, that "none are descended from Cham, but slaves, and tyrants, who are indeed slaves." But Mr. Mede's observation is more pertinent: "There hath never yet been a son of Cham, that hath shaken a scepter over the head of Japheth. Shem hath subdued Japheth, and Japheth subdued Shem; but Cham never subdued either. Which made Hannibal, a child of Canaan, cry out with amazement of soul, Agnosco fatum Carthaginis; —'I acknowledge the fate of Carthage.'" (Livy.)

*Patrick on Gen.* IX. 27.

Do not such historical facts, when found also in accordance with the present state of the world, look very much like the corresponding prophecy,—"*And Canaan shall be his servant?*" And if, His Word and Providence are the two witnesses to prove it His decree, is it wise to fight against it?

### THE EARLY CHURCH.

As in the early Church, it was unlawful for a Christian master to sell a Christian slave, or even a pagan slave, to Jew or heathen; so in our own days, no truly Christian master can be willing to sell a slave to an unbeliever. There are many such masters who would not do it on any consideration, or for any price. Why? The conscientious Christian requires no answer. Others might not understand the true answer, and this therefore is not the place to answer it.

## A SMALL SHARE IN THE INHERITANCE.

The author of Alton Locke, thus describes some of the miserable classes of proud old England:—"Such a visage as only worn-out poachers, or tramping drovers, or London Chiffoniers carry; pear-shaped, and retreating to a narrow peak above, while below, the bleared cheeks and drooping lips, and peering purblind eyes, perplexed, hopeless, defiant, and yet sneaking, bespeak their share in the inheritance of the kingdom of heaven;—savages without the resources of a savage—slaves without the protection of a master—to whom the cart-whip and the rice swamp would be a change for the better—for there, at least, is food and shelter. Slowly and distrustfully a dripping scarecrow of rags and bones rose from his hiding place."

This excellent English author, who is trying hard to shame England into something like the decencies of humanity, first exaggerates the condition of slavery, by the introduction of the cart-whip, as if an inseparable adjunct,—did he learn this of Lord Palmerston?—and then declares it preferable to the condition of the poor Briton, even physically, as well as morally degenerate. Did Mr. Kingsley know of the comfortable and happy condition of our southern slaves, —with goodly shares in the inheritance of the kingdom of heaven—would he not say with sorrowful indignation, "Oh, forbear, my country, from condemning an institution which feeds and clothes and protects the poor, and trains many for heaven, and take up a lamentation that you had not rather taxed labor for twenty millions to elevate the condition of your own *miserables*, than to condemn the West Indian slaves to theft, robbery and pauperism!"

## FOREIGN SLAVERY.

MADAM PFEIFFER finds herself quite agreeably disappointed to find the slaves of Brazil in a more comfortable condition than the laborers of Europe. "All work ceases at sunset, when the negroes are drawn up in front of their master's house for the purpose of being counted, and then, after a short prayer, have their supper, consisting of boiled beans, bacon, &c. &c., handed out to them. At sunrise they again assemble, are counted, and after prayers and breakfast go to work.

"I had an opportunity of convincing myself that the slaves are not by far so harshly treated as we Europeans imagine. They are not overworked, perform all their duties very leisurely, and are well kept. Their children are frequently the playmates of their masters' children, and knock each other about as if they were all equal. There may be cases in which certain slaves are cruelly and undeservedly punished; but do not like instances of injustice occur in Europe also?

"*I am certainly very much opposed to slavery, and I should greet its abolition with the greatest delight!* but, despite this, I again affirm that the negro slave enjoys, under the protection of the law, a better lot than the free fellah of Egypt, or many peasants in Europe—the principal reason of the better lot of the slave, compared to that of the *miserable* peasant, may perhaps partly be, that the purchase and the keep of one is expensive, and the other costs nothing. After all, slaves are far from being as badly off as many Europeans imagine. They are generally pretty well treated; they are not overworked, their food is good and nutritious, and the punishments are neither particularly frequent nor heavy.—Their lot is less wretched than that of the peasants of Russia, Poland or Egypt, who are *not* called slaves."

## HUNGER THE GREAT SOURCE OF CRIME.

"A large portion of the crimes punished by law, arise from hunger." So says a French Abbe already quoted. "They will disappear *when* the men whom it now besets shall be beyond the reach of its fatal suggestions."

Are the Abolitionists accelerating that important WHEN? What progress have they made in London, New York and Philadelphia, in the imperative duty of saving the poor—not from ordinary hunger merely but,—from *Death, death by starvation?*

"I hope to see the day," said Lord Brougham,—who seemed to have thought the ability to read an excellent substitute for meat—"I hope to see the day when every young man in England shall be able to read Bacon."

"Better hope for the day," replied Cobbett, "When every man in England shall be able to *eat* bacon."

This reply of Cobbett, Coleridge declared to be "the best speech of the session."

The southern negroes are able to eat bacon abundantly, though, probably, not always their entire allowance; for I well know a model master in Alabama,—one of the very best of men, whom I love as a brother or a son, whose allowance of bacon, in the working season, is four pounds a week, with all needful accompaniments. How many of abolition England's hard laborers would gladly exchange conditions with these bacon-eating negroes? Under other names, Great Britain has, on her own home islands, more slaves than all our South; and some of them may be able to *read*, but very few to eat bacon to that amount.

## A PET.

During my residence in the South, a maiden-lady-friend of ours, having arrived at that kindly age when it is pleasant to have a pet, had the rare good fortune to find among her acquaintance a little negro child of a year old that had lost its mother. She at once secured it to herself as a pet, as a lady might procure a lap-dog. It became a much more interesting pet than any lady's lap-dog ever was. No pet was ever more tenderly cared for, or more highly prized. Had it been the orphan of a princess it could not have been made more comfortable. There was nothing of the Topsy romance in the affair; but there is no occasion to doubt of its being now a far happier negro, than any that can be found among the snow-banks of the GREEN Mountains, where, in 1826, *twenty-four out of nine hundred and eighteen, were in the Penitentiary!*—one in 38¼!

## DIGNIFIED MODERATION.

A Northern divine, who some seven years ago denounced the Abolition party as extravagant and malignant fanatics,—the "Cold Steel party,"—I wonder if he still does?—wrote this of Southern servitude: "*It has produced unspeakable mischief and misery in the domestic relations.*"—And has nothing else done as much and far more, in this way, supposing this false charge to be granted to the full? "*It has transferred parental authority to a source that God never designed.*" Which is this, modesty, or profane presumption? "*It has deprived the ignorant of knowledge, and taken from the defenceless the shield of their protection.*" How so? Are not Southern slaves better instructed and protected than are the "Moyamensing blacks or their white companions, or even the poor generally?" "*It consigns him to toil as a beast of burden, without any just and adequate remuneration.*" He toils less, and he is better remunerated than the free laborers of any country. "*The avails of his labor is the property of his master, and cannot be made his own.*" Whose are the avails of the labor of the free man, who works far harder, without being able to procure half the comforts of the slave, for himself and family, and in sickness and age is in destitution and beggary, and in danger of DEATH BY STARVATION?

"*He is* HIMSELF PROPERTY, *and of course can own none.*"

Could the rank fetor of impiety be *chlorinized* out of it; so that we might handle it, secure against infection and offence, no doubt there might be found somewhat of psychological interest, together with a vast fund of amusement, in the abolitionistic notion of "*the property of man in man.*" It is a mental abortion. It is a profane fancy. It is the monster offspring of the infidel mother of a very gross materialism, whose father is an atheist.

"The property of man in man," says Rev. Dr. Thornwell—"a fiction to which even the imagination cannot give consistency—is the miserable cant of those who would storm by prejudice what they cannot demolish by argument. We do not even pretend that the organs of the body can be said strictly to belong to another. The limbs and members of my servant are not mine, but his—they are not tools and instruments which I can sport with at pleasure, but the sacred possession of a human being, which cannot be invaded without the authority of law, and for the use of which he can never be divested of his responsibility to God."

So much for this Key stone in the arch of Abolitionism. But, in common parlance—the most figurative of all parlances—and in the view of the carnal-minded materialist, neither is the slave's person or mind, the *property* of the master. They are both his *own* property; to which he may, and not unfrequently does, add largely; so as often to be able to command more ready cash than his master is able to command. And by a general public sentiment, stronger than law—without which laws are powerless—the slave's property is as sacred as the master's. The property of the master is the *obedience* of the slave to all his lawful commands. So much, no more. If the master be foolish and wicked enough to be a tyrant; and the slave to disobey lawful commands, they will be as unhappy as many foolish and wicked fathers and sons.

## A PLEASANT RECOLLECTION.

In St. Augustine, my excellent host, in his generous kindness, appropriated to my use and comfort, a servant boy of some fourteen years old, and as black as a jet. Peter was a good, amiable, and attentive boy. With the entire approbation of the master,—though I had been taught that an attempt of the kind would peril my life,—I taught Peter to read the Bible.

In my pleasant quarters, I was much alone with Peter, and had a good deal of talk with him; and at no time, for many years, did I ever hear Peter express the shadow of a wish to be freer than he was, in his easy and well compensated servitude. How great would be the increase of comfort if all services were as well paid. When he attained to the ability to read the Bible a little, so as to understand, in easy passages, something of its meaning, Peter's happiness, in the shadow of an orange tree, might have been envied by a prince or a poet.

## AN APHORISM WITH A COMMENT.

"Truth, Virtue, and Happiness, may be distinguished from each other, but cannot be divided."—COLERIDGE.

Are the Abolitionists happy? I met one in travelling through Ohio, who so raved and foamed, while denouncing slavery, as to frighten women and children. He could not have been happy. Happiness never takes that frightful form. Calmness and elevation are the attributes of that Truth which is the source and mother of happiness; and the child though sometimes joyous exceedingly, and sometimes indignant, never foams at the mouth.

## A SEDITIONARY.

"Block the locomotives!—Tear up the rails!—Law or no law, Constitution or no Constitution, resolve that this law shall not be enforced."—WENDELL PHILLIPS' ANTI-SLAVERY ORATION.

As if a hopeless evil, if not the only one of any account in the world, Mrs. Stowe had intended to keep silent on the painful subject of slavery, until "she heard, with perfect surprise and consternation," of the passage of the fugitive slave law, as if it were a quite new and unheard of, and unparalleled abomination. Then her sense of duty awakened her to the irksome task of teaching the people of the North "what slavery is. From this arose a desire to exhibit it in a living dramatic reality."

What a miserable pity that she had not been consulted at an early day by the Government; and especially, by Clay, Webster and Cass!

## ABOLITION PERVERSION OF SCRIPTURE.

Though often sufficiently revolting to all sober and reverent minds, the grotesque absurdity of the abolitionists' perversions of Scripture, are sometimes irresistibly ludicrous. It is a pity that they are not always as innocently simple as that of the Scotch mother and her good boy Sawney. The good mother and the good son were together hoeing their potato patch. The day was hot and thirsty. The ground was hard and foul. And long before the task was done, the poor boy, though "a lad o'grace"—felt as though he could stand it no longer without water from the *burn*. The good mother was strongly bent on its completion before leaving it; and so she delved away lustily, and with a good heart. She said many and cheering words of praise, encouragement and comfort to her boy, who sadly began to lag. He had often asked leave of her to go to the "*burn*" for a drink; but the burn was a good way off, and so poor Sawney was not permitted to leave the potato patch, lest it might not be finished so soon as desired. "We'll ha' done it, Sawney, my bairn in a wee bit; and then the burn will luik beautifu' Sawney, darlin'; an' it'll sing ye a bit ditty, my lad, an' gie ye a stoup o' its drink sweetened, Sawney, ay', my bairn, sweetened."

"But, guid mither, I'm muckle drouthy. An', mither, does na' the guid buik say, 'gi' drink unto the drouthy?'"

"Aye, mi bairn, and so saith it sure. That's unco true mi ain Sawney; but na' till the patch is done, Sawney."

"An' where, mither mine, does the guid buik say ony thing o' that like?"

"Aye, Sawney! Sawney! I could a wal be greetin' that ye shud forget that the Bible saith—Ho, every ane that thirsteth."

Sawney too was much distressed that he had forgetten it; and he hoed away lustily till the patch was finished. That Scotch mither no doubt raised up on her knees many a Bible expositor to do credit to her nurture.

With the mere amusing expositions of the abolitionists we ought not, perhaps, to find fault, unless they be also profane;—then indeed they would not be merely amusing. But when a learned divine of the *dignifiedly moderate class of abolitionists,* takes upon himself so flatly to contradict Holy Writ as to declare that "*masters cannot render to their servants that which is just and equal,*" he seems to extort rebuke for his impious presumption.

"*Masters cannot render to their servants that which is*

*just and equal,*" says a Philadelphia divine. Let him settle that with the apostle who commands it.

## NEGRO TRADERS.

Among negro slaves,—as often among white freemen,—there are found occasionally vicious fellows who are never safe—out of prison—from harm or harming. These are found out and bought up by the negro traders,—who sometimes corrupt them for the purpose—and taken off to New Orleans, or elsewhere.

So from London, men and women have been transported on the oaths of such as have led them into crime from selfish and sinister motives.

## CLEON AND I.

What this has to do with my subject, no one will guess, but such as have hearts with eyes in them. Is it a large class? I don't know. Some people think it a *very* large class; and some people think it a very small one. I cannot decide. I dare not. The truth, perhaps, lies between them, where it is usually found,—as it is said,—between extremes.

"Cleon hath a million acres,
Ne'er a one have I;
Cleon dwelleth in a palace,
In a cottage I;
Cleon hath a dozen fortunes,
Not a penny I;
Yet the poorer of the twain is
Cleon, and not I.

"Cleon, true, possesseth acres,
But the landscape I;
Half the charms to me it yieldeth
Money cannot buy.

Cleon harbors sloth and dullness,
Freshening vigor I;
He in velvet, I in fustian,
Richer man am I.

"Cleon is a slave to grandeur.
Free as thought am I;
Cleon fees a dozen doctors,
Need of none have I;
Health-surrounded, care-environed,
Cleon fears to die;
Death may come, he'll find me ready,
Happier man am I.

"Cleon sees no charms in Nature,
In a daisy I;
Cleon hears no anthems ringing
In the sea and sky;
Nature sings to me forever,
Earnest listener I;
State for state, with all attendants,
Who would change?—Not I."

Is it not a bright particular gem? Where did I *get* it? Why it came to me rolled up in a fresh copy of the CHRISTIAN WITNESS, of Feb. 11, 1853. *How* it found me,—away up here between the hills and beside the river, I am sure I don't know;—all the way from Boston. What a nice thing it would be—wouldn't it—to be able to enjoy and help to support such papers, that send out such nice things for the promotion of wisdom and happiness? Perhaps so. I don't know. It might be a nice thing; or it might not. It would be a blessing that might be abused. I hope it is right for me to think it best as it is.

## ABOLITION LOGIC.

How the Anti-Slavery authorities reconcile all their arguments against Southern Slavery is no affair of mine.

But that their notion, which happens to be a true one, that slave labor is less profitable than free labor, can be reconciled with their oft repeated assertion, that the slave gets nothing for his work, is a question which might gravel even the philosophy of the Hons. Greely and Sumner. To be consistent as a Socialist, Greely ought to feel kindly towards Slavery, as approaching nearer to Socialism, than any thing else, on a large scale, that he is likely ever to see in this world. And, indeed, in very many instances of this species of Socialism, the slaves know themselves to have the best of it; and the conscientious and grateful among them, often show, that they know and feel it, by kind and generous exertions to ameliorate the circumstances of their masters. Very many beautiful cases of this character might easily be catalogued, to the no doubt great surprise and wonder, not only of Abolitionists, but of the illiberal and selfish of all classes, who ought to blush, if able, that in real excellency of character they are inferior to many a slave.

## RUNAWAY SLAVES.

It is one of the usual arguments against the happiness of the negro slave, that sometimes they run away! And what an argument! As if people in all conditions of life were not generally discontented. Why are the overland routes to California lined with graves of New Englanders, fled from homes that would have been happy homes, but for the very bitter ingredient that makes not only negroes run away, but also apprentices, and sons, and even daughters, and occasionally, a husband, or a wife? Many a white man, and woman, too, have changed their condition, by removal, and otherwise, who would gladly change back again. And so is it with the Southern slave, who runs away. Many of them get back to their happier home than they find elsewhere; and many more would gladly retrace their steps, but are not able. From one plantation, with which I was well acquainted, two negroes ran away; and in a few months were right glad to find themselves at home again. They were both thoroughly cured of their discontent; and were, and still are, as recently I have learned, more faithful and happy, than before they tried the unsatisfactory experiment. "A few cold days in New York, among the free negroes of Anthony Street," Dick Downing used to say, "would be enough to content any Southern fellow with his own lot." Dick had never been in the Baker Street of another city.

## A STRIKING CONTRAST.

St. Paul put a letter into the hand of a runaway slave, and sent him back to his master.

A reverend New England divine put a Colt's revolver into the hands of a runaway slave, with a charge to use it with effect on the person of the first man who should dare to call or treat him as a slave; and afterwards he boasted of it in the pulpit!

## ENGLAND IN DANGER.

"Three and a half millions of the inhabitants of Great Britain—one-eighth about of the entire population, depend for subsistence on the various manufactures of cotton."—British Statistics.

What employment would they find, by which to earn their subsistence, in so crowded a population, and where "leave to toil" is granted as a special favor, should British abolitionism succeed in its zealous endeavors to ruin our cotton growing population, by insane intervention with its rights? And how *then* would England get on with her pauper difficulties?

Anomalies, varied as rainbow colors, are found every

where; but the strangest of all anomalies are those of British policy, and British public morals. Heaven grant that this anomalous state of things may not be a true foreshadowing of a swift coming event of deplorable evil to our race!

## NEGRO SECURITY FROM TERRIBLE EVILS.

There may be no people on earth, of their number, so secure against fearful accidents, disasters, calamities and violence, as are the colored peasantry of the South. They are very rarely exposed to great dangers of any kind. Steamboat explosions and collisions, and railroad crashes; and shipwrecks, and fires, and floods, and highway robbers, and assassins, and incendiaries, find few victims among them.

Is there no happiness in this? Read the newspapers, and then ask the maimed, and the mourning, and the dying, and the desolated,—and then answer me!

"All things are double, one against another." So saith the wise; and that it is so let me submit and be thankful.

What charming little dishes of whipt sillabub are often found served up by English writers for the benefit of our negroes. Look at and taste of this.

"Take an extreme case. Take the case of the slaves on American plantations. I dare say they are worked hard. I dare say they don't altogether like it. I dare say their's is an unpleasant experience on the whole."—*Bleak House.*

I dare say, Mr. Skimpole Dickens, you know very little about it. I dare say, that English writers who meddle with our affairs in this way, would often appear less ridiculous and damage their own country less, if they would try honestly to know more and write less about what they are shamefully and it seems blissfully ignorant. In their stolid ignorance of us, which shuts them out from even as much knowledge of our geography, as they ought to have of the geography of the moon, I dare say, on examination, it would be found that in their mind, there is mixed up the horrors of a piratical slave-trade, with the condition of the slaves on American plantations. And I dare say, if they would examine honestly into the truth of the matter, they would find the slaves on our plantations, as much better off than English farm laborers, as these are better off than were the cruelly treated galley slaves of the Dey of Algiers, when that dignitary reckoned it among his highest duties and dearest privileges, to torture the "Christian dogs" which his piratical corsairs had captured. I dare say that all this is so. The English seem rapidly to be getting to where they were in 1694 when Bishop Patrick said "they seemed to take pleasure in being ignorant of the most important truths." Let us hope better things of them, and that they only *seem* in love with error.

Now a closing word for the author. In charity with all, to all he would do good, and evil to none. If a little harshly he has sometimes chided, it has not been from hate, but love. Some things are not very praiseworthy, and he has not praised them. Some notions have done great evil. They cannot be good notions. With plainness of speech he has said so. For the holders of them he has charity. In return he asks theirs for himself; but not for any of his false notions. To the abolitionists at home and abroad, he has shown where they may employ their means to better than revolutionary ends. He has shown that the southern slave is in a happier condition than the negro in Africa,—than the free blacks here—than the suffering poor of all countries. He would gladly have done it better. He did what he could. He now concludes his task in the loving hope for all hereafter, of better counsels and kinder sympathies.

THE END.

## Theophilus Americanus; or, Instruction concerning the Church.

BY CHR. WADSWORTH, D. D.

Edited by H. D. Evans, LL.D. $1.50.

---

## Lectures on the Apocalypse, Critical, Expository, and Practical.

BY CHR. WADSWORTH, D. D.

8vo. $2.

---

## Maurice's Nine Sermons on the Lord's Prayer.

12mo. 50c.

---

## The Elements of Christian Science; a Treatise on Moral Philosophy and Practice.

BY WILLIAM ADAMS, D. D.

8vo. $1.50.

---

## The History of the Articles of Religion.

BY HARDWICK.

8vo. $1.75.

---

## Restoration of Belief;

A new and valuable work on the evidences of the Christian Faith.

12mo. 75c.

---

## Rev. Henry Blunt's Works,

In Four Volumes, 12mo. Price reduced to $3.

More than 40,000 of these works have been sold in England, at three times the cost of them here. How many will read them here—so cheap and yet so excellent!

www.ingramcontent.com/pod-product-compliance
Lightning Source LLC
LaVergne TN
LVHW010233110826
845151LV00004B/1276

* 9 7 8 1 4 2 5 5 2 4 8 2 1 *